The Evolution of Intelligence

Other Books by James H. Fetzer

As author:

Scientific Knowledge: Causation, Explanation, and Corroboration
Artificial Intelligence: Its Scope and Limits
Philosophy and Cognitive Science
Computers and Cognition
Philosophy of Science

As co-author:

Glossary of Epistemology and Philosophy of Science
Glossary of Cognitive Science
American Assassination

As editor:

Foundations of Philosophy of Science: Recent Developments
Principles of Philosophical Reasoning
Science, Explanation, and Rationality
The Philosophy of Carl G. Hempel
Aspects of Artificial Intelligence
Sociobiology and Epistemology
The Great Zapruder Film Hoax
Epistemology and Cognition
Probability and Causality
Consciousness Evolving
Murder in Dealey Plaza
Assassination Science

As co-editor:

Program Verification: Fundamental Issues in Computer Science
Philosophy, Language, and Artificial Intelligence
Philosophy, Mind, and Cognitive Inquiry
The New Theory of Reference
Definitions and Definability

The Evolution of Intelligence

Are Humans the Only Animals with Minds?

JAMES H. FETZER

OPEN COURT
Chicago and La Salle, Illinois

To order books from Open Court, call toll-free 1-800-815-2280, or visit
our website at www.opencourtbooks.com.

Open Court Publishing Company is a division of Carus Publishing
Company.

Printed and bound in the United States of America.

Fetzer, James H., 1940-
    The evolution of intelligence : are humans the only animals with
minds? / James H. Fetzer.
        p. cm.
    Includes bibliographical references and index.
    ISBN-13: 978-0-8126-9459-8 (trade pbk. : alk. paper)
    ISBN-10: 0-8126-9459-7 (trade pbk. : alk. paper)
    1. Intellect. 2. Psychology, Comparative. 3. Animal intelligence.
I. Title.
    BF431.F415 2005
    155.7--dc22

                                                        2005013754

For Sarah

Contents

Appendix

Tables and Figures

Preface

Human beings have nurtured many conceits about the exalted place of humanity within the scheme of things entire: that the Earth is the center of the universe or, if not that, then at least that the Sun orbits the Earth or, if not that, then at least that humans are the rational animals or, if not that, then at least that humans were created as the only animals with minds. The pilgrimage from Aristotle to Copernicus to Freud has been a revelation, where the cosmic insignificance of the human species has been further magnified by the relative unimportance of our solar system as a tiny feature of the Milky Way, which is merely one of billions of galaxies made up of billions of stars.

The progressive displacement of the species from its central position at the center of the universe, at the center of the solar system, or even as distinctively rational animals has been brought about by developments within science, especially advances in psychology as well as in physics and astronomy. Anyone today who proclaimed that the Earth was the center of the universe, that the Sun revolved around the Earth, or that humans were invariably rational would be widely regarded as displaying ignorance of the classic discoveries associated with the names of Kepler, of Newton, and of Freud. Yet a tendency remains to assume that humans are still the only animals with minds.

This book provides a systematic exploration of alternative theoretical hypotheses and recent empirical evidence with the objective of demonstrating that this conceit also should be relegated to the dustbin of intellectual history. The principal difficulties that have confronted investigations of animal mentality have revolved around the development of an adequate conception of mentality, on the one hand, and the emergence of a suitable methodology for investigating mental phenomena, on the other. Antiquated Cartesian conceptions of consciousness as the object and introspection as the method have severely constrained scientific studies of animal mind.

The presuppositions that have affected inquiries within this domain have been distinctively philosophical, including, for example, that knowledge must be certain, while consciousness remains private—at least, for anyone other than oneself! The privacy of consciousness may preclude others from direct access to mental states, but it does not preclude indirect access: we typically draw inferences about others on the basis of observations of their speech and other behavior. And the absence of certain knowledge is compatible with the presence of uncertain knowledge: scientific knowledge is typically inductive and uncertain. Sciences of the mind are possible.

Indeed, a hardy band of students of animal behavior have made contributions to this enterprise that deserve candid acknowledgment and further exploration. These scholars include pioneers in the application of scientific approaches to the study of social behavior among human beings as well as other species, including E.O. Wilson and Charles Lumsden, who first introduced (what is known as) "sociobiology" and its successor, "gene-culture co-evolutionary theory", but also those who are extending scientific techniques to the study of animal mind, Donald Griffin, Dian Fossey, Carolyn Ristau, Marian Stamp Dawkins, and Sue Savage-Rumbaugh, among others.

This book has the objective of discussing and advancing the scientific study of animal mind through the systematic elaboration of a philosophical framework that clarifies and unifies (what appears to be) a conception of the mind that applies to human beings, other animals, and even machines, if such a thing is possible. It is indispensable to such a conception that it should not "beg the question" by taking for granted that mentality is the exclusive property of a special group, even when that group is identified with humanity itself. The conception of minds as "semiotic systems" appears to possess precisely the properties that this framework requires.

In order to appraise the theoretical potential of the conception of minds as semiotic systems, however, it is indispensable to undertake a preliminary study of the empirical phenomena that are illuminated by its adoption. This includes the work of those students of animal behavior ("ethology") who have been willing to embrace its cognitive dimensions (as "cognitive ethology"), such as Griffin's studies of animal awareness, Ristau's studies of the piping plover, Dawkins's studies of animal cognition, Fossey's studies of the great apes, and Savage-Rumbaugh's studies of the mentality of chimpanzees. Their work reflects the phenomena science must explain.

The obstacles to progress within this domain, alas, have emerged, not from the work of scientists, but from the efforts of philosophers, such as Noam Chomsky and his conception of innate syntax, Jerry Fodor and his hypothesis of a mental language, and Stephen Pinker and his defense of the language instinct. Their publications have exerted an influence that appears to be grossly disproportional to the theoretical and empirical merits of their positions. Indeed, if the conception of minds that receives elaboration here is right, then their work is wrong—not simply in its details, which would be unsurprising, but to its core. Their work is fundamentally misconceived.

Thus, if the arguments offered here are well-founded, then Chomsky, Fodor, and Pinker are part of the problem, not the solution. And their work is only the tip of the intellectual iceberg. The entire field of cognitive science, which they have strongly influenced, has become infatuated with the computational conception of the mind, according to which minds operate on the basis of the same (or similar) principles as digital machines. One of the most memorable characterizations of this conception would have us believe that thinking is reasoning, that reasoning is reckoning, that reckoning is computing, and that the boundaries of computation define the boundaries of thought. That is wrong.

In order to understand the nature of animal mind, it is necessary to understand the nature of human minds. If the computational conception of human minds cannot be sustained, then its extension to animal mind—as Daniel Dennett, for example, has pursued it—cannot be sustained. But exposing the misconceptions that underlie so much of contemporary cognitive science—to the extent that at least one scholar has even defined the field as the study of computational models of the mind!—requires serious consideration of the elements implicit in that conception. If people are not computers and minds are not machines, then those contentions warrant refutation!

Thus, if minds are to bodies as programs are to machines, then the processes or procedures that relate minds to bodies must be similar (or the same) as those that related programs to machines. Programs turn out to be causal implementations of algorithms as "effective decision procedures", which are solutions to problems that are always applicable, always reliable, and always correct. They yield appropriate solutions to problems within a specific class that are always right and they do that within a finite number of steps. If the analogy is well-founded, then human thought must be governed by mental algorithms that serve the same (or a similar) function.

While the nature of computational systems has received considerable investigation, however, the nature of thinking things, even human beings, has not. It turns out that some of the most basic kinds of thought processes, including dreams and daydreams, perception, and memory—as well as ordinary thinking—do not satisfy the conditions for qualifying as "effective decision procedures". Even if there are modes of thought, such as the evaluation of proofs in logic, say, that do properly qualify as algorithmic, the computational conception no longer remains defensible. The analogy between human beings and digital machines cannot be sustained.

This misconception has also been imported into the study of what is known as "evolutionary psychology" in the work of Leda Cosmides and John Tooby, among others. This has an ironic aspect, since digital machines are cultural artifacts that are subject to artificial selection rather than members of species that are subject to natural selection. Their appeals to "Darwinian algorithms" not only suffer from defects inherent in the computational conception, which they embrace, but also in mistakes specific to arguments for their own position, addressed in the Appendix. This domain is better understood as devoted to the study of the influence of evolution upon psychology than as pursuing the study of the evolution of algorithms.

Indeed, although Cosmides and Tooby advance the notion of Darwinian algorithms as an improvement upon the counterpart conception of "epigenetic rules" that Lumsden and Wilson have proposed, there are excellent reasons to suppose that their earlier conception is also the more justifiable. It does not assume that mental processes are invariably algorithmic, which makes it a more encompassing conception. When "semiotic" epigenetic rules are distinguished within the general class of "epigenetic rules", it clarifies the nature of mentality. And it permits the evolution of mentality as a concomitant effect of the evolution of epigenetic rules.

One of the most important scientific hypotheses advanced in the pages of this book is the proposal that the general intelligence factor "g" discussed by Arthur Jensen, among others, should be identified with epigenetic rules that involve the use of signs. While Lumsden and Wilson introduced their notions of "selectivity" as of "penetrance" as properties of predispositions to acquire and to utilize one or another disposition within a certain range, an additional measure of "ease of learnability" appears to be required. Semiotic epigenetic rules then have three dimensions: the range of dispositions organisms could acquire, under suitable conditions (selectivity); the ease with which those dispositions would be acquired (rapidity); and the strength of the acquired dispositions to manifest themselves (penetrance).

Ultimately, distinctions must be drawn between "intelligence" and "mentality", because, although "intelligence" can be envisioned as a special kind of mentality associated with cognitive versatility and behavioral plasticity, it can also be employed to describe inanimate machines that display behavioral plasticity, not because of their cognitive versatility, but because of their capacity to "learn" or to "acquire" a wide range of different forms of behavior, which are consequences of their susceptibility to programming. When properly understood, therefore, it is perfectly appropriate to describe systems of this kind as "intelligent machines".

No doubt, the most controversial dimension of the evolution of intelligence addressed here is the hotly disputed contention—which, with important qualifications, I endorse—that cognitive abilities of human races have evolved in ways that differentiate them. In exploring this possibility, I have discussed work by Richard Herrnstein and Charles Murray as well as by J. Phillipe Rushton, who has summarized hundreds of studies that appear to support this conclusion. Though other scholars, such as Stephen Jay Gould, denounce their findings, so far as I am able to discern, they appear to have a firm foundation in these empirical studies.

While this aspect of my discussion may be discounted as politically incorrect, the subject is not political but scientific. Two questions demand differentiation, because the answer to one does not determine the answer to the other, namely:

(Q1) *What cognitive differences, if any, may distinguish the races?*; and,

(Q2) *If such differences exist, what attitude should we adopt toward them?*

The first is an empirical and scientific question, while the second is a moral and political question. Open and democratic societies should adopt public policies that benefit all of their citizens. But, absent such knowledge, which are those and how could we tell?

The range of alternatives extends from the pessimistic conception Herrnstein and Murray explore ("the custodial state") to the optimistic alternatives others have described (more enlightened options) that are discussed in the final chapter of this inquiry. There always remains the prospect that new hypotheses and new evidence may transform our understanding of the cognitive versatility not only of specific races but of the human species, as Richard Rothstein (2000) remarks. Indeed, recent research on the human genome has led some students of race to conclude that there is no genetic basis for distinctions between different races.

Natalie Angier (2000) has reported that the demise of a genetic basis for race has been endorsed by J. Craig Venter, the head of Celera Genomics Corporation, who suggests, "Race is a social concept, not a scientific one", where those traits often used to distinguish the races—such as skin and eye color, or the width of the nose—appear to be controlled by a relatively small number of genes. In a similar vein, Harold P. Freeman of North General Hospital in Manhattan, asserts, "If you ask what percentage of your genes is reflected in your external appearance, the basis by which we talk about race, the answer seems to be in the range .01 percent", which is a very small percentage of a person's genetic make-up.

But the existence of polygenic and of pleiotropic effects, where many genes interact to bring about single traits, on the one hand, or where single genes are responsible for many traits, on the other, hints that obituaries for race as a scientific category are probably premature. Human beings and chimpanzees share approximately ninety-eight percent of their chromosomes. That does not imply that significant differences between us do not exist. On the contrary, it indicates the importance of that two percent genetic difference. Genetic differences between the races of .01 percent or less may prove to be as important as they are subtle and complex.

The alteration of a single gene has been sufficient to change the sexual behavior of fruit flies from heterosexual to homosexual, which appears to be the first occasion where a single gene has been shown to control complex behaviors (Rosenthal 2005). Since female mammals possess two copies of the X chromosome while males possess one X and one Y chromosome, the X chromosome containing 1,098 genes and the Y only 78, it shouldn't be surprising if women display traits different from those of men across a broad spectrum of behavior. It may even turn out that Lawrence Summers, Harvard's President, was not actually mistaken in suggesting that there might be differences in aptitudes for science and mathematics between the sexes, but was targeted ideologically for advancing opinions regarded as being politically incorrect, because his critics knew no better.

A recent study has suggested that an unusual pattern of genetic diseases which occurs among Jews of central or northern European origin, called "Ashkenazim", may be an effect that accompanies natural selection for intellectual ability. While praising the scholarly qualities of the authors' research, Stephen Pinker has remarked that "It would be hard to overstate how politically incorrect this paper is" (Wade 2005). But surely empirical claims are properly appraised on the basis of logic and evidence, not by their capacity to conform to political preferences. On the basis of an investigation of ten categories of research, the latest review concludes that racial differences in IQ are as much as eighty percent genetic in character (Rushton and Jensen 2005). Political correctness, alas, can also exert a powerful negative influence upon the integrity of science, which may be more subtle than, but still has parallels with, that of religious fundamentalism.

Moreover, other studies substantiate the "out of Africa" hypothesis of the origins of *Homo sapiens*. Additional investigations of mitochondiral DNA substantiate the thesis that our species originated in Africa and dispersed across the continent to Europe and to Asia perhaps as recently as fifty thousand years ago (Donn 2000, Wade 2000). This work, based upon larger samples, reinforces earlier research that provided the foundation for concluding that the species had emerged from Africa less than two hundred thousand years ago, as this book explains. Traits that affect intelligence may be among those that were selected during the history of the species, even across an evolutionary past of fifty thousand years.

   The study of human differences is an important area of scientific inquiry, but we must be as tolerant of group differences as we are of individual differences. We cannot begin to understand the evolution of intelligence unless we possess a suitable conception of the nature of the mind and its origins in other species. While the computational conception has been shown to be mistaken, the conception of minds as semiotic systems appears to fare much better. Its broad scope and explanatory power are displayed relative to human beings and other animals as well as inanimate machines. And understanding the evolution of intelligence places us in a better position to appreciate where humans stand in the natural scheme of things and better able to promote our survival as a species.

   It also provides an indispensable foundation for understanding the nature of rationality. Once we understand the nature of rationality, we begin to appreciate that, as a transient property humans can be without and still remain members of the species, its emergence tends to depend upon the presence of conditions that are fortuitous, such as having reasonable and open-minded parents, benefiting from a broad education that develops critical thinking, and acquiring the strength of mind necessary to preserve independence of thought in a world increasingly dominated by the manipulation of information for political purposes. One of the most important reasons for studying the evolution of intelligence thus turns out to be that it can contribute to the exercise of our own rationality by providing us with a better-grounded understanding of our place as humans in a troubled world.

   The study of ethics, moreover, raises further important questions about relations between religion, evolution, and morality. The positions advanced in the pages of this book contend that religion alone cannot justify morality, but that morality transcends the boundaries of evolution as well. Neither religious-based morality nor evolutionary ethics are theoretically defensible conceptions, where the autonomy of morality offers a perspective from which the respective contributions of religion and of science may be more adequately understood and potentially reconciled. The study of science and its ramifications for public policies, however, suggests that commitments to theology that lie beyond any prospect of empirical testability should not be permitted to take precedence over scientific findings in relation to the determination of public policies.

   Ultimately, however, relations among ideas must also be reconciled with behavior among people. As Bertrand Russell observed long ago, probably more human beings have been slaughtered in the name of religion than have died from all other intentional causes. If we are to attain forms of organization that approximately something that might qualify as "the moral society", then we are going to have to practice forms of mutual respect and toleration for human diversity that have not been widely embraced in recent times. The moral society, which combines majority rule with minority rights, fulfills its destiny by embracing and defending freedom of religion and freedom of speech. The task may not be easy, but the goal is worthy. Our potential for doing the right thing depends upon it.

Acknowledgments

As in the case of most students of interdisciplinary subjects such as this one, my own intellectual debts are many and varied, including the books of authors who have made a special impact on my thinking. Throughout the chapters, in many important sections, I have discussed the work I have found to be especially valuable to the process in which I have been engaged of thinking things through. I envision research and scholarship on these subjects as a collaborative enterprise, where we have much to learn from each other. In the case of these books, I have made an effort to discuss their contents fairly explicitly so readers would have a clear idea of their contributions in contrast to my own. I have been unable to devise any more fair and open mode of acknowledgment.

It would be manifestly unjust, however, for me not to accent my intellectual indebtedness to two persons, one a colleague and one a student, who have had a profound impact upon the course of my thinking, albeit in very different ways. At New College of the University of South Florida, I enjoyed excellent colleagues and exceptional students. None of my colleagues had a more positive impact on the direction of my research than David Smillie, with whom I spent a summer's reading in the area of sociobiology and human behavior. The other was one of the most exceptional students of my career, Darwin Kurt Hoop, who displayed brilliance in thinking through conceptual and theoretical problems in this domain and from whom I may have learned at least as much as he has learned from me.

My interest in these problems is one of long standing. In my discussion of gene-culture co-evolutionary theory, I have drawn material from Fetzer 1985. On the nature of morality, I have drawn from Fetzer 1996b. On the nature of society, I have drawn from Fetzer 1998a. On the nature of mentality, I have drawn from Fetzer 1998b. I have also drawn from some lesser pieces of my own without specific attribution. Those who would like to pursue issues related to consciousness and cognition might want to explore my *Artificial Intelligence: Its Scope and Limits* (1990), *Philosophy and Cognitive Science* (second edition, 1996), or *Computers and Cognition: Why Minds Are Not Machines* (2001). Some may find the first too hard, the second too easy, and the third just right.

Chapter 3 includes material drawn from Appendix E, "Common Gorilla Vocalizations from Main Study Groups and Coco and Pucker, the Captive Juveniles," from *Gorillas in the Mist* by Dian Fossey. Copyright © by Dian Fossey. It is reprinted here by permission of Houghton Mifflin Company. All rights reserved. Chapter 4 includes two panels from "Cornish Game Clams: A False Start in Six Parts," from the book, *Two Guys Fooling Around with the Moon* by B. Kliban. Copyright © 1982 by B. Kliban. By kind permission of the Brentwood Funnies Company. All rights reserved. The Appendix, "Logical Reasoning and Domain Specificity: A Critique of the Social Exchange Theory of Reasoning," by Paul Sheldon Davies, James H. Fetzer, and Thomas R. Foster, first published in *Philosophy and Biology* (January 1995), pp. 1–37, appears by kind permission of Kluwer Academic Publishers. Copyright © 1995. All rights reserved.

PART I

Evolution and Cognition

1

Biology and Behavior

An evolutionary explanation for intelligence and mentality confronts profound problems, including accounting for the adaptive benefits of consciouness and cognition and their origins within biological species. If consciousness and cognition involved nothing more than experiencing colors, for example, as having certain intensities and hues, then the evolutionary explanation for their emergence would remain obscure. But if they are crucial components in acquiring information and beliefs about an agent's (or an organism's) environment, the evolutionary explanation for their emergence would become abundantly clear. Our beliefs have causal consequences for our behavior. We act on the basis of our beliefs and when they are true, our actions are, in those respects appropriately guided; when they are false, however, those actions may be inappropriate and misguided. The place to begin, accordingly, is with the character of mental states such as beliefs as properties of human beings.

Indeed, the property that links issues in the philosophy of psychology about beliefs with issues in the philosophy of biology is that some are true and others false. The fundamental distinction between "units" of selection and "levels" of selection matters here. The *units of selection* are that which is selected—that is, what is perpetuated during evolution—which appears to be individual genes as the transmissible entities underlying heritable traits. The *level of selection* concerns how those units are selected—especially, whether the causal mechanisms of selection operate exclusively upon individual organisms or perhaps upon larger entities, such as groups. While many prominent evolutionary theoreticians such as George Williams (1966), insist that selection operates exclusively at the level of individuals, others, such as David Sloan Wilson (1989) contend that some kinds of selection operate at higher levels.

The notion of level of selection is related in turn to a traditional distinction between "broad" and "narrow" conceptions of the content of mental states in the philosophy of psychology. Specifically, when *narrow content* is understood as consisting of (the content of) mental states with respect to their intensions, meaning, or sense, while *broad content* encompasses (the content of) those mental states with respect to their extensions, truth, or reference, the basic difference between actions and successful or unsuccessful actions becomes explicable. An agent may act on the basis of his beliefs, but his actions tend to succeed only when those beliefs are true. Even though any agent's *actions* must be based upon the narrow content of their mental states, the *success or failure* of those actions tends to depend on their broad content or their truth.

While I shall focus upon the explanation of human behavior as the most complicated and interesting, the consequences that follow from this analysis may apply to other species, especially those capable of *behavioral plasticity*, whose conspecifics can manifest specific behavioral tendencies that vary from organism to organism and from time to time as a function of their history and environment. While *genes* are principally responsible for an organism's innate cognitive capacity to acquire narrow content, *behavior* is primarily responsible for that organism's tendency to survive and reproduce. Organisms that have a propensity to acquire mental states that are appropriately related to the world, therefore, should possess obvious adaptive advantages. Though genes are thus the proper units of selection, behavior itself appears to be the appropriate level.

1.1 Behavior and Causation

In my book, *Philosophy and Cognitive Science* (1991/96) and elsewhere, I have suggested that a complete account of the kinds of factors that can affect human behavior should include motives, beliefs, ethics, abilities, capabilities, and opportunities. *Motives*, of course, might be biological or psychological in character, ranging from the need for food, shelter, and sex to the desire to be rich, famous, and exercise political power. *Beliefs* obviously include whatever we take to be the case, ranging from pedestrian beliefs about our own name, where we live and our social security number to theoretical beliefs about the nature and origin of the universe, the existence or non-existence of God, and everything in between. Although many discussions of human action focus on motives and beliefs as determinants of behavior, they are clearly incomplete.

The function of *ethics*, for example, is to exclude some behaviors as unacceptable on moral grounds, especially because they would cause harm or, in other ways, violate the rights of others. For most of us, the knowledge that money can be made robbing banks, counterfeiting credit cards, and trading in stolen merchandise does not influence our choice of careers, even though we aspire to make money. We thus tend to exclude those alternatives, not because they are ineffectual in securing that end, but because they violate (what we take to be) the rights of others. Those who are less scrupulous, of course, may not rob banks but manufacture unsafe products. A more complete account of human behavior thus has to take morality into account, too.

In ordinary conversational contexts, of course, we tend to take for granted that most persons have the ability to pursue their objectives, guided by their beliefs and consistent with their morals. That assumption, however, may be overridden when we discover, for example, that Eugenio did not understand the officer's warning when he ran the red light, because he knows no English; that Janice could not fix the flat tire, even though she knew how to use a jack, because she did not have a spare; or that Max was unable to call for help when the house caught fire, because the phone had gone dead. When we lack either the *ability* to perform an action or are *incapacitated* from performing that action—either because we lack the resources or are otherwise restrained—then we may find ourselves explaining why an act was not done rather than why it was.

Moreover, even when somebody has the ability to perform an action and is not physically incapacitated or morally inhibited from its pursuit, the success or failure of his actions tends to depend upon and vary with the completeness and accuracy of the beliefs upon which those actions are based. When Jim steps on the accelerator in order to pass a slower car, when Julia puts a cake in the oven to bake, and when Sarah answers questions on a physiology exam, each of them—we may assume—is guided by their beliefs about driving, cooking, and anatomy. When their beliefs are *true*, then their actions are, to that extent, at least, appropriately guided; when those beliefs are *false*, however, then their actions are, to that same extent, inappropriately guided. The effects of acting on those beliefs, even if false, however, may be no more serious than a lost point or a burnt cake.

On the other hand, of course, their consequences might be more serious. More than one motorist has died while trying to pass a slower car when a third automobile unexpectedly appeared before them, they lost control of their own vehicle, or other unanticipated factors intervened. Had they only known better, they might have endured a different fate. Their actions were brought about by the complex interaction of their motives, beliefs, ethics, abilities and capabilities. Thus, when our motives, abilities and capabilities are equal to the task, the consequences of our actions—their success or their failure—is then typically determined by the extent to which the situation in which we were in was the one we thought we were in, which in turn fixes our *opportunities*. Consider the case of predators and prey.

A hunter who wants to hit his target (motive) and who believes that his target is present (belief) and does not rule out firing at such a target on moral grounds (ethics) may hit his target only if his skills are equal to the task (ability) and his rifle and ammunition are available (capability). But success crucially depends on the presence of the target in the vicinity (opportunity), in the absence of which a hunter may have no chance to bag his prey at all. Indeed, speaking generally, it should be apparent that the *actions* we attempt are manifestations of the causal interaction of our motives, beliefs, ethics, abilities and capabilities, while the *success or failure* of our actions are manifestations of the causal interaction between our motives, beliefs, ethics, abilities, capabilities and opportunities—at least, when these events are brought about on purpose rather than merely by chance or luck!

That chance and luck often contribute to evolution has not escaped the notice of others. In a recent paper, "On Cognitive Luck: Externalism in an Evolutionary Frame" (Forthcoming a), for example, Ruth Garrett Millikan has observed that "the history of life is like a lottery," where, even though the vast majority of forms of life fail to survive and reproduce, nevertheless, some are bound to win "because so many bought tickets and there [are] so many different drawings". While it is perfectly appropriate to describe evolution as "a gamble with life", what I would add is that, as in life, there still can be no winners. She also affirms that, "Higher fitness lends only a higher *probability* of survival and reproduction", in relation to specific evolutionary contexts, with which I entirely agree. When she suggests there are no laws of evolution, only mechanisms, however, I must take exception.

When properly understood, the causal mechanisms that are the hard core of evolutionary theory include genetic mutation, sexual reproduction, genetic drift, and genetic engineering (as potential sources of genetic variety) and natural selection, sexual selection, group selection, and artificial selection (as mechanisms for separating between them). The causal processes of genetic mutation, sexual reproduction, and so on, qualify as the causal processes of evolutionary theory. Different versions of evolutionary theory may be distinguished on the basis of which subset of these mechanisms they take to be adequate to account for evolution. When these causal processes are applied to specific circumstances that obtain during the history of the world, historical evolutionary explanations result, where the set of events thereby described reflects the evolution of species.

The causal processes that define these causal mechanisms are (described by) the laws of evolution, which means that the laws of evolution tacitly correspond to those causal mechanisms. The presumption that there is a mutually exclusive disjunction between laws of evolution, on the one hand, and causal mechanisms, on the other, simply reflects misunderstanding about the nature of laws. Laws need not have infinite instances or many instances or even a few, when properly understood as logically contingent subjunctive conditionals that attribute dispositional properties (as single-case causal tendencies of variable strength) to everything possessing a corresponding reference property (Fetzer 1981, 1993). Indeed, the belief that there are no laws of evolution appears to be founded, at least in part, upon the popular view that species are not classes but individuals.

Millikan attributes the idea that species are "big, scattered, historical entities, enduring for longer or shorter periods though time" to Michael Ghiselin and to David Hull. Even if species are not "spatiotemporally unrestricted classes" within finitely many instances, however, they are not therefore *individuals* in some ontologically basic sense. Indeed, among the most fundamental laws of biology are those that relate genotypes Gi (where i ranges over $1, 2, \ldots$) to phenotypes Pi under the influence of environmental conditions EFi and that relate phenotypes Pj to behavioral tendencies BTj, under the environmental conditions EFj, which can be formalized by combining subjunctive conditionals ". . . $\Rightarrow$ ___" with (probabilistic) causal conditionals ". . $n\!\!\Rightarrow \Rightarrow$ ___" along the following lines:

Table 1.i Some Basic Laws of Evolutionary Theory

(L1) $(x)(t)[G1xt \Rightarrow (EF1xt = m \Rightarrow P1xt^*)]$

(L2) $(x)(t)[P1xt \Rightarrow (EF2xt = n \Rightarrow BT1xt^*)]$

---

where, for any genotype of kind $G1$ at time t, being exposed to environmental factors of kind $EF1$ would bring about (with strength m) its development into a phenotype of kind $P1$ at t^*; and, for any phenotype of kind $P1$ at time t, being exposed to environmental factors of kind $EF2$ in turn would bring about (with strength n) the development or acquisition of behavioral tendency $BT1$ at t^*; ..., the ranges of variation of which are "norms of reaction" (Sober 1984, p. 106). Indeed, if there were no such laws, there could be no science of biology.

The use of subjunctive and of causal conditionals (of universal or of probabilistic strength) becomes important in distinguishing merely accidental generalizations (as correlations) from genuine lawful relations, which may be simple or causal in kind. A non-definitional property A is a *permanent property* of R, when there is no process or procedure, natural or contrived, by means of which A could be taken away from something that is R without making it no longer R (Fetzer 1981, 1993). A property that could be taken away while that thing remained a thing of kind R is *transient*. Given the definition of a specific kind of thing, say, "gold" defined as whatever is made of an element with the atomic number 79, then the shape, the size, and the selling price of things that are gold are among their transient properties, while their melting points, boiling points, and specific gravity are not. This justifies the use of the subjunctive to assert, "If x were gold, then x would have a melting point of 1064° C", which would be true, while "If x were gold, then x would sell for $500 an ounce" would be false. And analogous considerations apply in contrasting correlations from causation.

   In his paper, "Rational Action" (1962), Carl G. Hempel observes that motives and beliefs are *epistemically interdependent*, insofar as testing for the values of variables of one of these kinds presupposes assuming values of the other. What we have discovered is that motives and beliefs are not the only variables whose values make a difference to behavior, where epistemic interdependence in Hempel's sense must extend across simultaneous values for motives, beliefs, ethics, abilities and capabilities (with respect to actions themselves) and opportunities (with respect to their success or failure). Consider, for example, the difference in possible values of variables of these kinds that could causally interact to produce as their effect a young man saying to a young woman, "I love you!", when they are on a date, when they are actors on a stage, and when they are in love.

   The interdependence of motive, belief, ethics, ability, and capability attributions has not been misunderstood by law enforcement officers across the U.S.A. In my neighboring state of Wisconsin, for example, more than one hunter has been brought before a judge charged with illegally firing a weapon from a vehicle as a consequence of a game warden's sting. Those entrusted with upholding the law in that vicinity have created tempting targets for hunters who are willing to employ illegal means to bag their prey in the form of stuffed dummy antlered deer, which are situated a few yards away from the highways at just the edge of the surrounding forests. When hunters stop in the road and take a shot, they are providing clear and convincing evidence that they possess the motives, beliefs, ethics, abilities and capabilities to perform actions of that kind.

   The notions of motive and belief as well as those of ability and capability, of course, are generalizable to other species. In his book, *The Evolution of Culture in Animals* (1980), for example, John Bonner reports that *E. coli* bacteria are able to detect the presence or absence of twenty different chemotactic substances, of which twelve are attractants and eight repellants. Specific receptor proteins located on the cell surface of these bacteria combine with these substances to bring about the rotation of their flagella, which move them toward or away from those substances. Assuming that *E. coli* are attracted to some substances because they are beneficial to them and repelled by others because they are detrimental, it makes sense, from an evolutionary point of view, to infer that *E. coli* have evolved these behavioral tendencies as adaptations that are still adaptive.

It may or may not make equally good sense, from a theoretical point of view, to attribute motives and beliefs to *E. coli* bacteria, even though their abilities and capabilities are not in serious doubt. When their environments are frozen or their flagella are removed, their responses to chemotactic substances are not the same. When "motives" are broadly construed as variables whose values determine the energy characteristics of organisms (intensity, persistence, and such) and "beliefs" as variables whose values determine the directional characteristics of organisms (regulating, organizing, and such), as Kurt Madsen (1960), among others, has proposed, then a distinction may be drawn between *motivation variables* understood as dynamogenic function variables and *cognitive variables* understood as directive function variables. In this case, even lowly bacteria can have motives and beliefs.

The possibility that bacteria might have motives and beliefs in some broad or technical sense, of course, does not imply that they possess mental states or have the capacity for cognition in narrower or stronger senses. It does suggest that at least one measure of the strength of a motive would be the frequency and intensity with which forms of behavior that tend to satisfy that motive are indulged, under suitable conditions, and that a comparable measure of the nature of a belief would be displays of behavior that are consonant with that belief, once again, under suitable conditions. Indeed, the conditions that are suitable for organisms whose behavior manifests the causal interaction of motives, beliefs, ethics, abilities and capabilities would be specific values for each of the other variables in relation to specific values of those very variables, an analysis that is broadly dispositional.

Thus, if we consider a complete set of specific values for each of the other variables that make a difference to behavior as a *context Ci* (where *i* ranges over 1, 2,. . . as diverse complete sets of specific values for those variables, which, as in the case of ethics, may be null), then what it means for an organism to be in a specific *motive state M1*, for example, would be the totality of differences to *response behavior of kinds R1, R2, . . .* that having this motive would make in varied contexts. When a person happens to be extremely thirsty, for example, they might walk out of a lecture to reach a nearby water fountain, even though, under normal circumstances, that is something they would not do; drink a glass of warm water, if that was the only thing available to drink, even though, under other circumstances, that is something they would not do; and so forth (cf., for example, Fetzer 1989, 1991).

1.2 The Matter of Meaning

Precisely the same pattern of analysis can be applied to specify the meaning, intension or sense of attributions of beliefs, ethics, abilities, and capabilities via this broadly dispositional approach, according to which factors of each of these kinds can best be understood on the basis of their causal influence on behavior. The meaning of a *specific belief B1*, for example, such as that I have fifty cents in my pocket, could then be explained using subjunctive and causal conditionals to stipulate the difference that that specific belief would make to my behavior:

Table 1.ii The Meaning of a Specific Belief

(D1) $(z)(t)[C1zt \Rightarrow (B1zt = m \Rightarrow R1zt^*)]$;

(D2) $(z)(t)[C2zt \Rightarrow (B1zt = n \Rightarrow R2zt^*)]$;

where, for any person z in context $C1$ at time t, having belief $B1$ would bring about (with strength m) response behavior of kind $R1$ at t^*; and in context $C2$,would bring about (with strength n) response behavior of kind $R2$ at t^*; ....

This broadly dispositional conception of the nature of meaning is motivated in large measure by *the problem of primitives*, which arises from the realization that units of language can be defined, explained, or otherwise understood on the basis of other units of language only if those other units are antecedently understood, which generates an infinite regress of previously understood units of language or circular definitions where antecedently understood units of language are used to define themselves. While Jerry Fodor has posited the existence of an innate "language of thought" that is both genetically determined and species-specific, he overlooks the possibility that primitive concepts might be acquired as non-linguistic dispositions of organisms and provide a foundation for learning a language without an innate language of thought (Fetzer 1989, 1991, 1991/96).

An account of the meaning of primitives in terms of their causal influence upon actual and potential behavior relative to different contexts suggests that different primitives that have the same causal influence upon actual and potential behavior relative to different contexts are causally eqipotent or equivalent in their meaning. The beliefs that you have *fifty cents* in your pocket and that you have *half-a-dollar* in your pocket would be causally equipotent for most if not all purposes relative to different contexts. But there are some with respect to which, say, having *two quarters* rather than *a fifty-cent piece* would make a difference. This approach supports the notion that analyticity in the sense of intersubstitutability *salva causalati* should be understood as a matter of degree, where similar considerations apply to motives, ethics, abilities, and capabilities.

The use of names and predicates to refer to individual things and specific properties allows the possibility of unique patterns of association between words and things that might vary from person to person and from time to time. It therefore permits *private languages*. In this respect, moreover, the account of meaning advocated here presupposes only that human beings are predisposed to acquire concepts to which words might be attached on the basis of (what turn out to be) *linguistic habits* rather than that human beings are disposed to have an innate mental language that does not vary from person to person or from time to time as a matter of *natural law* (Fetzer 1991). Indeed, among the reasons for preferring the present theory over Fodor's account is that mine makes unsuccessful translations between languages a theoretical possibility.

Even less appealing theories of meaning than Fodor's have arisen from what are known as *causal theories of reference*, according to which meanings are not really in the head, as it were, but rather in the external world, where intensions are specified by extensions, senses by reference, and so forth. The general idea is that meanings are dependent upon causal connections to the things for which words stand, such as thoughts of apple trees being causally dependent on apple trees. When thoughts of apple trees are taken to be *apple-tree-thought-tokens* and apple trees are taken to be *apple-tree-token-things*, this approach contends that what apple-tree-thought-tokens are properly understood to mean must be traced back to apple-tree-token-things to which they have been related causally by users of those thought-tokens by means of historical-causal linguistic chains.

Although this approach has been promoted and endorsed by Hillary Putnam, Saul Kripke, and others, there appear to be infinitely many notions for which there are thought-tokens that cannot possibly stand in causal connections to token-things for which they stand. These include *non-existent things* (such as werewolves or vampires, in the case of predicates; and Santa Claus or Mary Poppins, in the case of names), *abstract properties* (such as pi and the square root of -1), *theoretical properties* (such as gravitational attractions and electric currents), *non-observable properties* (such as conductivity and malleability, not to mention motives and beliefs). None of these token-things stands in any obvious causal relation to its thought-token, which suggests that this approach is rooted in confusion between intensions and extensions, sense and reference (Fetzer 1991/96).

The difference between broad and narrow content becomes readily apparent from this point of view. For a person who happened to be very thirsty and who observed a cold glass of a clear liquid might drink it down with a flourish, only to discover he had polished off a shaker of martinis by mistake. The action that he had attempted—of drinking a glass of ice-cold water—was not the one that he achieved. Thus, if we want to explain what he did and why, we must acknowledge an explanatory ambiguity, since an adequate explanation of why he drank *the cold glass of clear liquid* (believing by mistake that it was ice-cold water) is not going to coincide with an adequate explanation of why he drank *the shaker of martinis* (believing by mistake that a cold glass of clear liquid was a glass of ice-cold water). The latter explanation requires at least one additional premise.

The difference between what our actions are intended to achieve and what they may or may not achieve—their success or failure—reflects precisely the difference between narrow-based and broad-based conceptions of content. If we want to explain our successes and failures in coping with the world, we have to include those properties of the world that contributed to those successes, when we did succeed, and those failures, when we did not. Indeed, strictly speaking, a complete explanation for those successes and failures would not only have to account for our mistake in taking a cold glass of clear liquid to be a glass of ice-cold water but for our success in taking a thing to be a cold glass of clear liquid to begin with. The abilities and capacities that contribute to our successes and failures in coping with the world include perceptual as well as inferential ones.

The difference between broad and narrow content can be displayed even with respect to *E. coli* bacteria. It appears reasonable to infer that the explanation for the acquisition of the *E. coli*'s tendency to avoid eight chemotactic substances and to encounter twelve others qualifies as an *adaptation*, understood as a characteristic, property, or tendency that has proven beneficial in the past. Thus, the evolutionary situation appears to have been as follows. *E. coli* bacteria collectively have minor genetic variations, which give rise to minor phenotypic or behavioral variations. While initial encounters with different chemotactic substances in their environments may have occurred more or less in a random fashion, those encountering toxic substances were harmed, while those encountering nutrients thereby benefited. The subpopulation tending to avoid toxic substances and to encounter nutrients thus enhanced its prospects for survival and reproduction.

The evolution of the tendency to avoid toxic substances and to encounter nutrients thereby spread within the gene pool of *E. coli* bacteria because it had conferred adaptive benefits upon them in the past. But adaptations that have been adaptive in enhancing prospects for survival and reproduction in the past may ormay not remain adaptive in the future. Suppose, hypothetically, that the chemotactic substances that have been harmful in the past were to become beneficial and that the chemotactic substances that have been beneficial in the past were to become harmful. Then a previously adaptive adaptation would become maladaptive. Presumably, enough genetic variation would remain in the gene pool to permit evolution to bring about a corresponding change in future gene pools, which might occur fast enough for *E. coli* to survive rather than become extinct.

The conclusion these examples ought to bring home is that the behavior of bacteria, like that of human beings, is brought about by the interaction of specific values of motivational dynamogenic function variables and specific values of cognitive directive function variables. The motivational variables in both instances are broadly biological (in quenching thirst, for the human being; in avoiding toxicity and deriving nutrients, for *E. coli* bacteria). And even their cognitive variables, however different they may be in functional complexity, are surprisingly similar, since *E. coli* bacteria use specific receptor proteins at the bacterial cell surface to detect the presence of these substances as a primitive form of perception, where adaptations themselves function as a form of memory, while human beings use different forms of perception and memory—and inferences based on them—to fix the values of their cognitive variables.

No doubt, some of the similarities displayed by these examples are coincidental rather than invariable features, where the range of factors that affect the behavior of human beings is vastly larger and more complex, especially when alternative psychological motivations are taken into account, than is that for *E. coli* bacteria. From the perspective of the distinction between "broad" and "narrow" content, however, the striking feature appears to be the same, namely: that organisms of both kinds act on the basis of *expectations*, which are determined by the values of variables of internal states of the organisms. When motives and beliefs are properly understood as dynamogenic function variables and as directive function variables, it becomes apparent that *actions* are determined by the complex interaction of the internal states of organisms.

Since actions are determined by internal states of organisms, including beliefs understood as directive function variables, but tend to succeed or fail depending upon whether or not they are appropriate in relation to properties of the external world that affect their success or failure, the problem that confronts organisms of every species appears to be that of maintaining beliefs as directive function variables whose values stand in appropriate relations to the external world. The problem might have an evolutionary solution were it the case that the values of beliefs as directive function variables always track the values of corresponding environmental variables, such that beliefs as directive function variables were invariably appropriate in relation to those properties of the external world that affect the success or failure of an organism's actions.

But adaptations that have been adaptive in the past may or may not remain adaptive in the future, due to change. Indeed, within philosophy, the problem of anticipating the course of the future on the basis of information concerning the past is referred to as *the problem of induction*. We know that the future will not be like the past in every respect and that it will be like the past in at least some respects. If we assume that the future should be like the past in *every* respect, therefore, our expectation will be false. If we assume that the future should be like the past in *some* respects, however, our expectation will be trivial, unless we happen to know in which specific respects the world will or will not change. What we want to know are the respects in which the world will and will not change which make a difference to survival and reproduction.

The causal mechanisms that evolution has produced to cope with the problem of induction are those implicit in the cognitive capacities of various species. In his book, *Darwin Machines and the Nature of Knowledge* (1994), for example, Henry Plotkin has identified three capacities that nature has produced, namely: *the primary heuristic* of the biological process of genetic-developmental change through evolution by selection; *the secondary heuristic* of the immune system and intelligence that compensates for many shortcomings in dealing with rapid chemical changes and rapid physical changes; and *the tertiary heuristic* of culture that compensates for even more rapid forms of change than individual intelligence can handle. Species possessed of immune systems and intelligence, not to mention culture, thus may cope with problems that other species cannot.

Plotkin's scheme supports the realization that the evolutionary strategies of various species may be strongly affected by their respective cognitive abilities. Species whose members display the same behavior under the same conditions independently of their histories and experience are largely limited to the first heuristic of genetic-developmental change through evolution. Those with the capacity for variable behavior under the same conditions as a function of their histories and experience—under the influence of classic, operant, or other forms of conditioning—may be capable of benefiting from the second. And those with the capacity for teaching and learning from each other's history and experience—especially those who have some collective capacity for storing, processing, and transmitting information about the past—may benefit even more from the third.

The question is largely a matter of behavioral plasticity. Species such as *E. coli* bacteria are essentially constrained to coping with change on the basis of the primary heuristic, because their behavior does not appear to be influenced by classic, operant, or other forms of conditioning, for example, whereby *E. coli* might learn from experience. In the absence of changes in individual bacteria induced by their personal histories, therefore, biological evolution seems to be the principal if not exclusive causal mechanism that can bring about change in *E. coli* behavior. The case of human beings appears to be quite different, however, since we are not only capable of learning from our own experiences but also from the experience of others, which might be transmitted to us by means of teaching and learning via lectures, books, and other modes of communication.

Behavioral plasticity appears to depend upon cognitive versatility, insofar as organisms with greater cognitive capacities ought to be more competent at insuring that their beliefs as directive function variables are appropriate to guide their behavior in pursuing their motives as dynamogenic function variables than those with lesser cognitive capacities. The resources at our disposal include our capacity for imagination and conjecture, our ability to use language and other modes of communication, our deductive and inductive reasoning ability, and the information we are able to derive about the world on the basis of observation, experimentation and measurement. The strength and variety of the cognitive capacities possessed by human beings may be our most important difference from other forms of life, even if, relative to higher primates, this difference is merely a matter of degree.

In her paper, "The Mind and Its Ecological Niche, Its Language Community" (Forthcoming b), Ruth Millikan has correctly observed that we cannot expect (what she refers to as) *cognitive systems* to be infallible and never make mistakes, that is:

> . . . it is helpful to keep clearly in focus what the cognitive systems are for. Their mission is not, for example, the acquisition of justified certainty. As modern skeptics are aware, no one lives by justified certainty. (C)ognitive systems are not at fault or malfunctioning when they take risks, when they rely, as they must, on environmental statistics rather than on certainties.

Millikan thus suggests that reliance upon many different fallible methods for various cognitive activities—such as recognizing the same person, the same property, the same species, the same disease—where one method can be used under some conditions, while others can be used under others—is "the strategy that gets us by".

Or doesn't! Indeed, as Millikan herself repeatedly observes, the typical outcome of evolutionary processes is *not* the survival of a species but its extinction. Plotkin even estimates that ninety-eight percent of species ever to have evolved no longer exist. Since the conditions for successful cognition arise from causal interactions with the environment, we may count upon our "cognitive luck", as Millikan suggests, and hope we find ourselves within a "co-operative environment". But we might be able to do better. The strategies that have got us by in the past may or may not be the strategies that can get us by in the future. What naturalized theories of content and cognition do not provide are resources necessary for the consideration and evaluation of alternative cognitive strategies to determine whether or not we should adopt more efficient, effective, and reliable cognitive methods.

The relationship between naturalized theories of content and cognition and normative epistemology thus comes to this. Naturalized theories attempt to explore the cognitive methods that biological evolution has produced as cognitive dispositions and predispositions of organisms which belong to different species. Normative epistemology, by contrast, attempts to discover means and methods that are capable of attaining specific cognitive objectives, whether or not those strategies are ones that nature has produced. When it succeeds, the naturalistic approach provides a *description* of where we stand as an evolved species with respect to the cognitive strategies that we happen to presently employ. When it succeeds, the normative approach provides a *prescription* of where we ought to stand as a species with respect to cognitive strategies that we should employ if we want to enhance our prospects for reproduction and survival as a species.

Nothing about normative epistemology affords any guarantee that methods are available that guarantee success in attaining cognitive objectives. What we take to be the truth may not be the truth, and there are no infallible strategies. However, by exploiting the resources that normative epistemology can supply, it may be possible to better understand where we stand in relation to our evolutionary history. What we need in order to pursue this objective will include higher-order methods for evaluating the efficiency, effectiveness and reliability of various lower-order methods, which may be based upon their relative-frequency of success in attaining cognitive objectives. These success relative-frequencies, in turn, provide an evidential foundation for drawing inferences about the reliability of various methods as propensities of cognitive systems.

1.3 Cognitive Strategies

The place to begin, no doubt, is with the possibility that there might be infallible methods. If there were, after all, surely we would want to employ them. We therefore need to understand what an infallible method or cognitive strategy would be and why it does not appear to be available. In his book, *Philosophical Explanations* (1981), Robert Nozick considers principles such as these that capture species of cognitive infallibility:

Table 1.iii Two Principles of Logical Omniscience

(P1) If p were true, then z would believe p;

(P2) If p were false, then z would not believe p.

These principles describe (what might be referred to as) *logical omniscience,* insofar as they imply the possibility of the direct acquisition of true beliefs unmediated by any method of discovery. In this sense, it is a simple theory.

Several comments qualify the conception of logical omniscience thereby described. The first is that the distinction between (P1) and (P2) seems to be appropriate, insofar as, if z were to believe *everything*—of every p and its negation, $\sim p$, that it is true—then it would be the case that, if p were true, z would believe p; but, of course, that would be trivial, since z would also believe $\sim p$. Similarly, if z were to believe *nothing*—of every p and its negation, $\sim p$, z would believe neither—then it would be the case that, if p were false, z would not believe p. The problem is to believe all and only those things that are true, if possible. But principles such as these also imply the ability —the inevitability—of possessing true beliefs about the origin of the universe, the existence of God, and such, *automatically*—merely because they are true!

Since different people hold different beliefs about the origin of the universe, the existence of God, and so forth, it cannot be the case that everyone is possessed of logical omniscience, since otherwise their beliefs would have to be consistent as a necessary condition of their collective truth. It should therefore be obvious that truth is not solely a function of simplicity, insofar as at least one simple theory is false. Not the least of the problems confronting this approach, moreover, is the failure to distinguish between truths that reflect *relations between ideas* (which are more or less "analytic" in the traditional sense) and those that reflect *matters of fact* (which are more or less "synthetic", in the traditional sense). The properties of methodologies which might be appropriate to different kinds of true belief make a difference here.

Consider, for example, some alternative principles that are relative to the adoption of a specific methodology *SM* in application to this problem, namely:

Table 1.iv Two Principles of Methodological Infallibility

(P3) $p \Rightarrow [SMzt \Rightarrow B(p)zt^*]$;

(P4) $\sim p \Rightarrow [SMzt \Rightarrow B(\sim p)zt^*]$;

where, according to (P3), if *p* were true, then if *z* were to use method *SM*, then *z* would believe that *p*; and, according to (P4), if *p* were false, then if *z* were to use method *SM*, then *z* would believe that ~*p*. Even given a distinction between analytic and synthetic knowledge, the strongest methods that might be employed would be deductive reasoning applied to premises that are true by stipulation (as a matter of meaning or not does not matter here). The history of mathematics, however, suggests that even the most interesting theorems—such as Fermat's Last—do not satisfy this conception.

Neither logical omniscience nor methodological infallibility appear to be defensible conceptions that might apply to cognitive agents, human or otherwise. On the principle that *ought implies can*, which applies within epistemic and cognitive contexts as well as within ethical and moral ones, it would be unjustifiable to maintain that cognitive agents should aspire to logical omniscience or methodological infallibility. The more modest— and more appropriate—approach would be to consider methods for the acquisition of beliefs that are available to cognitive agents rather than those that are incapable of realization. Here some obvious alternatives include obser-vation, memory, and testimony as potential sources of justified belief. The problem becomes that of evaluating their respective degrees of reliability.

The manner in which this might be done would be to conduct empirical tests, under controlled conditions, to measure the relative frequency with which beliefs acquired by means of these methods happen to be true. Thus, calculate the relative frequency for the successful use of each such method:

Table 1. v   Comparisons of Relative Frequency of Method Success

---

(SM1)   Observation: # observe *p* & *p* / # observe $p = m1/n1 \ggg 0$

(SM2)   Memory: # remember *p* & *p* / # remember $p = m2/n2 \gg 0$

(SM3)   Testimony: # testimony *p* & *p* / # testimony $p = m3/n3 > 0$

---

where the relative frequency with which the method (observation, memory, testimony) yields *p* when *p* is the case relative to applications of each method produces a measure of their relative degrees of reliability, where I have made the empirical assumption that observation is more reliable than memory, and so forth.

The justification for supposing that observation is more reliable than memory and that memory is more reliable than testimony depends upon the causal connection between them, where observations do not depend upon memory or testimony, memories depend upon observation but not upon testimony, and tes-timony depends upon both observation and memory. Indeed, it turns out that observation proves highly reliable. According to recent studies, eyewitnesses are as much as ninety-eight percent complete and ninety-eight percent accurate in reporting their observations when what they are observing appears to them to be significant (Marshall *et al.* 1971). It qualifies as common knowledge, moreover, that memories tend to be less reliable with the passage of time and that testimony is all too often affected by causal factors that tend to bring about deviations from the truth.

Information about the relative frequencies of successful application of various methodologies not only provides a basis for evaluating their relative reliability in the past but also affords a foundation for drawing inferences about the reliability of the cognitive mechanisms that produce them. In general, if these relative frequencies prove to be stable relative frequencies that remain relatively constant across large numbers of tests under a wide variety of test conditions, it would then become appropriate to infer that these relative frequencies are manifestations of the cognitive propensities of the cognitive systems that produced them. Thus, if the success ratio of observation is $m1/n1$, it would be appropriate to infer that the success propensity for observation is $m1/n1$, and so forth, assuming data acquired under suitable test conditions.

With regard to higher-order cognitive strategies, the situation becomes one in which the exercise of rational criticism appears to be even more important than empirical tests to epistemic evaluations of alternative methodologies. With respect to the discovery of *natural laws*, for example, at least three methodologies qualify as alternatives: Inductivism, Deductivism, and Abductivism. The issue that arises within this context thus becomes whether one of these is a more efficient, effective, or reliable method for attaining that objective. The methodology known as *Inductivism*, which is widely popular, assumes science is a process that proceeds in four stages of Observation, Classification, Generalization, and Prediction. Mere observation, unconstrained by specific hypotheses, however, tends to produce scientifically insignificant findings (Hempel 1966).

The fact that many textbooks in scientific disciplines endorse this conception does not help. Inductivism is founded upon a specific rule of inference, known as *induction by enumeration* (IE) but it is also referred to as "the straight rule":

(IE) From "*m/n* observed *R*s are *A*s" infer (inductively) "*m/n R*s are *A*s", assuming that a suitable number have been observed over varied conditions.

This rule, unfortunately, suffers from serious defects. Because its application depends on the existence of both observable reference properties and observable attributes, it cannot be applied to theoretical properties (including gravitational attractions and electric currents) or non-observable properties (such as conductivity and malleability, not to mention motives and beliefs). Indeed, if there is more to causation than mere correlation, then (IE) cannot possibly provide a suitable logical foundation for inferences to law (Fetzer 1981, 1993).

The methodology known as Deductivism, by contrast, appears to be capable of overcoming some of the most important objections that Inductivism encounters. *Deductivism* likewise assumes that science is a process that proceeds in four stages, which in this case are Conjecture, Derivation, Experimentation, and Elimination. Insofar as Conjectures are not restricted to observational language alone, they may be formulated by means of theoretical and non-observable properties which have proven to be of enormous importance during the history of science. Classical mechanics, quantum mechanics, and special and general relativity are but four examples of scientific theories that Deductivism would permit but that Inductivism would prohibit. Moreover, Deductivism allows for conjectures that are causal, even if causation involves more than correlation (Fetzer 1981, 1993).

The rule of inference on which Deductivism is founded is *modus tollens* (MT):

(MT)   From "hypothesis h entails e" and "not-e", infer (deductively) "not-h".

That the logical relation between the theory h and its consequence e is deductive, where e must be true if h is true, does not undermine the fallibility that attends the employment of the rule (MT), precisely because the evidence on which the inference that e is false is based might be in error. It would therefore be wrong to assume that applications of Deductivism guarantee true beliefs (Popper 1963).

But while Deductivism enables us to draw justified conclusions about which of the available alternatives ought to be rejected as false, it does not—apart from the class of hypotheses we have yet to reject—tell us which we ought to accept! In that respect, it provides a negative solution but not a positive solution to the cognitive problem of establishing the values of directive function variables that are essential for appropriate actions. In this respect, therefore, Abductivism appears to provide a highly desirable methodological alternative, since it provides for the acceptance as well as the rejection of hypotheses and theories. According to Abductivism, science is once again a process proceeding in four stages, but now those of Puzzlement, Speculation,

Adaptation, and Explanation, where the stage of Adaptation incorporates the principles of Deductivism among its basic elements.

And Abductivism is based on *inference to the best explanation* (IBE), namely:

(IBE)   The alternative *h* that provides the best explanation for the available evidence *e* is the preferable hypothesis; and when the available evidence *e* is sufficient, the preferable hypothesis *h* is acceptable. Thus, under those conditions, infer (inductively) that *h* is true.

The conditions that must be satisfied for a hypothesis to qualify as a possible explanation for the available evidence *exclude* non-scientific hypotheses from consideration, but cannot be guaranteed to *include* every scientific possibility. (IBE) must therefore be regarded as a fallible methodology. Nevertheless, for the purpose of making inferences about laws of nature, it is the most efficient, effective, and reliable among the available methodologies (Fetzer 1981, 1993).

Evidently, different methodologies can be appraised by means of different methodologies, where the relative reliability of observation, memory and testimony were appraised on the basis of their relative frequency of successful employment based upon *empirical procedures*, while the relative reliability of the scientific methodologies of Inductivism, Deductivism, and Abductivism were evaluated on the basis of their theoretical potential for successful employment based upon *rational criticism*. On the basis of (what appear to be) their differing degrees of reliability as ordinary methodologies, it appears justifiable to infer that, in cases where their results conflict, observational findings should take precedence over remembrances of things past and remembrances of things past should take precedence over the recollections advanced by means of testimony.

On the basis of (what likewise appear to be) their differing degrees of reliability as scientific methodologies, moreover, it appears justifiable to infer that, whenever possible, the conclusions of scientific inquires ought to be based upon the methods of Abductivism rather than those of Deductivism or of Inductivism. Indeed, these findings reflect the more general consideration that, in the process of forming subjective expectations about the future on the basis of experience of the past, knowledge of *causal propensities* established by means of (IBE) should take precedence over knowledge of *relative frequencies* that is based upon (EI). Subjective expectations (or degrees of conviction) should be based on knowledge of causal propensities whenever possible. Subjective expectations that are not based on frequencies or propensities do not qualify as forms of rational belief.

Rationality of belief becomes especially important to higher species of organisms in permitting them to subject potential actions to rational criticism before they undertake them. In this sense, we are able to formulate hypotheses and theories on the basis of which we might act and kill them instead of ourselves, as Popper often emphasized (Popper 1978). When we embrace the method of *Inference to the Best Explanation*, for example, we acquire the disposition IBE, given evidence E at time t, to accept beliefs Bi (i ranges over 1, 2, ...) at t^*:

Table 1. vi   Cognitive Strategy IBE

(IBE1) $(z)(t)[IBEzt \Rightarrow (E1zt = m \Rightarrow B1zt^*)];$

(IBE2) $(z)(t)[IBEzt \Rightarrow (E2zt = n \Rightarrow B2zt^*)];$

We thereby adopt a cognitive strategy that promotes our prospects for survival and reproduction by establishing appropriate values for the beliefs we act upon.

Human beings, of course, are among the species that have the cognitive flexibility to embrace alternative strategies on the basis of their degree of empirical success or on the basis of how well they withstand rational criticism. A phenotype of the kind *Homo sapiens HSi* at time t might thus be such that exposure to environmental conditions of kind *EFj* (including lecture courses with specific assigned readings and in-class exams) could thereby induce disposition *IBE* at t^*:

Table 1. vii   Acquiring Cognitive Strategy IBE

(L3) $(z)(t)[HS3zt \Rightarrow (EF3zt = m \Rightarrow IBEzt^*)];$

(L4) $(z)(t)[HS3zt \Rightarrow (EF4zt = n \Rightarrow IBEzt^*)];$

He would thereby acquire the adaptive advantages that attend forming beliefs on the basis of methods of reasoning that transcend those otherwise available, which in turn maximize the rational expectation for the success of his actions.

These considerations shed light on the underlying problem of the units and the levels of selection, which possesses several dimensions. The first is that selecting which organisms survive and reproduce might be regarded as a function of genotype, phenotype, or behavior. Strictly speaking, however, genotypes Gi give rise to phenotypes Pi as (ordinarily unique) temporary organisms, whose adaptive fitness depends on their potential for successful interaction with their environment. As George C. Williams has observed, the fitness of most organisms rapidly moves toward zero, where environmental pressures overcome them, causing them to succumb (William 1992). What successful sexually reproducing organisms pass along to offspring, therefore, cannot be their unique genotypes and phenotypes, but specific sets of genes.

If genes are the units of selection as what is passed along during selection, however, the level at which selection itself occurs is not thereby determined. For species for which *the same* behavioral tendencies are properties of every member who possesses a similar phenotype, as in the case of bacteria, it may not be impermissible to consider the *phenotype* as the level at which selection occurs. For those species whose behavioral tendencies can vary from member to member even when they possess similar phenotypes, however, as in the case of human beings, *behavior* seems to be the level at which selection occurs. Indeed, the very existence of behavioral plasticity demonstrates that phenotypic properties alone do not determine success or failure. Acknowledging behavior as the level of selection yields a more suitable uniform standard across species.

The difference between broad and narrow content thus appears to have led us to consider the difference between rationality of action and rationality of belief, between behavioral plasticity and cognitive flexibility, and between naturalistic cognition and normative epistemology. The success of our actions, at the first level of explanation, appears to be explainable on the basis of the extent to which the situation we were in was the situation we took ourselves to be in as a matter of the opportunities that we actually confronted. At the second level of explanation, however, the situation we took ourselves to be in arose as a function of the cognitive strategies we employed in processing the information available. Whether or not we might have done better appears to be explainable in turn by exploiting the resources of normative epistemology.

Although languages can be private—and, to some extent, they always are—there are adaptive advantages to *public languages* that become obvious upon reflection. When different members of a community can speak the same language with the same intensions, meaning, and sense, they thereby contribute to enhancing their prospects for successful communication. The adaptive advantages of successful communication in turn represent (what may well be) the most important example of collective adaptation that evolution has ever produced, because successful communication promotes co-operation between conspecifics and co-operation between conspecifics promotes the attainment of shared objectives and goals. Those with the capacity to teach and learn from one another by means of language thus derive benefits that culture can confer.

Perhaps the greatest advantage of human beings over other species is that we have the capacity to exercise our rational faculties and to evaluate and improve upon our language, our theories, and our methods. Whether or not we are able to alter our motives (as values of dynamogenic function variables), we are capable of changing our beliefs (as values of directive function variables) and thereby potentially enhancing our prospects for survival and reproduction. The difference between human beings and other animals, especially the higher primates, may be a matter of degree, but it seems to be a difference of degree that properly qualifies as a difference in kind. We have behavioral plasticity, at least in large measure, because we have cognitive versatility. And we can exploit our cognitive versatility by taking advantage of our rational faculties.

Species whose members lack behavioral plasticity and cognitive versatility, of course, are creatures whose behavior remains completely under the control of the process of evolution. We, however, have the prospect of being able to influence the course that it will take. But that requires knowledge. To explain and to predict the behavior of organisms, we need to know not only laws that relate genotypes to phenotypes and to behavior (in the case of instincts), but that relate experience to behavior (in the case of conditioning), and beliefs to behavior (in the case of rationality). Knowledge of nature holds the key to our success. We need epistemology to understand biology even more than we need biology to understand epistemology. We have the chance to minimize luck as a factor in cognition, action, and evolution, which may be our greatest advantage and most important difference from bacteria.

2

Animal Mentality

No one has contributed more to the study of animal mentality, consciousness and cognition than Donald Griffin, whose work on this subject—including *Animal Thinking* (1984) and *Animal Minds* (1992)—virtually defines the field. The problem that confronts this discipline is the existence of the phenomena to which its investigations are directed. Different views about the existence of animal mind extend from the "common-sense" opinion (that animals think about their behavior and deliberate over their options) to the "behavioristic" position (that mental phenomena are no more than epiphenomena that may be correlated with but do not causally influence behavior). The range of views that have been advanced about the existence of animal mentality has therefore been very broad, indeed.

Thus, if behaviorism were correct, then there could be no science of *cognitive ethology*, understood as the analysis of the cognitive processes that affect the behavior of non-human animals, because cognitive processes do not affect the behavior of human or of non-human animals. And if mentality, consciousness or cognition does make a difference to behavior, then *behaviorism*, understood as the analysis of behavior strictly on the basis of the public properties of organisms and their environments (including their histories of reinforcement), has to be misconceived, insofar as cognitive variables lie beyond its scope. In his efforts to resolve this difficulty, Griffin provides numerous case studies that provide empirical support for the existence of the phenomena basic to this discipline.

The range and variety of behaviors Griffin describes provides grounds for inferring that the underlying problems that confront cognitive ethology are not empirical but are instead conceptual and methodological. Griffin—along with many other contributors to this field—varies between the *Cartesian paradigm* (according to which self-awareness is the criterion of mentality and introspection is the appropriate methodology) and the *computational conception* (according to which mentality is reducible to the manipulation of symbols for which written and verbal behavior provide suitable access). While Griffin supports the conclusion that animals may possess at least two kinds of consciousness, his conception of the nature of mentality remains unclear.

Griffin's distinction between *perceptual consciousness* (understood as the state or process of being aware of something) and *reflective consciousness* (understood as the state of awareness of one's own awareness) is a valuable contribution, but his work does not provide a definition of "mentality" that could be applied to humans, to other animals, and even to machines, if such a thing is possible. The purpose of this chapter and following, therefore, will be to explore the prospect of moving beyond the Cartesian paradigm and the computational conception in search of a more adequate theory of mind. The view that emerges from these reflections is that the conception of minds as *semiotic (or "sign-using") systems* affords a framework of this kind. Before introducing that approach, we shall consider further research in this domain.

2.1   Do Animals Have Minds?

In her remarkable work, *Through Our Eyes Only?* (Dawkins 1993), for example, Marian Stamp Dawkins advances a valuable study of the nature and existence of animal mind that both clarifies and illuminates relevant work. Perhaps no other issue in animal ethology has created as much controversy or generated as much disagreement as has this. With the appearance of this study, however, most of that controversy should subside and most of that disagreement disappear, where those who continue to deny the existence of animal mind are now seen to support a cause that is lost.

Dawkins has not only written an immensely readable study that ought to have appeal far beyond the bounds of academia, but has also produced an important synthesis of recent research on this problem that deserves to be taken seriously by everyone who is interested in cognition. While she mentions two specific groups as her intended audience—namely, those who reject the existence of any but human mentality and those who accept the existence of animal mentality as obvious—her potential audience encompasses most philosophers, psychologists, biologists, and ethologists.

Dawkins appears to appreciate what unreflective thinkers tend to overlook—namely, that without committing ourselves to some account of mind, we do not know what we are accepting or rejecting when we take a stand on either side. If we reject the existence of *non*-human kinds of mentality, for example, yet accept the existence of *human* mentality, what are we denying to other forms of life that we are ascribing to ourselves? Surely the first lesson of a scientific education is that we must understand the meaning of a hypothesis before we can subject it to test and accept or reject it.

The apparent hazard of any alternative approach is that literally we do not know what we are talking about. It can happen, however, that we, at least initially, only vaguely and incompletely understand the phenomenon that interests us, which arises when dealing with *consciousness*. Dawkins thus surveys (what she takes to be) varieties of consciousness that range from sensation and perception to recollection and abstract thinking, but confines herself (for the time being) to the conception of "consciousness" as *immediate awareness*, avoiding premature definitional commitments.

As Dawkins observes, the existence of consciousness even has ramifications for morality. If things that are conscious are things that deserve to be treated with respect, for example, then if non-human animals are also things that are conscious, then they deserve to be treated with respect. If non-human animals are not conscious, "then possibly we can get on with our meals and eradicate pests and do all sorts of things to them without being disturbed by the moral issues that might trouble us if we thought they were" (Dawkins 1993, p. 6). So the question has a moral dimension.

Even more strikingly, however, consciousness also poses a problem of explanation from the perspective of evolution. Since it exists, it must be either an *adaptation*, which has provided adaptive benefits in the past, or an *exaptation*, whose presence has to be accounted for on non-adaptive grounds. Virtually every adaptive benefit that consciousness can be supposed to confer, such as learning to avoid bodily damage, however, might instead have been secured by non-conscious organisms or even by programmed machines. The rationale for its existence is therefore obscure.

Dawkins acknowledges two properties of (even human) consciousness that appear to make it scientifically problematic. One is that it is an *essentially private* phenomenon: what goes on inside of your head is not something to which anyone else has access. The other is that it is therefore impossible for anyone to possess *certain knowledge* about conscious phenomena—at least, in the case of anyone other than myself! The first seems to be an ontic (or ontological) property of consciousness as a special kind of being, the second an epistemic (or epistemological) consequence thereof.

The ascription of these properties to consciousness has a history that dates at least from the work of Descartes, but longevity does not imply validity. The privacy of consciousness may preclude others from *direct* access but it does not prevent *indirect* access: we typically draw inferences about the mental and emotional states of others based upon our observations of their speech and bodily behavior. And the absence of *certain* knowledge is compatible with the presence of *uncertain* knowledge: scientific knowledge is characteristically inductive and uncertain.

The Cartesian paradigm, according to which beliefs must be certain to qualify as knowledge, could be sustained only if *knowledge* were limited to what can be deduced from premises that are syntactical or semantical truths, which would preclude the possibility of any empirical knowledge. Indeed, Descartes's position was even less defensible, because he interpreted "certainty" as *indubitability*, which is a subjective property that varies from person to person. The Cartesian paradigm, properly understood, is no more than a prejudice having no significance for scientific inquiries.

The Cartesian paradigm is often accompanied by methodological commitments to analogical reasoning as the only kind possible for acquiring knowledge of other minds. This association, however, appears to be unwarranted on several grounds. Analogical reasoning involves comparing two things or kinds of things, where because one possesses properties A, B, C, and D, for example, and the second possesses A, B, and C, the second is supposed to possess D as well. Since I am a human and I feel pain if I burn myself on a hot stove, I infer the same is true of other humans, and so forth.

When there are more differences than similarities or few but crucial differences or such inferences are taken to be conclusive, however, then analogical reasoning is fallacious. The similarities and differences which matter are supposed to be *relevant*, in the sense that they make a difference to the outcome. When comparisons are drawn between members of different species, there may be more relevant differences than similarities. Even when comparisons are drawn between members of the same species, there can still be crucial differences. Such reasoning is always uncertain.

Since analogical reasoning is always uncertain, while Cartesian knowledge is always certain, it cannot provide Cartesian knowledge. Fortunately, Dawkins commits herself to the common-sense position that, "despite the impossibility of never [sic] really knowing what other people experience, we all go about our daily business as though we were perfectly well able to do so" (Dawkins 1993, p. 10). She severs the Cartesian knot by not defining "knowledge" in terms of certainty, which makes her reliance upon the use of analogical reasoning consistent with her concept of knowledge. But her methodology may actually be far more sophisticated in practice.

Dawkins thus maintains that the fundamental difficulty in reasoning about other species is to ensure that there are sufficient relevant similarities to warrant analogical arguments. She also emphasizes that different species have different bodies and inhabit different environments, where:

> To be truly open to the discovery of what conscious experiences in other animals might be like, we must be prepared to go beyond the narrow-minded, rather arrogant anthropomorphism that sees human conscious experiences as the only or

even the ultimate way of experiencing the world and make ourselves open to the much more exciting prospect of discovering completely new realms of awareness. (Dawkins 1993, p. 14)

Indeed, she displays a refreshing sensitivity to the idea that other animals have "a point of view" that must be appreciated to fully understand them. Dawkins acknowledges the existence of an enormous barrier to understanding other species, which takes the form of *language*. Indeed, some thinkers have gone so far as to insist that language is essential to thought, where absence of language implies absence of mentality. Communication between humans and non-humans may be limited, in Dawkins's view, but is not therefore impossible. It would be a blunder to assume either that other animals cannot communicate with one another without language or that animal modes of communication must always parallel human modes.

As soon as Dawkins turns her attention to criteria that may be used as evidential indications of the presence of animal consciousness, it becomes apparent that her conception of consciousness may be somewhat broader than mere "immediate awareness". Her first criterion of consciousness, (CC-1), say, is *complexity of behavior*, where "the complexity of behavior and the ability to adapt to changed circumstances are some of the hallmarks of a conscious mind" (Dawkins 1993, p. 20). As an example, she offers vervet monkeys, who have different alarm calls for different kinds of predators.

Dorothy Cheney and Robert Seyfarth (1990) have studied the sound patterns that vervets make under a wide variety of different conditions. They have discovered that the monkeys use at least four types of grunts under specific social conditions, two of which are made when encountering socially dominant and socially inferior conspecifics, respectively, and two of which are made when moving into an open area and when observing unfamiliar monkeys from other groups. When tape-recorded sounds of these kinds were played to unsuspecting monkeys in the wild, moreover, they displayed responses appropriate to those particular messages.

Dawkins also discusses findings concerning female ostriches, red deer stags, and female black grouses that suggest ingenious strategies for raising chicks, picking fights, and selecting mates, where animal behavior is strongly influenced by subtle cues that are more complex but also more reliable than simpler alternatives. Dawkins's second criterion of consciousness, (CC-2), is *adapting behavior to variable conditions* (Dawkins 1993, p. 36), where the fulfillment of this condition is taken to imply the existence of "undeniable evidence of the ability to learn", which is exhibited by the pecking order of flocks of hens, the song-identification of white throated sparrows, and concealing-of-food behavior of marsh tits and chickadees.

Her discussion of marsh tits and chickadees, who tend to hide hundreds of food items in the course of a single day, displays a great deal of methodological sophistication. In order to establish that these creatures are actually remembering exactly where they stored these items of food, a variety of alternative explanations—which might explain their remarkable ability by means of other causal mechanisms—may have to be eliminated. Sherry (1982, 1984) and Shettleworth and Krebs (1986) have subjected these hypotheses to empirical tests by employing artificial trees and controlling for other conditions that might be relevant.

In order to accept the hypothesis (H1) that chickadees and marsh tits have phenomenal memories, it was necessary to eliminate possible alternatives, including (H2) that they locate hidden seeds on the basis of smell or other subtle cues and (H3) that they have simple rules or routines they use for hiding and recovering food. Insofar as chickadees and tit marshes do not search systematically and follow no apparent routines, their behavior undermines hypothesis (H3). And because they tend to search in just those locations where they have stored food even after that food has been removed from those locations, their behavior also defeats hypothesis (H2).

The methodology applied here goes beyond mere analogical reasoning. A set of alternative possible explanations—some of which may be inspired by analogies—is introduced and subject to systematic evaluation. Hypotheses that explain more of the available evidence are preferred over those that explain less. Those that are preferable when sufficient evidence has become available are acceptable as true. Hypotheses that are inconsistent with that evidence are rejected as false. Any hypothesis that is accepted might still be false, but is the most rational among the alternatives. This exemplifies *inference to the best explanation*, as introduced in Chapter 1.

Other students of cognitive ethology have employed this methodology without acknowledging it by that name. The most striking instance with which I am familiar is Carolyn Ristau's study of the piping plover (Ristau 1991), which apparently deliberately feigns injury to lead predators away from its young, where she systematically eliminates the alternatives that this behavior is explainable (H1) as a reflexive or a fixed action pattern response, (H2) as conflict behavior, (H3) as an approach/withdrawal tendency, (H4) as a preprogrammed sequence of behavior, or (H5) as a kind of learning, where only (H6) as purposive or intentional behavior remains.

Ristau's study, like those of Sherry, Shettleworth and Krebs, also illustrates that every relevant alternative explanation must be taken into consideration. Otherwise, the true explanation need not be a member of the set of possible alternatives. Thus, the discovery that some possible alternative explanation has been overlooked may necessitate reconsideration of the inferen-

Table 2.i Ristau's Inference to the Best Explanation

(h1) The bird's behavior is a reflexive fixed-action-pattern response.

(h2) The bird's behavior is a manifestation of conflicting motivations.

(h3) The bird's behavior manifests approach or withdrawal tendencies.

(h4) The bird's behavior is a pre-programmed sequence of behavior.

(h5) The bird's behavior has been acquired as a function of learning.

(h6) The bird's behavior is intentional or purposeful in its character.

The behavioral observations (observational evidence) includes that injury-feigning is not random, not simply away from the nest or from an intruder, not inconsistently leading away from the bird's nest, not rigid and inflexible, not acquired from repeated exposures, and so forth.

---

tial situation as a manifestation of the tentative character of scientific knowledge. Most importantly, however, it displays how hypotheses that make reference to cognitive variables are capable of being subjected to tests involving controlled experiments and focused observations.

The third criterion of consciousness Dawkins introduces (CC-3), is *learning from others* (Dawkins 1993, p. 45), which goes beyond learning from experience for oneself to include benefiting from the experience of others. It thus raises the prospect of communication and co-operation for the benefit of the community as a manifestation of the transmission of information from one generation to another as a form of "culture" or "tradition". What may be most surprising is that the example that Dawkins discusses is rats, who exemplify mental abilities that exceed what our preconceptions imply.

Dawkins discusses clever experiments involving pairs of rats conducted by Bennett Galef (1986, 1991), in which he would expose one member of the pair (the "demonstrator" rat) to food scented with cocoa or cinnamon. The second member of the pair (the "observer" rat) would notice if the demonstrator appeared to be healthy after having eaten and would associate the scent it detected with the palatability of the scented food. The presence of the smells thus function as useful indications of correlated causes (scented foods) and effects (healthy or not) where one rat could learn from another.

Even more elaborate studies suggest that information about potential dangers can be transmitted within whole colonies of rats. A colony was regularly fed food of two kinds, X and Y. Food of kind X was then treated with lithium chloride, which makes rats ill but does not kill them. As a result, the whole colony stopped eating food X and only consumed food Y, an effect that persisted through subsequent generations, even though food X was no longer being treated with lithium chloride and was just as palatable as food Y. Although Dawkins does not phrase it this way, the rats are apparently thereby perpetuating a "tradition" (Dawkins 1993, pp. 48–52).

Dawkins introduces two additional criteria of consciousness in the form of (CC-4) *behavior involving choice* and (CC-5) *behavior involving co-operation* (Dawkins 1993, p. 53). An example of "choice behavior" in this sense is that of cock house sparrows, who must decide whether or not to swoop after food on the lawn when a threat in the form of a cat might or might not be in the vicinity. Studies by Elgar (1986a, 1986b) found that sparrows would behave one way or another under various conditions and even seemed to be making calculations about their risks and benefits. The sparrows were confronting options, weighing alternatives, and then acting.

Dawkins also discusses Wilkinson's studies of vampire bats (Wilkinson 1984), who share their food with other vampire bats, especially with those who have shared their food with them in the past. They are not inclined to share their food with others unless the others have been willing to co-operate with them in the past. These creatures thus display behavior involving what is known as *reciprocal altruism*, where they help each other when they are in need in the expectation of reciprocation on other occasions. Vampire bats thereby rely on their knowledge of each other's past history to co-operate in ways that may turn out to benefit the community.

Dawkins provides convincing reasons to conclude that consciousness, properly understood, makes an important difference to the behavior of organisms that possess it, especially coping with problems that are novel or unpredictable, where unconscious and routine responses may not provide solutions that are adequate to handle adaptive problems. This generates a difference that enhances the relative fitness of organisms possessing this property in contrast with organisms that do not, which supplies a plausible explanation for the existence and evolution of consciousness.

If Dawkins has carried this off well, at least three ingredients appear to have been enormously important in contributing to her remarkable success. The first is that Dawkins did not allow herself to become embroiled in premature disputes over the precise nature and definition of "consciousness". The second is that Dawkins rejected the Cartesian conception of knowledge as certainty and substantially advanced tentative scientific understanding. The third is that Dawkins's belief in analogical reasoning complemented rather than interfered with her practice of inference to the best explanation.

Among the more striking features of her work is that many of the kinds of consciousness that Dawkins considers—including most of those satisfying (CC-1) through (CC-5) as well as others she discusses—go beyond mere "immediate awareness". We may even want to admit that some forms of consciousness exist that do not satisfy even this modest conception. If internal bodily processes, such as digestion and gestation, for example, can take place without having any "immediate awareness" of those internalized activities, then it might turn out to be important to distinguish between (what could be called) *sentience* from the stronger forms of *consciousness* she considers.

We may ultimately acknowledge a continuum of grades of consciousness from sentience to awareness on to awareness with the ability to convey the contents of awareness and self-awareness consistent with Dawkins's position. And there may be more adequate conceptions of mentality than to identify it with consciousness. But their benefits are ontic rather than epistemic. I happen to believe that minds are best defined as sign-using (or "semiotic") systems—an approach we are about to explore—but I also know there are no better methodologies for scientific inquiries than those she has employed.

2.2   The Nature of Minds

The place to begin is with the theory of signs of Charles S. Peirce (1839–1914). According to Peirce, *a sign* is a something that stands for something (else) in some respect or other for somebody. The sign relation is therefore triadic, involving (a) a *causal* relation between a somebody (a sign user) and a something that stands for something (a sign); (b) a *semantical* relation between that something (sign) and that for which it stands (the something else); and (c) a *pragmatical* relation between that something and that for which it stands (which may be itself or other things), and that sign user. This general conception may be diagrammed as a triangular figure for which the vertices are respectively the sign, "S", the user "z", and that for which it stands "x"; indeed, absent some user, nothing functions as a sign for anyone at all, namely: See Figure 2.1.

Peirce distinguished between three different grounds as kinds of ways in which things might stand for other things in some respect or other, namely: (i) resemblance relations, where things that resemble other things are therefore *icons*; (ii) cause-and-effect relations, where causes and their effects are therefore *indices*; and (iii) habitual associations, where things that are merely habitually associated with other things are therefore *symbols*. While iconic and indexical relations may exist in nature whether anyone has noticed them or not (as tree rings, for example, are effects of the age of a tree), they can only serve as signs when someone has noticed a relationship by virtue of

Figure 2.1   The Triadic Sign Relationship

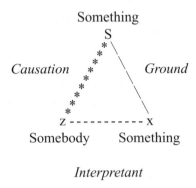

Interpretant

---

which those things (tree rings) can stand for associated properties of other things (the age of the trees).

Among the most familiar examples of symbols are the words that occur in ordinary languages, such as English, French and German. Words such as "snow" and "white" do not resemble the forms of frozen water and absence of color for which they stand, respectively, and therefore do not qualify as icons. And while speakers of English may use those words to describe aspects of their experience, the presence of snow by itself no more produces those words absent speakers of English than absence of snow inhibits the production of those words in the presence of speakers of English. Speakers of other languages, no doubt, would use other words under the same conditions, which indicates that words similarly cannot properly qualify as indices. They are properly characterized as symbols.

The relationship of habitual association that grounds symbols to things might be said to reflect an artificial rather than a natural connection, because, unlike resemblance and cause-and-effect relations, we must create them for them to even exist. Relations of resemblance and of cause-and-effect, by comparison, reside in nature whether we notice them or not. Habitual associations between words and objects are dispositions of sign users to use specific signs to stand for specific things in specific respects, where variations in usage between sign users are always possible. Indeed, there is no reason to reject the possibility that every sign user might use signs in ways that differ from any other user—not for every individual sign, necessarily, but for all of them considered together as a collection.

The prospects for what are often called "private languages" are therefore abundant (Fetzer 1989). Consider the case of a sailor, stranded on a deserted island, who decides to study the flora and the fauna he encounters, identifying and classifying them on the basis of a taxonomy of his own design and introducing names denoting specific animals and plants and predicates that designate their various properties. It would be unsurprising in the extreme for him to have thereby adopted a set of linguistic dispositions unlike those of any other botanist or zoologist the world has ever known. He would possess a constellation of dispositions for speech and other behavior that reflect a unique set of correlations between language and the world.

Although in this instance the sailor's language would be his alone, that condition might turn out to be temporary, for example, were another party to be stranded on the same island who adopted his novel taxonomy. That languages may be private does not imply that they are therefore unlearnable or could not be taught to someone else. An argument against the very possibility of private languages attributed to Ludwig Wittgenstein (1958) seems to hinge on the changeability of dispositions with each use of a word or an inscription, since their constancy cannot be guaranteed. It is logically possible for sign users to change dispositions from time to time, but if this were a frequent occurrence, even public languages would be impossible.

A similar argument could also be transferred to things in the world, whose properties might change arbitrarily from time to time and therefore be incapable of systematic prediction or explanation. Indeed, this was a thesis of David Hume, who denied the existence of "natural necessities" that could not be violated and could not be changed. Hume's position presumed that belief in the existence of non-observable properties and relations was never epistemically justifiable, thus overlooking the evident consideration that the existence of unchangeable and inviolable lawful regularities could be subjected to empirical test by attempting to falsify them, where unsuccessful attempts are positive evidence that they exist.

Without a certain degree of constancy in the properties of things in the world and of organisms in causal interaction with those things, not only language and perception but also communication and co-operation would be difficult to achieve. Communication situations, for example, typically involve two or more sign users interacting with the same sign, where they may or may not interpret it the same way by assigning it the same meaning. This becomes especially problematic with respect to symbols, since there are no resemblance relations or cause-and-effect relations to establish standards for comparing the degrees of similarity between one symbol and another until sign users arrive at some common understanding.

This general phenomenon may be represented by a pair of triangular figures that share at least one point, namely, a sign, "S", where user "$z1$" takes it to stand for "$x1$" and user "$z2$" to stand for "$x2$", where "$x1$" may not be the same as "$x2$":

Figure 2.2   Communication Situations

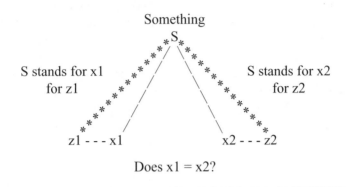

Something

S stands for x1   S stands for x2
   for z1   for z2

z1 - - - x1   x2 - - - z2

Does x1 = x2?

As a result, communities tend to be highly motivated to take measures to ensure that their members speak the same language through institutions that perpetuate specific linguistic practices distinctive of those communities as their *conventions*. Although, in almost every case, the members of these communities do not use all and only the same words exactly the same way—and thus have private languages—public languages are defined by the conventions adopted by those communities.

The use of the term "adopted", no doubt, must be understood historically insofar as many, perhaps most, of the linguistic dispositions that define these conventions are perpetuated as customs, traditions and practices of those communities, which may have a long lineage. Since these customs, traditions and practices can change across time, however, they require periodic reaffirmation as the current practices of their respective communities, whose study falls within the domain of empirical linguistics. But the normative significance of linguistic practices also falls within the province of philosophers, who attempt to demarcate between various aspects of their meaning and use. These conventions tend to fall into at least two domains.

The study of the meaning of words (sentences, paragraphs, and so on) falls into the category of *semantics*, which attempts to distill the meaning of words that are used by the members of language-using communities. Results of these studies are commonly codified in the form of *dictionaries*, which report upon the meanings of those words in practice during specific temporal intervals and may require revision as new practices are adopted and old ones discarded. The term "fuzz", for example, meant police officer to street gangs in New York City during the 1950s; but that use of the term has long since been abandoned. As a consequence, dictionaries that are not periodically revised may cease to describe current practice within a community.

The study of the use of language (to inform, to persuade, and so forth) falls into the category of *pragmatics*, which attempts to discern the conditions under which different uses of language occur. Many of these studies concern typical situations in which informative conversational exchanges take place, which are governed by *co-operative principles* such as maxims of quantity ("Say as much as but not more than is required") and of quality ("Say nothing you believe to be false or for which you lack adequate evidence"). But not all uses of language are for the purpose of the truthful exchange of information, since language may also be employed to mislead or to confound, for example, which may appropriately violate these standards.

Although dictionaries may be repositories of common practice, it has long been apparent that every word within a dictionary could be defined by means of other words within that dictionary only if either (i) some words are ultimately defined by means of themselves, thereby generating *circular definitions*, or (ii) old words are defined by new words, which are defined by new words, ad infinitum, generating an *infinite regress* (Fetzer 1991d). So long as vocabularies are finite, the only way to avoid circular definitions—where *a* is defined by *b* and *b* by *c* and so forth until *a* is defined by *a* again—would be by reliance upon some words that are not defined, where these words are *primitive* (or undefined) elements of a language.

The problem of primitives thus becomes that of explaining how it is possible to understand the meaning of words that are undefined. This difficulty has been appreciated by Jerry Fodor (1975), who has suggested that learning a language *L* presupposes understanding what it means. (Fodor's position is so instructive that I shall discuss it several times in this book.) Thus, learning that the meaning of *a* is the same as *b* can only occur for those who already understand the meaning of *b*—presumably, relative to their respective languages, *A* and *B*. Thus confronting the choice between an infinite progression of metalanguages *A, B, C, . . .* and the existence of a base case, an unlearned language, Fodor chooses the existence of an innate mental language called "mentalese" and known as *the language of thought*.

Fodor's position entails an initially appealing conception of perception according to which *perception* consists of the subsumption of experience by means of the private language of thought, which can be made public through speech. In order to have the ability to subsume every possible experience—past or future—however, its resources—from primitive man to *Homo sapiens*—must be sufficiently rich to encompass any innovation in art or literature or science or technology, no matter how technical and obscure, a scheme that precludes the gradual evolution of language or mind. For if mentalese lacks this property, there can be examples of learning new words that it cannot explain, which reinstates an infinite regress.

If learning new words implies the reinstatement of an infinite regress, then the language-of-thought hypothesis no longer provides the simplest or most adequate explanation of the phenomena of language learning, since it requires *both* an innate base mental language and an infinite regress of metalanguages, while its alternative posits *only* the existence of an infinite regress of meta-languages. Assuming that an adequate theory of language learning must be consistent with evolution, the language of thought must be rejected. But it also implies that every neurologically normal human being must have the same innate language and that unsuccessful translations between different languages must be systematically impossible, necessarily.

Even more importantly, the language-of-thought hypothesis and its regress alternative both appear to have been motivated by a misunderstanding on Fodor's part. Fodor's suggestion—namely, learning that the meaning of *a* is the same as *b* can only occur for organisms that already understand the meaning of *b*—implies the existence of their respective languages, *A* and *B*, only if that prior understanding has to be *linguistic* (Fetzer 1989)! Otherwise, learning that the meaning of *a* is the same as *b* may occur on the basis of prior *non-linguistic* understanding of the *b*-phenomenon that *a* might then be used to describe. Indeed, there are many commonplace cases in which we display the ability to understand phenomena prior to describing them with words.

The most familiar instances involve *ostensive definitions*, in which the meaning of words is explained by offering samples or examples of things of that kind. For those who are unacquainted with the meaning of "chalk", we might show them some pieces of chalk, write on the blackboard with them, break them into pieces and such, to convey the sort of thing meant by that word. In such a case, we are trying to convey the meaning (or *intension*) of the word by exhibiting examples that satisfy its meaning (and therefore fall within its *extension*). We may not always succeed, since incidental properties of the members of the sample, such as their size, shape or color, can be mistaken for necessary properties of everything of that kind. But we often do.

2.3 The Role of Concepts

Other cases appear to be analogous. Infants can learn to suck a nipple, bounce a ball, or draw with crayons *without knowing* that what they are sucking on is called "a nipple", that the thing they are bouncing is called "a ball", or that the marks they are making are made by "a crayon". Once they have acquired an understanding of the properties of things of those kinds, however, through causal interaction or even by observation and inference, neurologically normal *Homo sapiens*, under suitable conditions of acquisition, readily assimilate corresponding linguistic dispositions. They not only learn to *bounce balls*, *draw with crayons*, and so on, but also learn that what they are doing is "bouncing a ball", "drawing with a crayon", and so forth.

The non-linguistic understanding that comes prior to language learning appears to consist in the acquisition of specific sets of habits of action and habits of thought, which constitute corresponding *concepts*. Thus, the things that you can do with a ball (bounce it, roll it, squeeze it, throw it) become associated through experiences with things of that kind, such that seeing a ball (rolling a ball, and such) may bring to mind squeezing it (throwing it, and such), which in turn may bring about corresponding actions (of squeezing, throwing, and such). These patterns of association become mental habits because these properties come and go together as features of things of that kind, while others (such as where they can be found) may vary.

Since there might be infinitely varied conditions under which the properties of a ball would be displayed (by dropping it from greater and greater heights, for example), the content of our concepts may be strengthened through inference and the acquisition of knowledge about things of that kind, some of which (their behavior in weak gravitational fields, for example) may come as a surprise. This does not imply that the content of every concept has to be derived from experience, as some versions of empiricism may require. Our knowledge of which contingent properties of things are lawful properties of things of that kind and of which are not obviously requires empirical support, but it does not therefore have to be direct (Fetzer 1993).

These reflections are consistent with Peirce's analysis of the content of a concept by means of the causal role it would exert upon behavior under varied circumstances. Peirce thus distinguishes between verbal definitions and the concepts they are (very inadequately) used to describe, where the most adequate account of a concept that mere words can convey would consist of a description of the sets of habits of mind and habits of action that the presence of that concept would produce under various conditions. In the case of human beings, no doubt, those conditions would have to take into account not only motives, beliefs, abilities and capabilities in relation to thought processes, but those and ethics as well in relation to actions in the world.

The acquisition of linguistic dispositions that relate some signs to other signs (words to their linguistic definitions) on its own cannot overcome the problem of primitives, whose solution requires relating those signs that remain undefined to specific sets of habits of mind and of action, which determines their meaning (what they stand for). The relationship between signs and what they stand for thus has to be mediated by sign users, since, in the absence of corresponding concepts that are embedded within them, they have no meaning. And this includes icons and indices as well as symbols, since, even though resemblance relations and causal connections can exist in nature without having been detected, they cannot function as signs for anyone unless sign users are able to detect their presence and what they stand for.

These reflections raise the possibility that sign users may be precisely the kinds of things that properly qualify as "minds". This conception appears to be justifiable for many reasons, since without sign users, the problem of primitives could not be successfully overcome and nothing would stand for anything for anyone at all. Indeed, it is an anthropocentric prejudice to suppose that sign users have to be somebodies, when other animals or even inanimate machines might be systems of this kind. Let us therefore define *minds* as semiotic (or "sign using") systems, which are things (humans, animals, or machines) that can take something to stand for something else in some respect or other (Fetzer 1988a, 1989, 1990a, 1991/96).

It follows from the definition of minds as semiotic systems that there may be as many kinds of minds (or modes of mentality) as there are kinds of signs. Thus, systems that are capable of utilizing icons qualify as minds of Type I, those capable of utilizing indices as minds of Type II, and those capable of utilizing symbols as minds of Type III (Fetzer 1988a, 1990a, 1991/96). There are higher kinds of mentality, but for present purposes, these will do. These are successive stronger and stronger kinds of minds, insofar as the capacity to utilize symbols presupposes the capacity to utilize indices and the capacity to utilize indices presupposes the capacity to utilize icons. Systems of each type can differ in the number and variety of signs that they utilize.

It thus becomes obvious why the Fodorian conception of perception has to be rejected. Dreams and daydreams commonly occur as sequences of images and thereby exemplify iconic (or Type I) mentality. To the extent to which they include events that stand to other events as cause-to-effect, of course, they may also exemplify indexical (or Type II) mentality. While they may include the use of symbols, such as the occurrence of speech and other linguistic activities, which exemplifies symbolic (or Type III) mentality, nothing inherent in dreams or daydreams requires it. And similarly for perceptual situations, such as drivers encountering traffic lights at intersections. These activities involve signs but do not depend on the use of language.

Unlike the language of thought conception, this approach may also apply to other animals, such as bats, monkeys, or bacteria. Unless we are prepared to endow them with bat-language, monkey-language, and bacteria-language, those who accept that account must bite the bullet and deny that they are capable of thought or perception. This seems very odd if perception, for example, is indeed an adaptive function, since presumably it has evolved through successive species in a long evolutionary process over millions of years. Current studies suggest that many forms of animal life other than human display behavior exemplifying thought and perception. The problem has been to discover a framework that make the phenomena intelligible, which the conception of minds as semiotic systems appears to provide (Fetzer 1990a, 1991/96).

The nature of consciousness and of cognition has been the subject of many recent studies, including Daniel Dennett (1991), Roger Penrose (1995), and David Chalmers (1996). These works display the tendency to assume that "consciousness" involves "awareness", understood as the conscious subject's not only having experiences but being aware of having those experiences as well. This approach carries with it the temptation to assume that consciousness not only involves awareness of having experience but an awareness of the subject itself as that which is having experience. Although this tendency has a Cartesian legacy, it may not sufficiently distinguish between having sensations, interpreting them, and higher orders of consciousness.

Thus, when minds are defined as semiotic systems, consciousness is relative to kinds of signs that those systems use. Such a system (whether human, animal, or machine) is *conscious* with respect to signs of specific kinds (i) when it has the ability to use signs of those specific kinds and (ii) is not inhibited from the exercise of that ability. And *cognition* occurs as the effect of a causal interaction (i) when a system that is conscious with respect to signs of those kinds (ii) encounters signs of that kind within suitable causal proximity. Those specific effects depend on the system's other internal states, which constitute its *context* (Fetzer 1989, 1990a, 1991).

Consciousness is thus understood as a semiotic phenomenon involving (i) ability and (ii) capability, while cognition is a complementary semiotic phenomenon involving (i) consciousness and (ii) opportunity. When someone is suffering from a severe cold or has been blindfolded, their capacity to exercise their ordinary ability to use signs of specific kinds is thereby impaired. And when those who are not color-blind or otherwise visually impaired are within suitable causal proximity of red lights, for example, the effects that are thereby produced depend on their other internal states, including previously existing motives, beliefs, abilities and capabilities, which might variously yield perception of the presence of stop lights or of fire engines, and so on.

These reflections raise the possible existence of different kinds of consciousness. Insofar as the occurrence of the same stimulus (say, the presence of a red light) may bring about the occurrence of different responses (such as perception of a stop light, a fire engine, and so forth), these aspects of the phenomena of consciousness and of cognition require careful differentiation. The patterns of neural activation that are induced by an external cause (such as a red light within suitable causal proximity) might be qualified as *sensations*, in which case the ability to experience them might be regarded as the lowest level of consciousness. In that case, the interpretation of sensations by subsuming them under specific concepts should qualify as *perception*.

An alternative approach has been advanced by Dennett (1996), who raises the possibility that there may be no more to consciousness than its lowest level, which he identifies as *sentience*. Dennett suggests that, while sentience presumably combines (what he calls) *sensitivity* with some additional factor *x* to produce consciousness, perhaps there is no additional *x* factor and there is no more to consciousness than sensitivity. This may come as a rather peculiar claim given some of his own examples—photographic film, which is sensitive to light; thermometers, which are sensitive to heat; and litmus paper, which is sensitive to acidity—which appear to be appropriate illustrations of sensitivity *without* sentience. But, before pursuing this matter further, we may consider the nature of sensation in additional detail.

Neurologically normal human beings have the benefit of at least five sense modalities, including sight, hearing, taste, touch, and smell. Systems of the kind *Homo sapiens*, unlike bats, ants, and bacteria, are heavily dependent upon their visual abilities for information about their environments. From an evolutionary point of view, these sense modalities have evolved because of their adaptive contributions to the survival and reproduction of the species. Their cognitive function in acquiring and processing information about their environments matters not only because it positively affects the development of individual organisms but also because it makes a difference to the evolution of the species. These specific abilities have evolved because of their tendency to enhance fitness.

The neurology of perception is a complex causal process, which can be illustrated with respect to vision. Light rays pass through the cornea, a transparent membrane covering the eye, and through the lens to the retina at the back of the eyeball. The image is then sent to the brain by way of optic nerves, which induces the activation of patterns of neurons. Precisely which patterns are activated depends upon causal interactions between the patterns of light derived from some specific source—which, in ordinary experience, has an external cause—and the properties of the cornea, the lens and the retina, as well as the condition of the optic nerves and the state of the brain. Different effects are brought about by variations in the shape of the eyeball or curvature of the cornea, which may affect the pattern of activation (Vernon 1971).

When the eyeball happens to be elongated or the cornea is too steeply curved, for example, images are focused in front of the retina causing distant images to be blurry. When the eyeball is too short or the cornea too flat, images are instead focused behind the retina causing near images to be blurry. Thus, in cases of these kinds, patterns of neural activation that might otherwise be familiar and readily subsumed by means of present concepts remain blurry and indistinct. The effect may therefore be the occurrence of an impression rather than of a perception, where the sensations experienced are not capable of subsumption by more exact concepts but are unfocused and fuzzy. They may be subsumable only by those habits attending fuzzy and unfocused images.

From this perspective, therefore, perception can be characterized as a process that involves two or perhaps three separable stages. The first is the acquisition of some pattern of *neural activation*, which may have many possible sources (including internal causes, such as the influence of drugs or even brain damage). The second is the subsumption of that pattern of activation by *conceptualization*, whereby that pattern may or may not become an instance of a familiar kind. The third is that of *description*, where an instance of that kind happens to be described by the use of language. Mistakes of misidentification and of misclassification can occur between stage one and stage two, just as mistakes of misdescription or of miscalculation can occur between stages two and three. The prospect of non-linguistic perception, of course, motives envisioning the subsumption of a sensation by means of a concept as "perception". Perception thus requires concepts, but does not require language.

Thus, if Dennett (1996) were right—if there is nothing more to sentience (as the lowest level of consciousness) than sensitivity—then his own samples of sensitivity *without* consciousness—photographic film, thermometers and litmus paper—have to be conscious, after all, which is not an enviable position to defend. The missing ingredient x whose existence he doubts appears to be the subsumption of sensations by means of specific sets of habits of action and habits of thought. The reason why his examples are such appropriate illustrations of nonconscious things is that no one would be inclined to suppose that any causal interactions between photographic film and light (thermometers and heat, and so on) involve any subsumption by concepts.

The key to understanding consciousness and cognition specifically and mentality in general thus appears to be their distinctively semiotic dimension. Processes that involve the use of signs are properly qualified as *mental activities*, while those that do not are not. The term "sentience" appears to be perfectly appropriate in relation to the capacity to experience sensations. But unless those sensations are subsumed, in turn, by sets of habits of action and habits of thought with distinctively semiotic character, it does not properly qualify as "consciousness". And forms of consciousness that entail an awareness of the use of signs by a system, especially through the use of signs that stand for consciousness itself, may properly qualify as higher order.

The highest order of consciousness, from this point of view, may involve not only awareness of the use of signs by a system, but that system's own awareness that it is the system using those signs as "self-consciousness", a capacity that does not seem to be the exclusive prerogative of human beings.

Thus, *E. coli* bacteria swim toward twelve chemotactic substances and away from eight others (Bonner 1980), an evolved response that at least exemplifies sentience. *Bats* employ echo-location by means of high-frequency sound vibrations (Griffin 1984), an evolved response that appears to exemplify consciousness. And *chimpanzees* display forms of self-awareness that seem to properly qualify as kinds of self-consciousness (Cheyney and Seyfarth 1990).

None of these forms of consciousness—from sentience to self-consciousness—seem to be reducible to mere sensitivity. But it is fascinating to discover that precisely the same sensation as a pattern of activation of neurons in the brain might be interpreted iconically, indexically, or symbolically. Consider again, for example, a red light at an intersection. It might be taken *iconically* when the sensations that it brings about cause mental transitions to other patterns of activation that stand for other things that resemble its color (its shape, and so on), such as the dress that his wife wore the night before. Taken *indexically* it might cause a repair man to think about possible reasons why it is not working properly. Taken *symbolically* it might cause a driver to stop.

Indeed, as a generalization, it appears to be the case that for something to stand for something for a system presupposes a *point of view* relative to which something experienced as a pattern of neural activation becomes identified, classified or categorized as a thing of a certain kind. This function, of course, can be fulfilled when the system possesses corresponding concepts, in the absence of which it has no "point of view". These sets of habits of action and habits of thought occur as preexisting inner states of that system, which affect the tendency for the activation of one pattern of neurons to bring about the activation of another, which might be iconic, indexical, or symbolic. The strength of the tendency for specific patterns of neural activation to bring about other specific patterns has the nature of a propensity (Fetzer 1991/96).

As properties of semiotic systems, mental dispositions might be deterministic or probabilistic. They are deterministic when, under precisely the same (internal and external) conditions of stimulation, the system would respond in precisely the same way by effecting the same transitions between mental states and bringing about the same behavior as an outcome. They are probabilistic when, under precisely the same (internal and external) conditions of stimulation, the system would respond by effecting one or another transition between mental states and bringing about one or more behaviors as its outcome, each with constant probabilities. The system, in this case, possesses mental and behavioral propensities as probabilistic dispositional properties.

3

The Minds of Primates

Perception is obviously a cognitive function and, more importantly, an adaptive cognitive function, namely, one that contributes to the survival and reproduction of organisms. Thus, the adaptive virtue of perception is its *tendency toward veridicality* (truth), which is not the same thing as *veridicality*. The term is commonly used as a success term, where perceiving thing x implies the existence of thing x. Yet misperception is always a possibility, such as when I look into the refrigerator and see what I take to be a bottle of beer, later to discover it was instead a new fruit drink my daughter brought home that comes in bottles that look like bottles of beer, a difference I ascertain only when I actually have the chance to drink it.

This approach, of course, tends to explain at least one of the differences between direct realism and phenomenalism, since the process of interpretation by subsuming specific sensations as instances of specific concepts and thereby identifying, classifying, and categorizing them by relating them to specific habits of mind and habits of action allows for the possibility of misidentification, misclassification, or miscategorization as varieties of mistakes. The *ability to make mistakes*, moreover, appears to be a general criterion of mentality as an evidential indicator of the presence of mentality for minds as semiotic systems, since systems that can commit mistakes must have the ability to take some things to stand for other things, albeit wrongly.

As a consequence of the causal influence of evolution, perception (in normal organisms) is usually reliable for the purpose of acting within their environment, but things are not always the ways they are taken to be, not just as a matter of accident but sometimes quite deliberately. This extends to the deception of other members of the community, such as a lioness who behaves as if everything were normal with other lions in her pride in order to avoid sharing her new kill and to save it for her own cubs (Dawkins 1993). Cases of this kind illustrate the role of deception in animal life and offer evidence that other animals, as well as human beings, are capable of making mistakes and therefore appear to possess minds.

Errors that arise from faulty perceptions or misinterpretations of experience include when parallel lines appear to converge, dreams are mistaken for reality, or mirages induce false beliefs. Illusions can be said to differ from hallucinations, where *hallucinations* involve beliefs in the existence of things which do not exist, while *illusions* involve the belief in non-existent properties of things that do exist (Fetzer and Almeder 1993). These kinds of mistakes are highly interesting theoretically, because they exemplify the possibility of patterns of neural activation that are brought about by the influence of factors other than their typical causes, such as the influence of hallucinogenic drugs (hypnotic suggestions, and so forth).

3.1 The Great Apes

Another important contribution to understanding the nature of animal mind has been made by Merlin Donald, in his *Origins of the Modern Mind* (1991). Donald attempts to describe and to explain the emergence of successively stronger and stronger forms of cognitive ability by means of what he takes to be three primary transitions between distinct stages in the evolution of animal life. These are represented by shifts from what he refers to as "episodic" to "mimetic" to "mythic" to "theoretic" modes of thinking. Although, strictly speaking, each mode qualifies as a different response to a distinct evolutionary niche, each mode appears to be stronger than its predecessor, suggesting a kind of evolutionary progress regarding the evolution of minds.

The evolutionary forms of animal life Donald characterizes in terms of these dominant types of cognitive ability are the great apes, *Homo erectus*, *Homo sapiens* (early), and *Homo sapiens* (late). The episodic mentality of the great apes, for example, is dominated by stimuli in the immediately-present environment, where gestures are the prevalent form of communication. By the time of *Homo erectus*, however, the capacity for re-enacting events that have occurred in the past has emerged, which represents a new kind of communicative capacity that depends upon enhanced neural memory abilities.

The novel cognitive capacities represented by *Homo sapiens* (early) are somewhat more complex, involving two transitional stages. The first involves the use of varying "tones of voice", which he (following Darwin) tends to interpret as "song". The second involves the use of speech, especially as it is reflected by differences in vocal apparatus. The novel cognitive capacities represented by *Homo sapiens* (late) are typified by the emergence of reading and writing, which vastly extends the ability of a species to record and transmit information between members, as other authors have noted.

The principal theme that emerges from this study, which appears to be its main thesis, is that these transitions in cognitive capacity are primarily differences in memory storage and information retrieval abilities, where the computer revolution represents yet another great leap forward in our storage and retrieval abilities and thereby marks yet another step in the evolution of *Homo sapiens* (modern). The broadest features of the position that is developed in this book can therefore be outlined roughly as follows:

Table 3. i   Donald's Four Stages of Cognitive Evolution

Stage	*Level* (A)	*Level* (B)
I. The Great Apes	Episodic	Gestural (stimulus bound)
II. *Homo erectus*	Mimetic	Gestural with re-enactment
III. *Homo sapiens* (early)	Mythic	(1) Song (tones of voice) (2) Speech
IV. *Homo sapiens* (late)	Theoretic	Reading and Writing

This is merely an outline, which does not begin to do justice to the supporting evidence that he produces, including studies of neurophysiology and various kinds of paleoanthropological and other evidence. Thus, there is much more to Donald's position than I have outlined here. Nevertheless, if I have understood him correctly, then these are the major features of the stages of cognitive evolution as he presents them, where the difference between "Level (A)" and "Level (B)" is simply that between the general conception of cognition at that stage and a counterpart analysis of capabilities.

My basic criticisms of this approach are two-fold. In the first place, the distinctions that he draws between episodic, mimetic, mythic and theoretic do not appear to be fully developed and adequately justified. I should add that I am more intrigued by the episodic-mimetic distinction than I am by the mythic-theoretic distinction. The former strikes me as far more plausible than the latter, especially because primitive myths can be viewed as prototypes of theories. In the second place, the referential (or "propositional") conception of language that he relies on requires further refinement. The central problem about language, I believe, is better envisioned as the problem of meaning rather than as the problem of reference. While some words and sentences have referents, others can be meaningful even without them.

What I have in mind is the difference between a model of language that focuses upon names and predicates as standing for objects and properties in the world (which seems to be the conception Donald adopts, although I am unable to claim this with certainty) and models which do not. The primary function of language on a referential model is therefore that of making assertions that are either true or false. The most important kind of sentences for a model of this kind are declarative sentences, which are the only type of sentences that are ordinarily supposed to be either true or false. Other kinds of sentences assume a subservient role, if they are considered at all.

In my estimation, an adequate understanding of the nature of language from an evolutionary point of view requires abandoning a referential model of this kind in favor of a "speech-act" conception, where different kinds of sentences are acknowledged to fulfill different linguistic roles. From such a perspective, declarative sentences may turn out to be far less important to the evolution of cognition than other kinds of sentences, especially exclamatory sentences (which express attitudes or emotions) and imperative sentences (which issue directions or commands). "Ouch!" and "Look out!" are not sentences in the declarative mode and are neither true nor false, but their evolutionary significance might still qualify as extremely important.

These are kinds of sentences, moreover, for which "tones of voice" can make a tremendous difference. Consider the various degrees of emphasis that can be placed upon the same sentence, such as "Be quiet!" When said softly, it can have one kind of meaning; when uttered more forcefully, an other kind of meaning. The functions that sentences of these kinds can fulfill include alerting, warning, encouraging, discouraging, entreating, soliciting, and so forth, where their role in shaping behavior appears to be undeniable. More importantly, they appear to be forms of communication that are already exhibited by the great apes, a point we are about to discover.

In lieu of the interpretation Donald and Darwin would place upon differences in tones of voice as forms of "song", therefore, I interpret them as different kinds of emphasis that can be employed to convey different degrees of seriousness or importance with respect to corresponding behavior. I also conjecture that the use of sounds that originate as effects of various causes (such as those of pleasure or of pain, under specific circumstances) can be separated from their original stimulus-bound conditions and begin to function as conventional signs that stand for experiences of that kind.

This, of course, is very much as he proposes in separating the mimetic from the episodic, which I applaud. If we embrace the far broader conception of minds as sign-using (or "semiotic") systems elaborated in my *Philosophy and Cognitive Science* (1991/96), it becomes fairly obvious that, even if we want to restrict the concept of language to apply strictly to declarative and to interrogatory sentences, there are other communication modes involving signs that precede those involving declarative sentences and which appear to be even more important in effecting transit ions from lower cognitive forms to higher cognitive forms among animals.

Moreover, although Donald does not elaborate a theory of the mind, he does provide examples of the kinds of functions that he takes to be characteristic of cognition. They include imitation, focused attention, memory, dreaming, imagination, reasoning, caution, tool usage, abstract intelligence, self-consciousness, and various social and moral capacities, encompassing social co-operation, mutual defense, social bonding, and social intelligence (Donald 1991, pp. 28–31). Among these, the one on which Donald places greatest emphasis is memory, where his "stages" in the emergence of the modern mind involve increased memory storage and retrieval capacities.

Donald's use of these specific aspects of human and animal activities may be appropriate as examples of human and animal cognition, but without an explicit conception of the nature of mind that he does not provide, it is impossible to tell. A more adequate account of the emergence of the modern mind, therefore, might benefit from the introduction of a modern conception of the nature of the mind. An account that promises to serve the function of providing a framework for understanding cognition as an evolutionary phenomenon can be developed on the basis of the theory of signs proposed by Charles S. Peirce, which we have explored in Chapter 2.

According to Peirce, a *sign* is a something that stands for something (else) in some respect or other for somebody. By inverting and generalizing Peirce's account, the conception of a *mind* as a something for which other things can stand for other things is made available. Minds thus be come the kinds of things that are capable of utilizing signs. Indeed, since Peirce suggested that there are three basic kinds of signs—where *icons* stand for other things because they resemble them, *indices* because they are their causes or effects, and *symbols* because they are habitually (or conventionally) associated with those other things—there seem to be at least three corresponding kinds of iconic, indexical, and symbolic minds.

Things that are capable of utilizing signs that stand for other things because they resemble those other things (as different instances of the same shapes and sizes, for example) thus possess the most basic kind of *iconic mentality*. Things that are capable of utilizing icons and signs that stand for other things because they are causes or effects of those other things (such as food standing for satiation of hunger, for example) have a higher grade of *indexical mentality*. Things that are capable of utilizing icons, indices, and signs that stand for other things because they are merely habitually associated with those other things (such as the words of ordinary language) have an even higher grade of *symbolic mentality*.

An extension of Peirce's conception suggests that there are higher modes of mentality, where the capacity for formal reasoning, especially inductive and deductive reasoning on the basis of rules of inference, distinguishes *transformational mentality,* and the capacity for criticism (of ourselves, our methods, and our theories) exemplifies the highest grade of *metamentality* within the scope of this conception. For all five kinds of mentality, the same criterion serves as a usually reliable but not infallible indicator of the presence of mentality, namely: *the capacity to make a mistake*, because, in order to make a mistake, something must have the capacity to take something to stand for something, while doing so wrongly.

This framework can be applied to Donald's examples of cognitive functioning. Mental functions such as focused attention, memory, and dreaming could be properties of iconic minds (of Type I), since the objects of focused attention, of memories, and of dreams might be merely images—per haps sequences of images—that resemble what they stand for. Functions such as tool usage, imitation, and self-consciousness, by comparison, seem to require indexical minds (of Type II), since they involve comprehending cause and effect relations of various kinds. Imitation is an interesting ex ample, since it also appears to involve some analogical reasoning capacity.

Social co-operation, mutual defense and social intelligence (which ants, termites, wasps and bees display) may or may not require mentality that goes beyond the indexical, especially when they are instinctual behaviors. Indeed, the difficulty encountered in evaluating whether or not functions of these sorts involve mentality and to what degree is that it depends upon their sign-using (or "semiotic") character. Abstract intelligence and reasoning appear to go beyond indexical mentality to the level of symbolic minds (of Type III). Indeed, when reasoning takes the form of dependence upon rules of inference (as in the construction of deductively valid or inductively proper arguments), then transformational minds (of Type IV) are involved.

What turns out to be most intriguing about caution, from this point of view, is that it appears to exhibit the exercise of the critical capacity indicative of metamentality (of Type V). Since prudent behavior can result from behavior-shaping experiences (of the kind that operant conditioning, especially, can produce) as well as from critical reflection on alternative beliefs and behavior, however, this case too requires further contemplation. The distinctive feature of metamentality is the use of signs to stand for other signs (using words to talk about cinema, for example). Unless signs are being used to stand for other signs, prudent behavior need not be of Type V.

If birds can mistake vinyl owls for the real thing, if dogs can salivate at the sound of a bell as if it were going to satiate their hunger, and if pigeons can press bars in the false expectation of receiving pellets, for example, then things of each of these kinds can make mistakes and have minds. From this perspective, I would suggest, the conception of minds as semiotic (or "sign-using") systems affords a framework for understanding the evolution of minds of successively stronger and stronger kinds that promises to go far beyond the distinctions that Donald has drawn in his extremely stimulating work.

It seems plausible that different species possess distinct semiotic abilities in the form of distinctive ranges and capacities for the utilization of signs of various kinds. Some of these semiotic abilities may be inborn (or innate), while others are learned (or acquired). Presumably, if the semiotic systems conception is right-headed, lesser forms of life should exhibit lesser kinds of mentality and higher forms of life higher forms of mentality, where their exact range and variety depends upon specific social and environmental variables. The semiotic abilities distinguishing various species may even turn out to be the key to their behavior.

One of the most fascinating aspects of my study of his work, I should add, was the dawning realization that Donald's approach could benefit—perhaps greatly benefit—from adopting a speech act model of language in lieu of the referential model which is presupposed. Indeed, it is never really clear that Donald is wholly comfortable with the model of language he relies upon, in part because of his ambivalence about the work of Noam Chomsky and Jerry Fodor and in part because he often seems to want to go beyond it without feeling confident about how to do that. Whether or not the semiotic systems conception is ultimately embraced, too much work in philosophy and psychology, including this book, which reflects a clear understanding of the evolutionary problem, continues to be dominated by a preoccupation with propositions when speech acts are more fundamental.

From the semiotic systems perspective, in other words, the great apes are already engaged in the use of iconic and indexical forms of communication, where the emergence of mimetic uses out of episodic uses seems to represent an important transitional stage, as he suggests. The use of gestures with re-enactment also appears to provide a crucial bridge between non-symbolic (or non-conventional) uses of signs and what seem to be the first symbolic (or conventional) uses of signs. The transition to *Homo sapiens* (early) from *Homo erectus* thus appears to depend upon the use of (more or less) conventional exclamatory and imperative signs (first stage) and declarative and interrogatory signs (second stage), where reading and writing come with *Homo sapiens* (late), as Donald here maintains.

Table 3.ii The Theory of Minds as Semiotic Systems

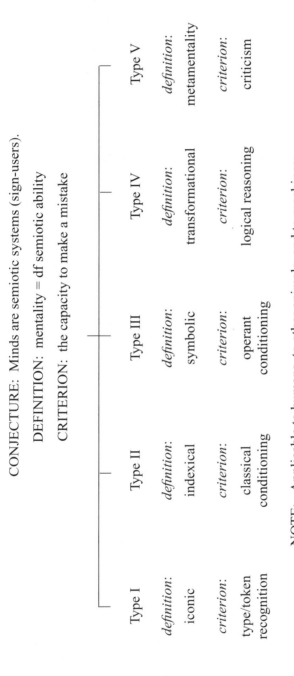

CONJECTURE: Minds are semiotic systems (sign-users).

  DEFINITION: mentality = df semiotic ability

    CRITERION: the capacity to make a mistake

Type I	Type II	Type III	Type IV	Type V
definition: iconic	*definition:* indexical	*definition:* symbolic	*definition:* transformational	*definition:* metamentality
criterion: type/token recognition	*criterion:* classical conditioning	*criterion:* operant conditioning	*criterion:* logical reasoning	*criterion:* criticism

NOTE: Applicable to humans, to other animals, and to machines:

(1) species are predisposed toward types of mentality;

(2) machines have mentality if they are semiotic systems;

(3) a thing has a mind if it is capable of making a mistake; etc.

3.2 The Mountain Gorilla

The adequacy of the conceptual framework that the semiotic systems approach provides can be tested on the basis of studies of the mountain gorilla that have been undertaken by Dian Fossey in *Gorillas in the Mist* (Fossey 1983). As Fossey observes, *Homo sapiens* and the other three members of the Great Apes—orangutan, chimpanzee, and gorilla—are alone among primates without tails. Only about 240 mountain gorillas were still alive when she lived among them in the vicinity of the intersection of Zaire, Uganda, and Rwanda. Recent upheavals there make it highly unlikely that this number survive today. But we continue to benefit from Fossey's studies.

In particular, she recorded nine distinct sounds that they make and use to communicate, which are reported in Appendix E, "Common Gorilla Vocalizations from Main Study Groups and Coco and Pucker, the Captive Juveniles" (Fossey 1983) as follows:

Figure 3.1 Roar

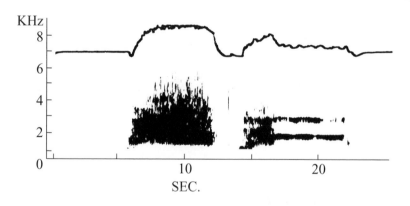

Roar. This monosyllabic loud outburst of low-pitched harsh sound lasted from 0.20 to 0.65 seconds, beginning and ending abruptly. As may be noted in Figure 1, there were individual differences in the frequency concentrations of a roar.

Figure 3.2   Scream

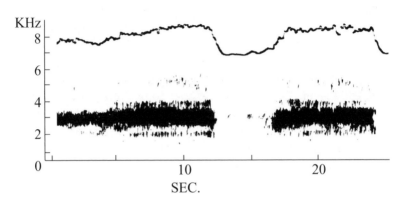

Scream. This shrill and prolonged emission of extremely loud sound could last up to 2.13 seconds and be repeated as often as ten times. Unlike with the roar, individual differences in screams could not be denoted, either spectrographically or subjectively.

Figure 3.3   Wraagh

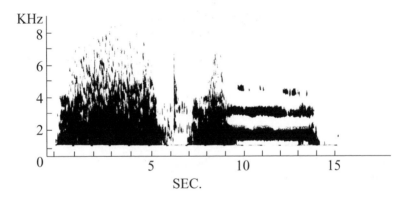

Wraagh. This explosive monosyllabic loud vocal outburst was not as deep as a roar nor as shrill as a scream. Like roars, wraaghs began and ended abruptly and lasted between 0.20 and 0.80 seconds. As may be noted in Figure 3, there were individual differences in the frequency concentrations of the sound, which was more harmonically structured than were roars.

Figure 3.4 Question Bark

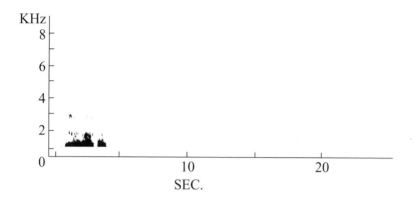

Question Bark. This vocalization is best described by its characteristic composition (both subjective and spectrographic) of three notes, with the first and third lower than the middle. The sound was short, lasting between 0.20 and 0.30seconds, and was heard more from silverbacks than from gorillas of any other age or sex.

Figure 3.5a Cries Going into Shrieks

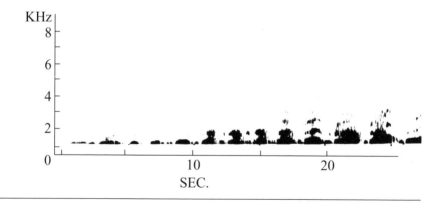

Figure 3.5b   Cries Subsiding

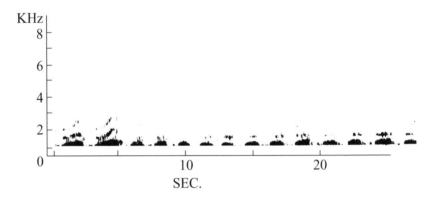

Cry. This sound, resembling the wail of a human infant, could build up into a shriek much like a human's temper tantrums. (Figure 3.5a shows cries going into shrieks; in 3.5b they subside.) Cries were emitted between 0.03 and 0.05 seconds apart and could last for nearly 19 seconds at a time. The wails had four distinct frequency concentrations, but the shrieks were much less structured.

Figure 3.6   Pig-Grunts

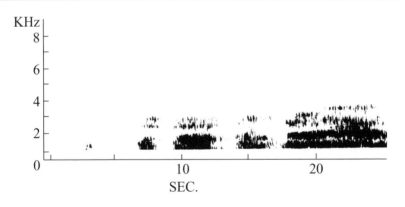

Pig-Grunts. A series of short, rough, guttural noises, pig-grunts are usually delivered between 0.15 and 0.40 seconds apart in sequences of nine or ten outbursts. The sounds, resembling the grunting of pigs feeding at a sty, tended to become louder and more closely spaced if prolonged.

Figure 3.7a Belch Vocalizations

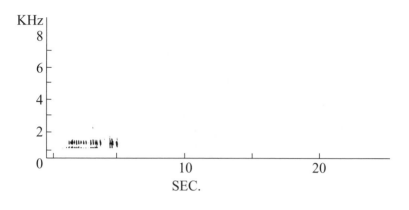

Figure 3.7b

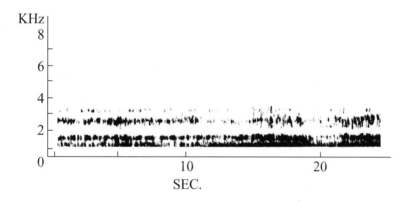

Belch Vocalizations. These sounds resemble deep, prolonged rumbles (naoom, naoom, naoom) rather like throat-clearing utterances. The sound, as recorded from both free-ranging and captive gorillas, had two frequency concentrations and gradated into crooms, purrs, hums, moans, wails, and howls if prolonged in situations of maximum contentment.

Figure 3.8 Chuckles

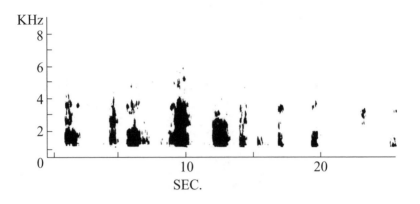

Chuckles. These raspy expirations of noise were irregularly spaced spurts of sound varying in length from 0.02 to 0.10 seconds with a low frequency concentration. No individual differences were noted.

Figure 3.9a Hootseries

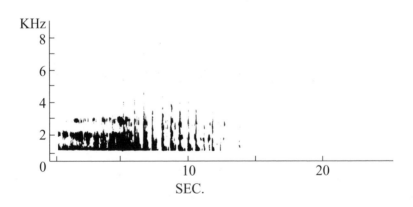

Figure 3.9b

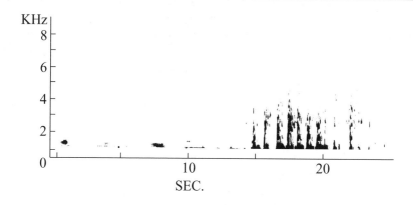

Hootseries preceding chestbeats. The hootseries, given with or without a terminating chestbeat, consists of prolonged distinct *hoo-hoo-hoos*. These were low-pitched, often undetectable to the human ear at the beginning of the series, but usually built up into plaintive-sounding and longer hoots toward the end. The lengthier the series, the more individual the fluctuations in harmony and phasing. Frequencies ranged between 1.4 and 1.8 kilocycles per second for as many as eighty-four hoots per second.

The first point to notice about these sound patterns, no doubt, is that they are among the possible sound patterns that organisms with the physiology of mountain gorillas can make. These sound patterns are known as "phonemes" as sound patterns to which meanings might be attached. The meanings that might be attached, in turn, are known as "morphemes". Apart from the contexts within which those phonemes are expressed, however, it is impossible —at least, virtually impossible—to understand their function as morphemes. Let us therefore consider the context within which each of these phonemes occurs and attempt to ascertain the meaning, if any, that they may convey.

Roars, for example, "were heard only from silverbacks in situations of stress or threat and were primarily directed at human beings, although occasionally at buffalo herds. The vocalization was always followed, on the part of the emitter, with varying degrees of display, ranging from bluff charges to small forward lunges" (Fossey 1983, p. 251). Searching for an analogue in human speech and behavior, it does not appear inappropriate to regard these *aggressive calls* (as Fossey describes them) as serving the same function as "Get away!" or "Don't mess with me!" in human contexts.

Screams "were heard from gorillas of all ages and sex classes, but more frequently from silverbacks. The vocalization was most often heard during intergroup disputes, though it could be directed toward human beings or even ravens if alarm, rather than threat, was the motivation for the call" (Fossey 1983, pp. 251–52). These *alarm calls* appear to serve a function analogous to that of "Damn it!" or "Watch it!" in human contexts. Observe, in particular, that both the use of the roar and the use of screams seem to fulfill functions that are similar to those of imperative and of exclamatory modes of speech.

Wraaghs "were heard from all adult gorillas but far more frequently from silverbacks. They were usually precipitated by sudden situations of stress— the unexpected arrival of an observer, duiker alarm calls, rockslides, thunder claps, or loud wind noises. The vocalization was most effective in scattering group members and, unlike the roar, was never accompanied by aggressive display behavior" (pp. 252–53). Fossey considers wraaghs to be another kind of *alarm call*, whose closest analogue in human speech may be "Look out!" as a form of warning that might be employed in a variety of different contexts, depending upon the nature of the problem encountered.

Question barks, consonant with its characteristic composition of sounds— three notes with the 1st and 3rd lower than the middle—were as if asking, "Who are you?" Fossey observed, "It was usually given in situations of mild alarm or curiosity and was a common response to discovery of an obscured observer or to branch breaking noises by gorillas not readily visible to other group members" (p. 253). Thus, it functions as a third kind of *alarm call*, which mildly inquires, "Who are you?" or perhaps "What's up?"

Cries, which resemble wails of human infants, "were heard only from infants or young juveniles and most frequently occurred when they had been left alone, thus temporarily separated from their mothers, or, in the case of [captives], when one was separated from the other or from myself. In both the free-ranging and the captive young gorillas, the cries built up into tem per tantrums if a stressful situation was prolonged" (p. 254). Indeed, cries not only resemble wails of human infants but appear to have precisely the same function as vivid and vocal expressions of unhappiness.

Pig-grunts "were most frequently heard when individuals were traveling, for this was when trail disputes and altercations over limited food re sources were more apt to occur. On such occasions, pig-grunts were effective rebuttal vocalizations and also served as disciplinary enforcements between adults and young" (p. 255). Thus, pig-grunts fall into the category of (what Fossey refers to as) *co-ordination vocalizations*, which function to induce misbehaving youngsters to mind themselves better, just as humans attempt to control their offspring by saying "Stop!" or "Behave!"

Belch vocalizations, which were "most frequently heard from stationary gorillas at the end of a long, sunny resting period or when in a lush feeding site" or from silverbacks "as a means of establishing location in dense vegetation" (p. 255), like chuckles, which were emitted from young engaged in play activities, such as wrestling, tickling, and chasing each other, were expressions of contentment, in the first instance, or of happiness or joy, in the second. There is an ambiguity for belch vocalizations, since they have an alternative (locational) significance, which is settled by context. Their human analogues in belching and laughing, no doubt, do not require explanation.

Hootseries, which were far more frequently emitted by silverbacks, were often concluded with "mechanical noises such as chestbeating, ground thumps, branch-breaking, or runs through thick foliage. . . . The farther the distance between callers—the hootseries may travel for roughly a mile—the less frequently the intergroup vocalization was terminated by mechanical noises. Hootseries thus functioned well as a type of vocal probing that did not reveal the precise location of a group or of a particular gorilla (pp. 256–57). The function of the hootseries followed by chestbeats, for example, thus seems to be analogous to that of humans affirming "I'm here!" or perhaps "My space!"

Table 3. iii Phonemes, Morphemes, and their Semiotic Type

Sound	Meaning	Type	Kind
1. Roar	"Get away!" "Don't mess!"	Imperative	Symbolic
2. Screams	"Damn it!" "Watch it!"	Exclamatory/ Imperative	Symbolic
3. Wraag	"Look out!"	Imperative	Symbolic
4. Question Bark (Curiosity)	"What's up?" "Who are you?"	Interrogatory (?)	Symbolic
5. Cries	Expressions of unhappiness	Exclamatory	Indexical
6. Pig-Grunts	"Stop!" "Behave!"	Imperative	Symbolic
7. Belch Vocalization	Expression of Contentment	Exclamatory	Indexical
8. Chuckles	Expressions of Joy	Exclamatory	Indexical
9. Hootseries Preceding Chest beats	"I'm here!" "My space!"	Declarative (?)	Symbolic

The benefits that may be derived from a speech-act approach toward understanding communications between conspecifics thus become quite evident in cases of this kind. The roars, screams, wraaghs, and pig-grunts, for example, have decidedly *imperative* character as instructions, directions, or commands intended to influence the behavior of others. Cries, belch vocalizations (in one of its forms), chuckles, and screams (again) clearly have *exclamatory* functions as expressions of unhappiness, contentment, happiness, or anger. Hootseries and question-barks are especially interesting from this perspective, insofar as they exemplify (what appear to be) *declarative* functions of making assertions and *interrogatory* functions of asking questions, respectively, as we have seen.

Perhaps even more important from the perspective of the theory of minds as sign-using systems, however, is that Donald's analysis can be supplemented by an analysis of the kind of connection that obtains between these respective sounds/phonemes (as signs) and their meaning/morphemes (as other things). While cries, belch-vocalizations, and chuckles are clearly *indexical* in their character (as effects that are related to corresponding causes of which they are in variable or probabilistic manifestations), roars, screams, wraaghs, question-barks, pig-grunts and hootseries with chestbeats all appear to be merely habitually associated with that for which they stand, which makes their character *symbolic*! This is a fascinating outcome, since it suggests that there may be an alternative analysis that emphasizes the semiotic quality of these modes of communication:

Table 3. iv   Four Alternative Stages in Cognitive Evolution

Stage	*Level* (C)	*Level* (D)
I. The Great Apes	Gestural*	Iconic/indexical/symbolic/ mentality
II. *Homo erectus*	Gestural* with Re-enactment	Iconic/indexical/symbolic/
III. *Homo sapiens* (early)	1. Exclamatory/ Imperative	Iconic/indexical/symboli/c mentality
	2. Declarative/ Interrogatory	Iconic/indexical/symbolic/
IV. *Homo sapiens* (late)	Reading and Writing	Iconic/indexical/symbolic/ Transformational/critical mentality

*Gestural** means already including some imperative and exclamatory ability.

Indexical and symbolic modes of semiotic mentality, of course, presuppose iconic mentality, since the recognition of different instances of sounds as instances of the same sound (phonemically) or of the same meaning (morphemically) in relation to their context implies the capacity to recognize them as the same. Insofar as the mountain gorilla already exemplifies the use of symbols, there appear to be grounds here for inferring that the most important stages in the evolution of mentality predate any transitions from episodic to mimetic to mythic and theoretic forms of cognition. More importantly, it offers evidence that the semiotic conception can clarify and illuminate the nature of animal minds.

3.3 A Precocious Chimpanzee

Kanzi: The Ape at the Brink of the Human Mind (Savage-Rumbaugh and Lewin 1994) reports the results of years of research at the Yerkes Regional Primate Center located near Atlanta, Georgia, where Sue Savage-Rumbaugh and others have conducted painstaking and systematic studies of higher primates, especially chimpanzees and bonobos, in an attempt to uncover what properly should be envisioned as the mental abilities of other animal species. Her work not only provides insights about the modes of operation of the minds of other animals but also explores reasons why scientific research in this area has been plagued and inhibited by mistaken paradigms and inadequate methodologies.

These mistaken paradigms have revolved about various doctrines that have been widely accepted in the past, especially theses about the nature of language as a distinctive attribute of *Homo sapiens*, a view that derives principally from the work of Noam Chomsky, who has dominated theoretical linguistics for most of the second-half of the twentieth century. Chomsky's emphasis on syntactical structures has encouraged the conceit that the study of these structure has the ability to lay bare the nature of the human mind and its corollary that all languages can be properly unified only by appealing to Chomsky's innate universal grammar.

From this point of view, the phrase, "human mind", assumes a certain kind of redundancy, insofar as Chomsky has cultivated the notion that languages are unique properties of humans, which implies that minds, as language-dependent information-processing mechanisms, are likewise uniquely human—where any "mind" must be human. As Savage-Rumbaugh observes, this attitude appears to be incompatible with evolution, where the emergence of adaptations crucially depends upon multiple sources of genetic variation and mechanisms of selection, where higher-level properties typically have lower-level antecedents.

Chomsky's approach would be plausible, therefore, only if it were reasonable to suppose that *Homo sapiens* should be expected to have abilities and capacities of fundamental importance to its successful adoption that differ from those of its evolutionary ancestors not merely in degree but in kind. This conception calls to mind the image of Athena, full-grown and armed, springing from the head of Zeus without the benefit of gestation. Strictly speaking, outcomes of both kinds might not be logically impossible (inconsistent with the laws of logic) but they appear to be highly improbable if not physically impossible (inconsistent with natural laws).

Her reservations about Chomsky's approach, moreover, have received powerful support from the research of Thomas Schoenemann (1999), who observes that the principles of evolution suggest that syntax is more adequately understood as an emergent property of the explosion of semantic complexity that occurred during hominid evolution, where the grammars that typify ordinary languages should be envisioned as conventional features of cultural practices rather than as the result of a genetically-based universal grammar of the kind Chomsky and Pinker (1994) have proposed. Schoenemann provides striking confirmation for the conception of human beings as possessing predispositions in the form of conceptual abilities for the acquisition of semiotic abilities of diverse kinds under suitable conditions.

Indeed, Savage-Rumbaugh's studies provide extensive evidence for capacities and abilities that, superficially, at least, look like modes of mentality exercised by bonobos and chimps. Sherman and Austin, for example, young male chimpanzees, proved quite adept at the use of lexigrams as arbitrary combinations of geometric forms arranged in a sequence on a keyboard, each of which stands for one word, including verbs, nouns, and adjectives. These two chimps were then exposed to samples or examples of things of the kind for which specific lexigrams stood in an effort to teach them the names of various objects through a process of association.

Savage-Rumbaugh soon discovered that Sherman and Austin were not learning the meaning of the banana-lexigram, for example, when she showed them bananas. On the contrary, they were preoccupied with the reward they would received when they pressed the symbol key. Instead of the physical banana serving as "stimulus" for a banana-lexigram press "response", the chimps were pressing the lexigram as a "stimulus" for their investigators to give them food. Once the researchers began to *reward* them after they displayed appropriate responses, however, the process of mastering lexigrams proceeded smoothly and immediately led to rapid learning.

The difference involved here appears to be that between classical conditioning and operant conditioning, which makes a great deal of sense, especially since the process of association was not followed by reinforcing rewards. When examples were no longer displayed, the chimps experienced frustration, until they grasped (what Savage-Rumbaugh calls) the referential use of lexigrams, namely: their use to refer to objects and events even when those things were not physically present. This ability was manifest, for example, in the form of requests, where one chimp might request a banana, another juice, even when they were inaccessible to view.

Savage-Rumbaugh was thus motivated to distinguish at least four aspects of lexigram learning: (1) that "words" are more than simple associations between symbols and objects; (2) that even complex utterances can be produced without implying comprehension; (3) that developing comprehension entails violations of stimulus-response chains; and (4) that comprehensions are manifest, in part, by requests for food and other indications of future behavior. Subsequent studies with Kanzi, a male bonobo, who proved quite adept at learning English words as well as lexigrams, often without explicit instruction, were even more impressive.

One of the most remarkable of these studies involved comparisons between Kanzi and Alia, the daughter of a colleague, when Kanzi was 7 1/2 and Alia was 2:

> Over a nine-month test period, both Kanzi and Alia had demonstrated a well-developed ability to comprehend all types (and subtypes) of sentences [including conditionals], with Kanzi scoring just a little ahead. Overall, Kanzi correctly answered 74 percent of the sentences, while Alia's figure was 65. (p. 171)

Other results were extremely interesting in different ways. Sherman and Austin, for example, were able to use food lables (package wrappers) for *Doritos*, *M&Ms*, and *Velveeta* cheese when lexigrams were unavailable, even though this was not something that either of them had been taught. And bonobos turned out be highly skilled in using hand gestures to indicate the motions desired of others, including communicating to sex partners the positions that they wanted them to assume.

Ultimately, Savage-Rumbaugh concludes that comprehension is more essential or fundamental to language than is production, while offering the hypothesis that comprehension drives language learning as an alternative to Chomsky's account of an innate grammar. She observes that Chomsky's position has been widely regarded as the "default" option in the absence of reasonable alternatives, even though no anatomic evidence for innate language modules has been discovered. Envisioning languages as forms of symbolic communication appears to provide a more adequate conception, which can be subsumed within the theory of signs.

Peirce, of course, as we know by now, distinguished between three different ways in which things can stand for other things (in some respect or other) for sign users, namely: when that something resembles that something else; when that something is a cause-or-effect of that something else; and when that some thing is habitually associated with that something else. Signs as things that can stand for other things thus fall into three types as *icons* (including photographs and statues), *indices* (smoke, fire and ashes), and *symbols* (words and sentences). Ordinary languages involve the use of symbols, which are only one among three kinds of signs, and thus involves the highest but not the only kind of mentality.

All symbols are signs, but not all signs are symbols. All symbol users have minds, but not all minds are symbol users. Anything that has the ability to use signs by taking something to stand for something else in some respect or other qualifies as having a mind, whether iconic, indexical, or symbolic in kind. It is therefore essential in the study of the mind not to *presuppose* whether human beings, other animals, or inanimate machines can or cannot possess minds. That explains why, in defining "minds" as sign-using systems, it is indispensable to say "for something", and not "for somebody", to avoid precluding possibilities.

The chimpanzees and bonobos that Savage-Rumbaugh studies exemplify the use of signs of all three kinds: lexigrams, for example, are arbitrary signs that are merely habitually associated with that for which they stand (and therefore qualify as *symbols*); package wrappers may be viewed as (admittedly artificial) causes of the contents for which they stand (and therefore qualify as *indices*); and hand gestures to indicate the motions desired of others (in specific ways) resemble them (and therefore qualify as *icons*). Savage-Rumbaugh thus adduces evidence that these are sign-using (or semiotic) systems.

Indeed, some of her descriptions are exactly what ought to be expected from the perspective of the conception of minds as semiotic systems. If the use of symbols presupposes the use of indices, then we should expect outcomes such as this:

> When apes produce symbols, they are attempting to affect the behavior of others—for example, to ask for a banana. When apes comprehend symbols directed toward them, they are expected to bring about the effect intended by the user of the symbols. (p. 126)

This passage, after all, illustrates that symbolic mentality presupposes indexical, where the use of symbols can function as causes-or-effects in social interaction. This relationship is more subtle than that indexical mentality presupposes iconic, because the use of signs as causes-or-effects presupposes the ability to recognize different instances of uses of signs as instances of uses of signs of the same kind.

An even stronger indication that the theory of minds as semiotic systems fits the empirical data that Savage-Rumbaugh has obtained with chimps and bonobos emerges from her finding that the language of apes was unlike human language:

> It wasn't a complex language, not a language with syntax. It was more a culture language, a complex set of behaviors that was the way the chimps' lives were lived in the laboratory. It made one think of *Homo sapiens* without sophisticated spoken language—intelligent, sensitive creatures, able to communicate and co-ordinate their behavior in a collective subsistence effort. (p. 85)

And this is exactly what ought to be expected, because understanding the meaning of a sign is a process of acquiring habits of action and habits of mind relating signs to behavior, where the meaning of a sign should be viewed dispositionally.

Consider a simple case, such as a red light at an intersection. What this sign means for those who have mastered the rules of the road and understand road signs is to apply the breaks and come to a complete halt. When a driver comes up to a stop sign, of course, his behavior may not conform to those expectations, precisely because he is affected by other internal states, such as other beliefs, motives, and ethics. Felons with the police in hot pursuit would be expected to run the light and risk a collision, even though they understand its meaning, just as a husband whose wife has gone into labor might cautiously continue without stopping, because he is eager to get her to a nearby hospital for a safe delivery.

Thus, these internal states constitute a *context* in relation to which the meaning of signs must be understood, where the same sign means the same thing to other sign-users just in case they would have dispositions of the same or similar strength to display all and only the same behavior under the same conditions if they were in the same context, which includes their abilities and capabilities as well (Fetzer 1989, 1991, 1996). Savage-Rumbaugh is therefore entirely correct to maintain, as she does, that "Unlike chemicals, [animal] behaviors cannot be reasonably separated from the entire context in which they occur" (p. 254).

Savage-Rumbaugh concludes that comprehending and producing language turn out to be very different things, which is precisely what we should expect from the semiotic point of view, because *comprehension* is roughly analogous to the totality of uses to which signs might be put, while *production* is the use of specific signs on specific occasions for specific purposes.

Thus, focusing on production rather than on comprehension (understanding or meaning) appears to be a misconception as serious as taking the use of signs of one kind—namely, the use of human language—as essential to mentality. Mentality is far broader.

During the course of her closing chapter, Savage-Rumbaugh also makes several astute observations about inadequacies of methodology. She rightly rejects the Cartesian conception of other animals as mindless automata and challenges the applicability of experimental methods employed by the physical sciences. Descartes's influence on the study of behavior has been uniformly detrimental; it is therefore refreshing to find that she, like Marian Stamp Dawkins, among others, is not bound by the tradition of misconceptions discussed above in Chapter 2.

But it does not follow from her work that the methods fundamental to the natural sciences do not apply within the social science, including this domain, when properly understood as inference to the best explanation. Her own work, from this point of view, convincingly displays that the methods of inquiry that apply within physics, chemistry, and biology apply within cognitive ethology. In the final analysis, Savage-Rumbaugh has provided a brilliant *tour de force* supporting her conception of Kanzi as an ape at the brink of the human mind that further illustrates the power of the theory of minds as semiotic systems.

PART II

Evolution and Intelligence

4

Computers and Cognition

The conception of minds as semiotic systems provides an alternative to some prevalent—even paradigmatic—views for understanding language and mentality. These may be considered to be alternative hypotheses or possible explanations of linguistic and mental phenomena, provided that the notion of "language" receives sufficiently broad interpretation to encompass the communicative mechanisms that might be employed by lesser species (including termites, bees, and ants) as well as by higher species (including *Homo sapiens* and the Great Apes). Among the prevalent blunders of philosophers and other students of the nature of mind tends to be the presumption that thought cannot occur in the absence of language and that language has to be understood as it emerges in human forms.

The simplest of these alternatives may be viewed as *the propositional model*, with its focus on declarative sentences that make assertions. These communicative forms, which refer to or describe objects and their properties, are therefore either true or false: true when those objects to which they refer have the properties they ascribe to them and otherwise false. The most obvious limitations of the propositional model are overcome by *the speech-act model*, which expands coverage beyond declarative sentences to the multiple uses of language in achieving different effects, such as directing (amusing, misleading, . . .) with various intentions (motives or purposes). While a propositional model tends to identify meaning with reference, a speech-act model tends to identify meaning with use.

Indeed, from the speech-act perspective, it becomes obvious that declarative uses of language are only one special function within a family of functions. Thus, the conception of minds as semiotic systems not only shatters the myth that sentences are the basic units of communication in favor of signs but also transcends even the tendency to identify meaning with use. *The dispositional model*, which it implies, focuses instead upon the causal influence of signs upon behavior as a function of contexts, where those contexts include other motives, beliefs, ethics, abilities and capabilities and where the success or failure of an action depends (if not exclusively, at least in large measure) upon opportunities. Meanings are now identified, not with reference or even with use, but with dispositions to behave in various ways within different contexts in the presence of specific signs.

The scope of this approach easily ranges from the mountain gorilla (Fossey 1983) to marsh tits and chickadees (Dawkins 1993) and promises to deliver for every other species. The capacity of marsh tits and chickadees to hid hundreds of food items in the course of a single day, indeed, even suggests that memory plays a crucial role in their successful survival and reproduction, which lends support to Merlin Donald's emphasis on the importance of information storage and retrieval (Donald 1991). If the computer revolution marks (as it certainly must) yet another great leap forward in our information storage and retrieval abilities, then perhaps computers have something to teach us about the nature of mind. The most important alternative to the semiotic conception turns out to be what is known as the computational conception of language and mentality.

4.1   The Computational Conception

The fields of computer science, artificial intelligence, and what is known as cognitive science are dominated today by *the computational conception* according to which thinking is reducible to reasoning, reasoning is reducible to reckoning, reckoning is computation, and the theory of computability defines the boundaries of thought (Haugeland 1981). This approach receives support from analogies between digital computers and human beings, insofar as computers receive inputs, which are processed in accordance with a program to yield outputs, while people receive stimuli, which are processed in accordance with cognition to yield responses. The package is quite concise and very appealing in suggesting that cognition is nothing more computation.

Some of the most fundamental premises adopted in AI and cognitive science, however, seem to be fraught with ambiguity or to trade on equivocation. An especially striking instance is *the physical symbol system hypothesis* that Alan Newell and Herbert Simon have advanced, according to which being a *physical symbol system* (in their sense) is both necessary and sufficient for mentality or "general intelligent action" (Newell and Simon 1976). The problem with their conception appears to be that something can qualify as a "symbol" (in their sense) whether or not it stands for anything else for anyone at all. Consequently, Newell and Simon's "symbols" might or might not be *signs* of the kind Peirce called "symbols", which stand for other things on the basis of habitual associations, but may be merely meaningless marks that might be processed on the basis of their shapes, their sizes and their relative locations.

Their conception thus defines what ought to be called "syntax process-ing" or "string manipulating" systems, where the meaningfulness of that syn-tax or of those strings is not thereby guaranteed. Newell and Simon may have thought they captured the necessary and sufficient conditions for mentality, but they manifestly have not. If a system can be a physical symbol system (in their sense), yet not be processing meaningful marks, it can still have no semantic capacity essential to mentality. Consequently, it might not qualify as a semiotic system of Type III, which has the ability to use signs that are symbols (in Peirce's sense). Even without assuming that minds are semiotic systems, therefore, it is evident that their physical symbol systems are not minds. While the syntax processing capacity that Newell and Simon define might be necessary for the possession of mentality, it is not also sufficient.

The inspiration for the computational conception of language and men-tality has always been the presumptive parallel between computers and minds, namely: that hardware is to software as bodies are to minds. This has been succinctly captured by John Haugeland's recommendation, "Why not sup-pose that people *just are* computers (and send philosophy packing)?" (Hauge-land 1981, p. 5). What has now become evident, however, is that the capacity to process syntax might not be sufficient for mentality. Even Haugeland seems to concede this point by defining "computers" as *automatic formal systems*, which automatically manipulate the marks of formal systems according to the rules of those systems as self-contained, perfectly definite and finitely checkable systems, but where the meaningfulness of the marks subject to manipulation is a matter lying beyond their scope (Haugeland 1981, p. 10).

Upon initial consideration, Haugeland seems to have formulated a con ception going far beyond Newell and Simon's by imposing the requirement that the rules for mark manipulation should be self-contained, perfectly def-inite and finitely checkable, which Haugeland takes to define what makes a system "digital", but which perhaps more closely approximate "algorithmic". When algorithms are defined as *effective decision procedures*, for example, they have the properties of being completely reliable routines, procedures or processes that can be carried out in a finite number of steps to solve a prob-lem, as the Preface, for example, has already explained. Newell and Simon's conception and Haugeland's converge at this point, however, in view of the consideration that the conduct of physical symbol systems is supposed to be governed by programs as implementations of algorithms for these machines.

Algorithms are available to solve a rather large class of problems, includ-ing, especially, problems of mathematics. But an important distinction must be drawn between "algorithms" and "programs", where *programs* implement algorithms in a form suitable for execution by machine. This requires that an algorithm be translated into a progamming language (such as Pascal, LISP, or Prolog), where the corresponding program might be loaded into a computing machine and then compiled into machine language for execution. Ultimately, therefore, distinctions must be drawn between at least four different senses of "program", namely: (a) as algorithms, (b) as encodings of algorithms, (c) as encodings of algorithms that can be compiled or (d) as encodings of algorithms that can be compiled and executed by a machine (Fetzer 1988b, p. 1058). The sense appropriate to Newell and Simon and Haugeland thus corresponds to (d).

While Haugeland's assertions about his conception seem to be weaker than Newell and Simon's about their conception (since he acknowledges that marks manipulated in accordance with the encoding of an algorithm may or may not be meaningful), it should be evident that the underlying objection still obtains, namely: that the marks that are manipulated by means of programs might be meaningful for the *users of* that system—especially, presumably, for those who program them—but are not therefore meaningful for use by that system itself. It may sound appealing to suggest that people *just are* computers, but so long computers are nothing more than syntax processing mechanisms as automated formal systems or even as physical symbol systems, the meaningfulness of the marks they process appears to derive from those who use and who design them.

If people have minds but computers do not, people cannot *simply be* computers. According to (what is known as) *the thesis of strong AI*, computers actually possess mentality when they are executing programs. On the assumption that programs as encodings of algorithms are capable of providing solutions to the problems to which they are being applied, the executions of programs by computers are purposeful activities in relation to their users. But that no more implies that computers therefore have minds than the fact that having an unmowed lawn is a problem that can be solved by cutting it with a lawnmower, which is also a purposeful activity in relation to its user, implies that a lawnmower has a mind. Certainly, neither the physical symbol system conception nor the automated formal system conception satisfies conditions that might plausibly qualify as being enough for mentality. They have the ability to manipulate marks or to process syntax, but that is not sufficient to infuse those marks with meaning.

According to what is known as *the thesis of weak AI*, by comparison, computers are simply tools, devices or instruments that are or may be useful, helpful or valuable in the study of mentality but do not possess minds, even when they are executing programs. Indeed, from this perspective, automatic formal systems and physical symbol systems may be envisioned as physical counter parts that at least partially realize the logical properties of Turing machines in the form of complex causal systems of those very kinds. As long as these machines are constructed to appropriate specifications and subjected to appropriate empirical testing, including quality controls that ensure their reliability or trustworthiness, they need not possess the least inkling of the faintest whiff of the slightest trace of mentality at all. Perhaps automatic formal systems and physical symbol systems define "computational systems" rather than "minds".

Haugeland concedes as much when he maintains that automatic formal systems that consistently make sense—where the semantics follows the syntax, under an appropriate interpretation—are *semantic engines* and that *intelligent beings* are things of that kind (Haugeland 1981, pp. 24, 31). But it should be obvious by now that this formulation trades upon the same ambiguity as before, namely: that an automatic formal system might consistently make sense to the users of that system without consistently making sense—or making any sense at all—to that system itself. It should come as no surprise that formal systems that are constructed with an interpretation in mind consistently make sense—where the semantics follows the syntax, under some appropriate interpretation—when the syntax was intended to sustain that interpretation by the designers of that system. Only confusion arises from confounding interpretability with mentality.

Indeed, as most students of formal logic are aware, even the construction of simple arguments in sentential and in predicate logic assumes that marks and sequences of marks that occur more than once—that appear in both conclusions and premises, for example—must have the same meaning or stand for the same thing throughout the formulation of those arguments. Otherwise, fallacies of ambiguity arise, where conclusions that follow from premises on the basis of the syntactical rules of inference may have conclusions that are false even when their premises are true. If "John has lost his marbles" occurs in both places, for example, then it must be assigned the same interpretation, lest we infer from *John's loss of some small, round balls used in children's games* to *John's loss of mental capacity*. This semantical condition—the requirement of a uniform interpretation—must be satisfied, not only by semantic engines, but by every formal system, that is consistent.

Neither the conception of physical symbol systems nor the conception of automatic formal systems supports the thesis of strong AI rather than its alternative, where these conceptions properly apply. Even the conception of semantic engines does not appear to salvage the situation, since the properties that distinguish computers under that designation are precisely those we would expect them to have as formal systems that can be designed and constructed for the purpose of executing algorithms by means of machines. Neither conception is able to overcome the objection that causal systems with the capacity to manipulate marks or to process syntax—even on the basis of programs that have the capacity to solve problems—do not satisfy conditions sufficient to qualify them for possession of mentality. While the users and designers of these systems must be capable of interpreting them, we have found nothing that would enhance the credibility of the thesis of strong AI.

A stronger blow against the computational conception, however, might be struck if it could be shown that the conditions it would impose are not merely *insufficient* for mentality, as we have already discovered, but are *unnecessary* for mentality, as well. The appropriate strategy in adopting this approach would be to discover some properties—preferably, of a general kind—that are satisfied by any kind of thought that properly qualifies as computational, yet are not always satisfied by thinking things. There appear to be such features. One of the more appealing features of formal proofs for most students, I have observed, is that they begin at a definite starting point—given *premises*—and end at a definite stopping point—the desired *conclusion*. Similarly, algorithms begin with a *problem*, which is given, and end with a *solution*, while programs begin with *input* and end with *output*. What goes on in between, of course, involves the application of rules, processes or procedures.

Moreover, the application of those rules, processes or procedures has the property that they are supposed to be *appropriate* to derive those conclusions from those premises (in the case of proofs), to obtain that solution for that problem (in the case of algorithms) and to generate that output from that input (in the case of programs). Not only are such rules, processes or procedures designed to produce results when when they are applied, they are supposed to yield *the right result* (as valid proofs, correct solutions, or accurate outputs). And, of course, securing the right result has to be something that can be accomplished in a finite number of steps. Otherwise, the system would not satisfy the conditions either for being a semantic engine (as an automatic formal system that is self-contained, perfectly definite, and finitely checkable) or for being algorithmic (as a completely reliable routine, process, or procedure that can be carried out in a finite number of steps to solve a problem).

On the assumption that nothing causal interferes with its physical operation, the execution of software by hardware has the effect of creating a system whose behavior conforms to special *normative* constraints defined by these properties. Indeed, that is precisely what we should expect of a computational system that has been designed to fulfill the requirements of an automatic formal system or of a physical symbol system. Computational systems thus appear to be properly envisioned as complex causal systems that are designed and constructed as syntax-processing or mark-manipulating systems, which conform to the restrictions imposed upon semantic engines or physical symbol systems. They have the ability to execute algorithms encoded into the form of programs by means of a programming language that enables them to function properly. They thus appear to be normatively-directed, problem-solving, syntax-processing causal systems.

On the assumption that the kind of syntax-processing systems under consideration are classic (or "von Neumann") digital machines, there are many indications that regarding them as normatively-directed, problem-solving causal systems is appropriate within in this context. Robert Cummins and Georg Schwarz (1991), for example, define "computing" as the *execution of functions*, which entails the execution of algorithms: "computing a function *f* is executing an algorithm that gives *o* as its output on input *i* just in case f(*i*) = *o*" (Cummins and Schwarz 1991, p. 62). Executing an algorithm, in turn, involves *disciplined step satisfaction* or satisfying various steps "in the right order". This conception thus presumes the existence of a beginning (input) and an end (output), where the application of an appropriate routine, process or procedure (algorithm) yields the right result in a finite number of steps. They are normatively directed, problem-solving systems.

Moreover, as Eric Dietrich has observed, the same function may be implemented in more than one way. Indeed, "Computer scientists frequently distinguish between *computing a function* and *executing a procedure* because every procedure realizes exactly one function, but the same function can be realized in several different procedures" (Dietrich 1990, p. 192, emphasis added). This distinction has great merit, not only because the same algorithm can be implemented in various different programs but also because "computing a function" appears to be a more abstract description than is that of "executing a procedure". Indeed, pure mathematics may perhaps be best understood as a domain of abstract entities between which only logical relations can obtain, while applied mathematics concerns a domain of physical entities between which causal relations can obtain (Fetzer 1988c). It might be helpful to entertain "functions" as abstract and "procedures" as causal.

The multiplication tables of my youth affords an appropriate illustration. My fifth-grade teacher was concerned because I had not learned multiplication and the functions thereby defined, such as that 0 x 0 = 0, that 8 x 7 = 56, that 8 x 8 = 64, and so on, which map values in a domain onto those of a corresponding range: See Figure 4.1

Strictly speaking, I suppose, it would not have mattered to him whether I had internalized this function by means of addition (where the value of < 8, 8 >, for example, is obtained by adding 8 to itself 8 times) or by some other procedure, as long as it gave the right results. What mattered was whether I had mastered multiplication by becoming a normatively-directed, problem-

Figure 4.1   Multiplication Tables

Domain	Range
< 0 , 0 >	0
< 0 , 1 >	0
. . .	. . .
< 8 , 7 >	56
< 8 , 8 >	64
. . .	. . .
< 9 , 9 >	81

solving system of a special kind by implementing this set of functions as a set of mental procedures.

Dietrich (1990) and Cummins and Schwarz (1991) go much further, however, and define "cognition" as the computation of functions. On their view, *cognition* implies the execution of procedures, which, of course, can be causal counterparts of functions in an abstract domain. Thus, the kinds of things that are capable of cognition are the kinds of things that are capable of the computation of functions (abstractly described), which entails the capacity for the execution of procedures (implemented causally). If the capacity for cognition is the distinctive characteristic of things that have minds, then the kinds of things that are capable of the execution of procedures are also the kinds of things that have minds. Insofar as the execution of procedures entails disciplined step satisfaction, therefore, minds are a species of normatively-directed, problem-solving syntax-processing causal systems.

So if our minds satisfy this conception, perhaps people *just are* computers, after all.

4.2   Minds and Machines

It is fascinating to observe, therefore, that many kinds of thought processes of human beings as thinking things fail to satisfy these conditions. *Dreams and daydreams*, for example, fail to satisfy them because they have no definite starting point and no definite stopping point: they begin and they end, but they have no given premises or conclusions. The sequence of events between their beginnings and their endings has a causal character that is neither normatively directed nor problem solving in kind. They do not have to satisfy appropriateness conditions, and there are no right results for them to yield. They may contribute to solving problems—emotional or otherwise—but when that occurs, it is incidental to rather than constitutive of thought processes of this kind (Fetzer 1994a). Some dreams and daydreams may be pleasant or enjoyable, while others may be frightening or even terrifying. But these thought processes are certainly not computational.

Perception appears to be another case of this kind. Properly understood, of course, the results of perception arise as a consequence of causal interaction between the perceiver and the perceived. As a human phenomenon, it may often involve the use of language to describe the contents of experience. The completeness, accuracy and detail with which experience can be described thus depends upon our ability to use language, but it also depends on our perceptual abilities and the circumstances under which perceptions are acquired. All of these factors vary tremendously from new-born infants to toddling tots to the elderly and the senile and from case to case. Even assuming that perceptual episodes have a beginning and an end, what transpires in between lacks the normative character of always yielding the right result. Perception is a fallible activity, which makes perception a second kind of non-computational thought process.

Memory is yet another case. Since memories are retained as effects of the occurrence of past perceptions, there are at least two ways in which they can be faulty: our original perceptions may be mistaken or our retentions of those original perceptions may be wrong. The very idea of remembering something that never occurred may initially sound anomalous, but when you consider the influence of the multiple conditions that affect perception—including ones both internal and external to the perceiver, including attention span, state of awareness, and perceptual access—as well as the multiple conditions that affect memory—including physical age, temporal proximity to the original occurrence, and presence or absence of impairment—it should be obvious that there is no algorithm for remembering. There is no finite sequence of steps such that, if those steps are followed, then a specific memory will be recalled—not even hypnosis.

One underlying factor that may contribute to confusion about the scope and limits of computational procedures arises from failing to systematically differentiate causal processes that *implement the normative procedures that distinguish the execution of algorithms* from those that do not. Laws of nature that are causal rather than non-causal—no matter whether they are deterministic or probabilistic in kind—bring about changes in systems across time from state *S1* at time *t1* to state *S2* at time *t2*. There are no doubt causal laws of dreams and daydreams, perception and memory, just as there causal laws for physical, chemical and biological processes and systems. But special constraints must be satisfied by computational systems that do not have to be satisfied by other kinds of causal systems. Thought processes that do not invariably yield definite solutions to problems in a finite number of steps can still be non-computational properties of thinking things.

What is most striking about dreams and daydreams, perception and memory within this context is that they are familiar phenomena from the life experience of human beings. When we reflect upon our experiences in life, it seems obvious that many if not most of our ordinary thought processes do not properly qualify as the execution of procedures. There are no algorithms for when to start looking and when to stop looking or even how to look such that, if only you follow this procedure, then your perceptions must be accurate and you cannot make a mistake. There are no algorithms for when to start remembering or for how to go about remembering. Saying to yourself, "Remember!", certainly will not do. The very idea of compelling yourself to remember is at least faintly ridiculous. The case of dreams and daydreams is even more compelling as an example of a causal process each of us experiences that is not a computational procedure.

The question might therefore be posed, "Why should the computational conception be taken seriously at all?", to which I conjecture there are at least three possible answers. One is that we may be uncertain about the nature of thought and of thought processes themselves. If dreams and daydreams, perception and memory are not processes involving thought, then they do not count as counterexamples to the computational conception. Indeed, if cognition turned out to be computation, then they would not be examples of cognition. Such a result, however, would surely strain the plausibility of the computational account severely. Not least of the benefits to be derived from adopting the conception of minds as semiotic systems is that any kind of sign-using system possesses mentality, no matter whether the signs such a system is processing are dreams or daydreams and no matter whether those processes conform to normative constraints or not.

A second possible reason for taking computationalism seriously may be that we have not adequately understood the properties that separate computational procedures specifically from causal processes generally. If changes in systems from state $S1$ at time $t1$ to state $S2$ at time $t2$ in accordance with causal laws always qualified as *disciplined step satisfaction*, for example, then the difference between computational procedures and causal processes remains obscure. Any causal process could be cognitive. Another benefit to be derived from adopting the semiotic conception of mentality, therefore, is that it can explain why causal processes in physics, chemistry and biology, for example, can involve changes in systems from state $S1$ at time $t1$ to state $S2$ at time $t2$ without displaying mentality on that account alone. Causal processes qualify as "cognitive" only when they involve the use of signs by a sign-using system. Most of them are not cognitive.

A third reason for taking computationalism seriously may be the conjecture that, if some of our cognitive processes are computational procedures, perhaps all of our cognitive processes are computational procedures. Haugeland exemplifies this attitude when he suggests that thought "obeys (at least much of the time) various rules of inference and reason" (Haugeland 1981, p. 3) and covertly implies that thinking is reducible to reasoning. Indeed, if thinking is reducible to reasoning and reasoning is reducible to computing, then perhaps the boundaries of computation exhaust the boundaries of thought. Such an approach, however, not only runs the risk of *begging the question* by assuming that human reasoning is a computational process but the risk of *overgeneralization* by assuming that the kinds of routines, processes or procedures that operate in one domain of thought operate in every other. Computationalism thus seems to be founded on fallacies.

Perhaps the most striking effort to bolster the computational conception has been advanced by Barbara von Eckhardt (1993), who adopts the strategy of taking the central aim of cognitive science to be "the human adult's normal, typical cognition (ANTCOG for short)" (von Eckhardt 1993, p. 6). The ANTCOG approach thus excludes from consideration variations in cognitive capacities and abilities ranging from those of new-born infants and toddling tots to those of the elderly and senile. The domain of human cognition is taken to be capacities or abilities that are intentional or purposeful, pragmatically evaluable as more or less successful, coherent when they are successful, usually reliable, and productive in having potentially unrestricted applicability (von Eckhardt 1993, pp. 47-48). The effect of adopting these conditions is to constrict the range of pragmatical phenomena within the domain to which cognitive science is supposed to apply.

The rather flexible character of the properties that von Eckhardt adopts to define the properties of human cognition seems initially promising within the scope of its limited domain, where the course of science should decide whether typical, normal adult human cognition is computational or not. She diminishes the tenability of her own position, however, by adopting (what she refers to as) *two major substantive assumptions*, namely: that cognition is computational and that cognition involves representations (von Eckhardt 1993, p. 8). Her account of the general character of cognitive science thus implies that non-computational phenomena or non-representational phenomena cannot possibly be cognitive. The basic conception of von Eckhardt, therefore, is that cognition is computation across representations, which is true by stipulation. She thereby precludes the logical possibility that there might be non-computational cognitive phenomena.

From the perspective of the philosophy of science, von Eckhardt's work thus exemplifies the historical dilemma encountered by normal scientists, who have a paradigm in which they believe but are also confronted by anomalies. In this case the paradigm is defined by the conception that *cognition is computation across representations*. The anomalies are displayed by phenomena—such as dreams and daydreams, perception and memory—that appear to involve representations but also seem to be non-computational. von Eckhardt's account entails that phenomena of this kind cannot possibly be cognitive, which appears to be a rather difficult position to defend. Those who take the phenomena seriously, after all, already have empirical evidence that falsifies the computational paradigm, while those who adhere to the paradigm have only a definitional stipulation to justify its dismissal. Surely the phenomena have to be taken seriously.

von Eckhardt thus begs the question in taking for granted that cognition must be computational. This is difficult to understand, since she acknowledges that the concepts of computation and of representation "are (for the present, at least) quite open-ended and vague" (von Eckhardt 1993, p. 9). Indeed, her position is untenable in at least two respects. First, she appears to have succumbed to the almost irresistible temptation to identify the discipline itself (as a field of inquiry) with one of the theories that inspired it (the computational conception), a fatal defect in a work that pretends to define the field. The second is that less open-ended and more precise concepts of computation—involving algorithms, functions and disciplined step satisfaction—imply that computational procedures always yield definite solutions to problems in a finite number of steps. Her "flexible" conception of the domain of cognition appears to be inconsistent with her substantive commitments.

Ultimately, von Eckhardt also adopts the conception of computers as devices that are capable of accepting, storing, manipulating, and outputting data or information in accordance with a set of effective rules, characterizing minds—"if they are computers at all"—as automatic formal systems, very much as Haugeland envisions them (von Eckhardt 1993, p. 113). If she senses a tension in her implicit commitment to the twin theses that computers do not have minds, even though minds are computational systems and operate the same way computers operate, which apparently implies that even minds do not have minds, she does not reveal it. Indeed, occasionally she suggests the possibility that the computational model of the mind might be no more than a metaphor; other times, she hints that it has to be taken literally. But she also states that the seriousness with which it should be taken depends upon the level of theoretical detail that is available and desired.

A better definition of "cognitive science", of course, would be that of the science of cognition—whether in human beings, other animals, or even machines, if such a thing is possible—which appears to be the appropriate conception. The constraints that von Eckhardt imposes on the pragmatical phenomena of cognition combined with her substantive assumptions guarantee the emergence of a semantical model of cognition as computation over representations, *no matter what the phenomena*, which is unscientific. Indeed, dreams, daydreams, perception and memory appear to be typical cognitive experiences of even most normal adult human beings, which is evident from the perspective of Peirce's theory of signs. The images, events and words that are the stuff of dreams, daydreams, perception and memory are things that stand for other things in various respects for somebody, which qualifies them as "representatives" that are components of non-computational cognitive processes.

Even though von Eckhardt adopts Peirce's theory of signs in the guise of a theory of representations, a term that Peirce himself employed—which I applaud—her commitment to computationalism apparently precludes her from appreciating what the theory of signs has the potential to reveal about the nature of cognition. The triadic sign relation, for example, implies (1) the existence of a causal relation between a sign and a sign user; (2) a semantic relation between the sign and that for which it stands; and (3) a behavioral relation between the sign, its user and that for which it stands. The existence of a semantic (or "grounding") relation between signs and what they stand for is significant, first, because it offers an explanation for how a thing *can stand for something else* (by virtue of a relation of resemblance, of cause or effect, or of habitual association) and, second, because it also explains how something can stand for something else *in some respect or other* (by virtue of a relation of partial resemblance, of partial cause or effect, or of partial habitual association).

More significantly within the present context, these considerations are able to explain the underlying difference between semiotic systems and symbol systems and automatic formal systems, where genuine mentality presupposes *the existence of a grounding relation* between signs and that for which they stand. If minds of Type I can use icons as signs that are grounded in resemblance relations, minds of Type II can use indices as signs that are grounded in cause and effect relations, and minds of Type III can use symbols as signs that are grounded in habitual or conventional associations, while symbol systems in Newell and Simon's sense and automatic formal systems in Haugeland's sense cannot, then this can account for their difference with respect to semantics and meaning. Semiotic systems have the ability to use things to stand for other things as signs for those systems, an ability that symbol systems and automatic formal systems do not possess. This property distinguishes between systems with minds and without (Fetzer 1988a, 1990, 1991/96; cf. Searle 1992).

The differences between semiotic systems and symbol systems are not confined to the fact that symbol systems have the capacity to process syntax in the form of meaningless marks, while semiotic systems have the capacity to process signs that are meaningful for those systems. This might be described as a difference in *semantic content*: semiotic systems process signs that have semantic content for those systems themselves, but symbol systems manipulate marks that are meaningful, if they are meaningful at all, only for the users of those systems. There is, however, another difference at stake here, which is displayed by the fact that dreams, daydreams, perception and memory are processes that do not involve the execution of procedures. This might be described as a difference in *causal processing*: symbol systems process marks by the execution of computational procedures, but semiotic systems also have the capacity to process signs by non-computational procedures.

The difference in content that exists because semiotic systems have an ability which symbol systems lack can be displayed by means of the following diagram:

Figure 4.2 Semiotic Systems versus Symbol Systems

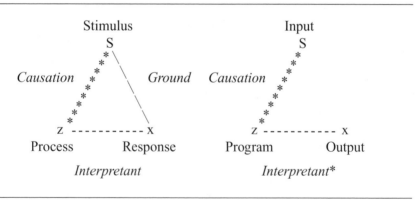

Some of the differences between symbol systems and semiotic systems are obvious from these diagrams. A grounding relationship between signs and what they stand for for a sign-user does not appear in the symbol system diagram, precisely because the absence of such a relationship is the most important feature distinguishing between systems of these kinds. Indeed, even when something affects the behavior of another thing (as causes bring about effects or as stimuli bring about responses), unless that causal connection obtains *because* that thing functions as *a sign* relative to those effects—unless it functions as an icon, an index or a symbol for that system—that connection cannot be semiotic.

"Interpretant" thus stands for a dispositional account of the meaning of a sign for a semiotic system, where the totality of ways in which that system would (invariably or probably) behave in the presence of that sign in relation to different (possibly infinite) specific contexts—including preexisting motives and beliefs but also other abilities and capabilities—is *the meaning of that sign* for such a system. "Behavior" in this sense includes changing one's mind, where two systems, even when confronting the same sign with the same meaning for them both, would be expected to display the same behavior only when they were in the same context.

> When drivers approach an intersection and notice a red traffic light, they tend to apply the breaks and come to a complete halt until the light turns green, but possibly not when they are frantic husbands with wives in labor, felons who are fleeing the police, or driving emergency vehicles. (Fetzer 1989, 1990, 1991, 1998)

"Interpretant*", instead, stands for a dispositional account of input processing by a symbol system, which is the totality of computations that that system would perform, relative to a specific program—assuming that other components of that causal system function properly—which, however, is not a semiotic phenomenon. von Eckhardt embraces a conception of this kind, which she extends to (what she calls) *mental representations*, where "The interpretant of a mental representation R for some subject S consists of the set of all possible determinate computational processes contingent upon entertaining R in S" (von Eckhardt 1993, pp 297-298). By virtue of its restriction to computational consequences, however, this conception has the effect of delimiting the causal consequences of cognition to its logical consequences. Human beings are complex semiotic causal systems rather than normatively directed, computational causal systems of the kind she has defined.

4.3   Consciousness and Cognition

Other benefits of the semiotic approach may be less obvious. The theory also implies a conception of consciousness (relative to signs of specific kinds) according to which a system is *conscious* (relative to signs of specific kinds) when it (a) possesses the ability to use signs of that kind and (b) is not incapacitated from exercising that ability. When a system is anesthetized, intoxicated, blindfolded or otherwise impaired, it may be incapacitated from the exercise of some of its semiotic abilities. Moreover, when properly understood, *cognition* is an effect that is brought about by a causal interaction between the presence of signs of specific kinds (within suitable causal proximity) and a system that is conscious with respect to signs of that kind in relation to its *context*, consisting of its other internal states, including preexisting motives and beliefs. Rather than computation across representations, *cognition is a causal process that involves signs*.

This approach also appears to resolve "Block's problem". Ned Block (1995a) has made a plausible case for drawing a distinction between *P-consciousness* (phenomenal-consciousness) and *A-consciousness* (access-consciousness), but he has been unable to locate their "real difference" (Block 1995b). However, Block's conception of P-consciousness appears to apply to the causal relationship between *possible* signs and semiotic systems, while his conception of Aconsciousness appears to apply to the causal relationship between *actual* signs and semiotic systems. P-consciousness thus appears to be the experience of a (potentially semiotic) phenomenon, while A-consciousness is an interpretation of its significance. A semiotic system can have P-consciousness without A-consciousness whenever it is subjected to things that are not signs for that system. P-consciousness thus turns out to be necessary but not sufficient for cognition.

The semiotic theory also compares favorably with that of minds as semantic engines. The difficulty confronting the conception of minds as automatic formal systems that consistently make sense—where the semantics follows the syntax, under an appropriate interpretation—has always been the source and character of that interpretation. The most popular candidates for that role among current alternatives have been the *language of thought hypothesis*, which posits a genetic species-specific semantics of in-born concepts (especially Fodor 1975), and *causal theories of meaning* (Schwartz 1977, for example), which effect an interpretation by means of reference, which we encountered in Chapter 1. The first supplies an internalist account for which meanings are innate, the second an externalist account for which meanings are acquired. Neither seems to qualify as a viable alternative to the semiotic theory that languages, for example, are systems of signs that are gradually learned to describe innate or acquired concepts.

The language of thought hypothesis, for example, presumes that understanding a language presupposes understanding another language, which invites the introduction of *a base language*—the language of thought—relative to which any other language might be acquired. This account not only overlooks the prospect that language learning might be rooted in *non-linguistic* understanding instead, an approach the semiotic conception embraces, but also implies that unsuccessful translations between different languages must be a theoretical impossibility. Causal theories of meaning, moreover, presuppose the existence of causal chains that connect names and predicates to their referents, an assumption that seems appealing for ordinary uses of familiar terms but appears appalling in any case where causal chains cannot or do not exist: non-existent objects, abstract entities, theoretical relations, and non-observable properties, as Chapter 1 explains.

Perhaps the most far-reaching discovery that has emerged from the pursuit of the semiotic conception of mentality, however, concerns the nature of the laws of thought. While it appears unproblematical to maintain that perception and memory, for example, are semiotic activities governed by causal laws, the conception of cognition as an effect brought about by causal interaction between a sign user and a sign may appear inadequate in comparison with the computational conception of cognition as the execution of procedures, which are causal counterparts of functions in an abstract domain. The causal processes that relate signs to other signs and meaning and behavior for ordinary thought, however, which is neither normatively-governed nor problem-solving in kind, appear to be associationistic rather than computationalistic. They do not satisfy the conditions of disciplined step satisfaction but rather approximate the free association of ideas.

Consider, for example, the following panels drawn by the humorist B. Kliban, which are the first and second in a series entitled "Cornish Game Clams: A False Start in Six Parts" (Kliban 1982). These capture the typical thought processes of ordinary human beings. Panel 1, for example, shows a fellow responding to the waiter's presentation by saying, "Ah! Cornish game clams, my favorite seafood!", where the meal itself was an icon that resembled other meals of a certain kind, which, in turn, caused the effect of bringing to his mind symbols by which food of that kind is described. His use of the phrase, "cornish game clams", in turn, is a cause that trigger's off another diner's recollection of related experiences as an effect, where he and Professor Jimbob were exploring an incredibly ancient temple. Thinking of this experience causes him to become pale, which functions as an index for his dining companion, who uses symbols to inquire about its cause, and so on.

Panel 2 is, if anything, even more revealing. As he and Professor Jimbob proceed to the temple to rescue Lydia, he hears her cries for help, symbols functioning as causes intended to bring about an effect. Hearing her cries reminds him of similar sounds made by the brakes on his old convertible on the basis of a resemblance relation, which, in turn, was an effect brought about by that cause. Thinking about the car, he recalls associated experiences indexically related to that car, including the night that Shirley's dress got sucked into the carburetor, where she is identified symbolically by her first name, which causes him to try to remember her last name, "Wozzle? Winkle? Workle?", which, successfully recalled, in turn, reminds him of her activities as associated effects thus brought to mind, which included singing at the Pancake House on Thursdays, for example, where one sign causes cognitive connections with other signs as a series of semiotic associations.

Figure 4.3   Panel 1 of "Cornish Game Clams"

Figure 4.4   Panel 2 of "Cornish Game Clams"

These panels (about which a great deal more could be said) provide vivid illustrations of the associative character of ordinary thought. In these cases, what we are observing are themselves iconic and symbolic representations of a series of semiotic associations, which displays an absence of the kind of disciplined step satisfaction characteristic of computational systems. These thought processes do not satisfy the computational conception and therefore properly count against it. It should also be observed that *the same thing*, such as the presentation of food, can function as an *icon* (by virtue of resembling other things of that kind), as an *index* (by virtue of being a cause of a future effect, for example), or as a *symbol* (by virtue of being habitually associated with things of other kinds). The cognitive effects of a sign within suitable causal proximity of a sign-using system that is conscious with respect to signs of that kind, therefore, appears heavily dependent upon context and may be either an indeterministic or a chaotic phenomenon.

Moreover, a distinction parallel to that between intension and extension may be drawn according to which a person's *connotation* (relative to a word, phrase, or expression) consists of their emotions or attitudes toward things of that kind, while a person's *denotation* (relative to that same word, phrase, or expression) consists in the subset of the class of things thereby described with which that person has acquaintance (iconically or indexically). Then ordinary thought also differs from logical reasoning insofar as the former is strongly affected by subjective connotations and denotations, as a function of their personal histories, while the latter is generally dominated by objective intensions and extensions, as a function of their language framework. This is a crucial dimension on which (psychological) semiotic associations differ from systematic (logical) reasoning.

It also undermines even the most enticing attempts to defend computationalism, such as Steven Pinker, *How the Mind Works* (1997), which envisions minds as information processing mechanisms of brains for effecting logical transitions between different "configurations of symbols". Pinker goes so far as to contend that a computational conception of mind is indispensable for understanding the evolution of the mind, where "evolution equips us . . . with a neural computer" (Pinker 1997, p. 27). But it should be evident that an adequate understanding of animal minds, primate minds, and human minds—much less their evolution—is most unlikely to be supplied by the computational conception, which appears to have arisen from an almost irresistible temptation to appeal to a domain in which a great deal is known (formal systems and computability) as a repository of answers to questions in a domain about which very little is known (mentality and cognition), an approach that can no longer be sustained (Fetzer 1994a, p. 25).

The semiotic conception of the mind also supplies a criterion for mentality in the form of *the capacity to make a mistake* (Fetzer 1988a, 1990, and 1991/96). A system can make a mistake just in case it has the ability to take something as standing for something (else) in some respect or other, but does so wrongly (by taking one individual thing for another individual thing, a thing of one kind for a thing of another kind, the false for the true, and so forth). Insofar as the semiotic conception is intended to apply to systems that have minds, no matter whether they are human, other animal, or even machine (if such a thing is possible), it is indispensable that the very idea of mentality should not beg the question by implying the applicability or inapplicability of this conception to systems of any of these kinds on the basis of a mere stipulation. If other animals or computing machines are capable of making mistakes, then they are possessors of mentality.

It should be observed, moreover, that misdescriptions, faulty inferences, and the like qualify as "mistakes" only if they are unintentional. If we distinguish between *standard cognitive situations* in which our intentions are truth-directed (in seeking to discover the truth, speak the truth, and so forth), then we tend to make mistakes when the available evidence does not support an appropriate inference— although, of course, even when sufficient evidence is available, we may still make mistakes when reasoning is inductive. A pragmatical condition—the requirement of total evidence—thus insists that, in arriving at conclusions, we must take into account all of the available relevant evidence. When we are in *non-standard cognitive situations*, however, where our intentions are not truth-directed (in desiring to mislead, to amuse, to insult, and so on), misdescriptions, miscalculations, and misdirections might then not actually qualify as "mistakes" (Coates 1997, pp. 171–197).

The realization that many if not most thought processes—including dreams and daydreams, perception and memory, and ordinary thinking—do not fulfill the conception of being normatively-governed, problem-solving causal activities does not mean that we never function in that capacity. As I and other students of symbolic logic have found, when *syntactical procedures* are adequately understood (within the context of constructing and evaluating formal proofs, for example), human beings seem to be capable of functioning (more or less) as though we were computational systems. Indeed, as Carol Cleland (1993) has observed, there exists a class of *mundane procedures* that are often employed to achieve specific effects, such as recipes for cooking and instructions for assembling. When implemented under appropriate causal conditions, these step-by-step routines bring about their effects as an especially interesting class of non-syntactical but still effective procedures.

It should have been apparent from the start, however, that the computational conception—according to which thinking is reducible to reasoning and reasoning is reducible to computing—casts a shallow net in relation to human cognitive abilities. The semiotic activities of human beings are barely tapped by deductive reasoning, where conclusions are drawn from premises and arguments are appraised. The use of declarative sentences that are true or false is not even representative of human linguistic abilities, which include the use of imperative sentences to issue directions and commands, exclamatory sentences to express emotions and attitudes, and interrogatory sentences to ask questions and make inquiries. Once we abandon a propositional paradigm and embrace a speech-act paradigm, where the diversity of human cognitive activities can be more adequately appraised, we soon discover that the dispositional conception that attends the conception of minds as semiotic systems offers an even broader and more powerful theory of meaning and mentality.

Even though human beings are indeed capable of disciplined step satisfaction in formal reasoning and in mundane procedures, activities of this kind seem to be special cases that are not representative of most human cognition. If the theory is taken to assert that *all* human cognitive activities are computational, it is false; but taken to assert that only *some* human cognitive activities are computational, it is trivial. Even our own experiences in life display that the computational conception cannot be sustained. Thinking is not reducible to computing, and minds are not merely digital machines. In abstracting from the pragmatic phenomena, its proponents have begged the question by assuming that procedures that may apply in one domain must apply in every other, where the theoretical model that they provide is neither sound nor complete. "Our best theory" is either trivial or false, where the conception of minds as semiotic systems offers something better.

5

Gene-Culture Co-Evolution

In his admirable study, *Sociobiology, Sex, and Science* (1993), Harmon Holcomb III has made the crucial observation, "Sociobiology does not explain behavior *per se*. It explains the evolution of behavior, that is, the evolution of behavioral preconditions (whether physical or psychological) and their effects upon behavior. This limits sociobiology's scope, placing limitations on its pro- per implications". These "behavioral preconditions" typically take the form of *predispositions* toward the acquisition of specific dispositions, where "A disposition of an organisim to do something is its tendency to behave in a certain manner under given circumstances" (p. 341). It is these organismic capacities and the conditions that trigger their effects that are the appropriate phenomena for sociobiological explanation, relative to their evolutionary determinants.

In Holcomb's view, it was no accident that Wilson's *Sociobiology* (1975) was written in three parts (on processes of social evolution, on social mechanisms, and on the social species), because those parts correspond to ideal explanations in evolution: "Evolutionary explanations ideally explain (a) past and present distributions of characters in local populations of organisms of various species in terms of (b) the effects of evolutionary processes, given (c) relevant parameters, (d) on mechanisms for survival and/or reproduction operative in the course of the evolutionary past". Thus, Holcomb maintains that "evolutionary theory would be complete if everything in category (a) could be derived as expected from exhaustive specifications of explanatory factors in categories (b), (c), and (d)" by means of explanations of the kind that I discussed in Chapter 1.

Holcomb thus properly rejects Wilson's presumption that sociobiology must subsume the social sciences and denies both the reductionistic and the anti-reductionistic theses "that a completed social science either would or would not be reducible to a completed evolutionary biology" (pp. 297–98). The scientific success of sociobiology, in Holcomb's view, depends upon continued progress in moving from anecdotal evidence and popular beliefs to statistical generalizations and lawful hypotheses about human behavior. The future of the discipline thus hinges upon the discovery of additional causal factors, intervening variables and auxiliary theories that close the gap between sociobiological theory (hypothesis/explanans) and observed patterns of behavior (evidence/explanandum). Holcomb thereby avoids the pitfall of embracing reductionism or other unworthy ideologies.

Indeed, to the considerable extent to which the social sciences and humanities study emergent properties of human beings, they cannot properly be reduced to biology and evolution alone. Even though there may be genetically-based predispositions for broad ranges of social behavior, the emergence of social behavior in specific forms, including specific social organizations and specific group behavior, appears to hinge upon the transmission of customs, traditions, and practices as a manifestation of cultural evolution as opposed to genetic evolution, where cultural evolution employs different mechanisms of transmission than genetic evolution. In particular, as we shall discover, cultural evolution permits the inheritance of acquired characteristics (and is therefore Lamarckian), whereas genetic evolution precludes the inheritance of acquired characteristics (and is therefore Darwinian).

5.1 Minds and Their Bodies

The last few chapters have been devoted to the elaboration of a theory of the nature of mentality that might apply to human beings, other animals, and inanimate machines, if such a thing is possible, without belaboring the connections between minds and their bodies. In her stimulating work, *The Roots of Thinking* (1990a), Maxine Sheets-Johnstone has advanced a conception of hominid evolution that emphasizes concepts rather than words and communication rather than language. Indeed, she focuses upon the role of the body in understanding the mind, where their interrelations have gone largely unappreciated in theoretical work up until now, especially at the hands of philosophers. She endorses J.S. Haldane's fundamental axiom of biology: that the life sciences are properly devoted to the study of the life of organisms as *Darwinian bodies*.

In criticizing mainstream philosophical research on the nature of mentality, Sheets-Johnstone castigates the artificial separation of the mind from the body:

Because "the mental" can be conceived as estranged from, and even [as] thoroughly independent of "the physical" (not as a brain in a vat but as a pure spirit or "thinking substance"), and in consequence, because the Darwinian body can easily fall through the crack, it is most reasonable to begin an investigation of the roots of human thinking from the perspective of the Darwinian body, that is, with interacting living creatures in the throes, pleasures, industries, and curiosities of their everday lives. (Sheets-Johnstone 1990a, pp. 304–05)

Thus, from her perspective, Darwinian bodies as products of natural selection should be understood as subject to further transformation by means of other kinds of selection, which include sexual, cultural, and metacultural varieties.

This point of view supports the conception presented in previous chapters of the emergence of *Homo* as more or less continuous with that of other forms of animal life, where many of our differences are properly viewed as matters of degree rather than as matters of kind. This is especially the case with respect to concepts and communication, which are presupposed by and not dependent upon words and languages as such. Indeed, the most fundamental tenet elaborated in her work may be the existence of *a biological disposition to use one's own body as a semantic template in communicating with other members of one's species or of one's group* (Sheets-Johnstone 1990a, p. 308).

This species-specific biological disposition manifests itself especially in the form of *signals* which are common to the members of the species or the group by virtue of reflecting common behaviors. The set of signals common to a specific species or to a specific group, as Sheets-Johnstone reports, are referred to "comsigns" by Stuart Altman. Some comsigns appear to arise as a consequence of analogical thinking hinging upon some commonality of animate form and of tactile-kinesthetic experience, which presupposes the existence of tactile-kinesthetic invariants by every normal member of a species. The common neurophysiology of Darwinian bodies thus creates the potential for similar sensations under similar conditions within species.

Examples that she explores include hardness as a property of teeth and also of stones. The use of the teeth for chewing and biting as well as other tactile-kinesthetic sensations involving the tongue or fingers running over the teeth give rise to the concept of hardness and of the uses to which hard things might be put. In a similar fashion, the association of a bipedal gait and what she calls "recognition counting" involves the recognition of similarities between bodily parts and bodily behavior, where walking involves making one step after another, where each normal member of the species possesses two arms, two legs, and so on, as aspects of their "animate form". Features of our body and behavior thereby provide the roots for thinking.

The role of analogical thinking can be illustrated by Sheets-Johnstone's analysis of hardness. The contact of our tongue with our teeth provides a tactile-kinesthetic introduction to hardness as a property of teeth, which gives rise to the concept of hardness as a property that teeth possess. In broadening our experience of the world to encompass other things which are also hard, such as stones, we tend to reason by analogy that, since our teeth are useful for biting and chewing, perhaps stones are useful for similar purposes. Reasoning by analogy is never conclusive, which means we can sometimes be surprised to discover that we are wrong. But it affords a process of thinking by means of which such concepts can be generalized.

The discovery of hardness may also have been promoted by observing that some things can be used to break other things, but not *vice versa*. This suggests that ordering relations between different degrees of hardness may have emerged early in hominid experience, more or less as a reflection of operational definitions of that kind. Similarly, the ability to count might have been nurtured as much by the need to determine if there is enough food (tools, clothing, and so forth) for the members of a group as much as by our bipedal gait. Yet there little room to doubt that different units of measure have been strongly affected by aspects of animate form.

Henry I of England, for example, defined a yard as the length from the tip of his nose to the end of his arm. One inch was the length of three barley corns laid end to end. And the instructions found in an old textbook for land surveyors specified the length of a rod as follows: "Stop 16 men coming out of church on Sunday, and line them up with their left feet touching. The distance from the toe of the first man to the heel of the last is one rod" (Bernstein *et al.* 1978, p. 1). Comparative concepts of *harder than* and *as hard as* and *not as hard as*, for example, and quantitative concepts of *how many* or of *how much* thus appear to have been closely related to or even directly dependent upon specific features of hominid bodies and behavior.

Sheets-Johnstone maintains further that tactile-kinesthetic invariants predispose organisms toward forms of communication that involve (what she calls) "iconicity", precisely because "the most easily formulated, consistently utilizable, and readily understood signals are those that are similar to bodily behaviors and experiences shared by all the members of the species" (Sheets-Johnstone 1990a, p. 126). Biological tendencies toward the use of the body as a medium of communication by means of gestures, expressions, and other movement, however, should not be supposed to be ones of which the members of a species are invariably conscious or aware. Sometimes these signals involve involuntary behavior, but sometimes not.

Although Sheets-Johnstone tends to focus upon the role of the body as a semantic template for individual members of a species, the commonality of the experiences that different members of the same species share itself supplies a foundation for understanding how communication between the members of a species might be rooted in their similar bodies and in their similar experiences. Some basic forms of thought seem to arise when experiences of one kind come to be associated with experiences of another, for example when tactile-kinesthetic experiences of one kind come to be associated with tactile-kinesthetic experiences of another, which supplies a foundation for anticipating or expecting that one will attend the other.

The prospects for an adequate theory of animal communication and for a more appropriate appreciation of non-verbal modes of communication in relation to the human species are greatly enhanced by Sheets-Johnstone's synthesis of a wide and diversified body of research on animal behavior. Indeed, much of my enthusiasm over the discovery of Sheets-Johnstone's work is that it tends to provide answers for one of the most difficult problems in the theory of language, namely: how did hominids first begin to use language as a form of communication? For it may be that the origin of language can be found in the use of sounds that are naturally connected to that for which they stand (compare Sheets-Johnstone 1990a, Chapter 6).

She focuses attention on the gratuitous and question-begging stance involved in adopting the alternative hypothesis that human speech first began with symbols as sounds that were arbitrarily related to the things for which they stand, which appears to be a wholly untenable contention. As an extension of her approach, it is not difficult to imagine that cries of pain, shouts of anger, laughter and such must have been some of the more basic elements of primitive forms of auditory communication. Thus, some sound that resembles the sound that one hominid would make were a wild animal to attack could readily have come to stand for an attack of that kind, where it might later be replaced by other sounds having the same meaning.

While Sheets-Johnstone tends to emphasize features of "semanticity" or meaning and of "iconicity" or resemblance as essential to comsigns which were utilized by early hominids, at least one more ingredient appears to have played a fundamental role, namely: relations between causes and effects. That different instances of specific sounds are both instances of the same sound depends upon the capacity to recognize resemblance relations between them. Cries of pain, shouts of anger, laughter and the like, however, are surely important as causes or effects of that for which they stand. Their meaning ("semanticity") is not a matter of resemblance at all.

Of course, this qualification may be viewed as little more than a refinement of Sheets-Johnstone's conception, since the reason why cries of pain, shouts of anger, laughter and such are able to function as comsigns within a community of conspecificies appears to be due to analogical thinking of the kind I have already described. Indeed, once we have mastered the relationship between sounds that are cries and sensations of pain, sounds that are shouts and feelings of anger, and sounds that are laughs and experiences of joy, it no longer seems difficult to imagine that the members of a community of conspecifics could tend to communicate on such a basis.

Many of the examples that Sheets-Johnstone employs to illustrate her theses tend to support such an interpretation. When a male pygmy chimpanzee wants to invite a female to join him in sexual activity, for example, he tends to approach within five yards or so and lie back while exposing his erect pink penis and gazing intently in the female's direction (Sheets-Johnstone 1990a, pp. 98–99, which is based upon N. Thompson-Handler, R.K. Malenky, and N. Badrian 1984). The pygmy chimpanzee thereby focuses attention upon his preparation for copulation. Unsurprisingly, through the use of his body this way, everyone gets the message.

Sometimes, however, the body is used to conceal rather than to reveal. In a paper, "Taking Evolution Seriously" (1990b), for example, Sheets-Johnstone reports other observations which George Schaller has made of lions. Thus, in one field study, he asserts that a female lioness, after a kill, may sometimes behave as though nothing has happened, to avoid sharing her bounty with other members of her pride (Sheets-Johnstone 1990b, p. 15, n. 22). In many ways, the lioness's behavior may be even more interesting than the penile displays of the pygmy monkey, not least of all because it involves using bodily gestures to deceive other conspecifics and thereby prevent them from doing something that they otherwise would tend to do.

Because thinking in terms of symbols appears to presuppose the capacity to think in terms of causes and effects, and thinking in terms of causes and effects appears to presuppose the capacity to recognize relations of resemblance, these abilities may well represent three stages in the evolution of mentality. While they can be viewed vertically as a hierarchy of modes of mentality of increasing strength, they can also be viewed horizontally as a sequence of stages in the evolution of minds of successively stronger and stronger kinds. Stronger kinds of minds would appear to afford obvious evolutionary benefits, where the capacity to use symbols, especially, supports the capacity to think about any subject, no matter how abstract.

If such an approach is right-headed, then organisms must develop the capacity to detect resemblance relations before they can develop the ability to detect causal connections. And they must have the ability to detect causal relations before they can acquire the capacity to use ordinary language. That the ability to think in terms of causal relations presupposes the capacity to recognize instances of similar kinds should not be difficult to understand, since inferences from causes to effects on various differerent occasions requires the ability to recognize various events as distinct instances of that kind of cause and others as distinct instances of corresponding kinds of effects, presumably because they resemble one another.

That the ability to use words presupposes the capacity to think in terms of causes and effects may be more difficult to appreciate, but it seems to be the case, nonetheless. The association of the word "Stop!", for example, with ceasing to do whatever one is doing presupposes that words can function as commands, which are special kinds of causes in influencing human behavior. The most likely candidates for the rudimentary vocabulary of early humans may be directives and exclamations, where expressions of both kinds tend to function as causes or effects of their meaning. "Oh, no!" can be an effect of a certain kind of situation, just as "Go on!" might be a cause of another.

Although Sheets-Johnstone tends to focus her attention upon things that appear to be important to human forms of life, such as tool making, ways of counting, hominid bipedability in relation to primate sexuality, the origin of cave art and the concept of death, her work appears to be compatible with the thesis that the meaning of a gesture, expression, or word is determined by the totality of behaviors that would be brought about by an organism that has the ability to use gestures, expressions, or words of that kind when aware of their presence. Their meaning as *signs* is their causal role in affecting behavior under various conditions.

That more than one sign or more than one kind of sign can stand for the same thing or have the same significance is not difficult to discern. When the male pygmy monkey displays his erect penis for a nearby female, his erection stands as a partial cause to the effect which he would like to bring about. It functions as a causal invitation to copulatory activity, which the pygmy female can accept or not as she prefers. When a human male on the make in a bar asks a human female, "Your place or mine?", those words may be only conventionally and indirectly related to that for which they stand, but their meaning is unmistakable.

It appears important in this context that a theory of minds as things that can use signs supports *the capacity to make a mistake*—to mis-take a sign as standing for other than that for which it stands—as a general criterion of mentality. As a criterion, the capacity to make mistakes affords a usually reliable, but not therefore infallible, evidential indicator of the presence of the property in question. The successful application of this criterion, however, is not therefore unproblematic, since it may be as difficult to decide whether a mistake has taken place as it would be to decide whether or not something has a mind (Fetzer 1990, p. 66).

Nevertheless, some of the cases that Sheets-Johnstone reports are remarkable when considered from this point of view. The lioness who deceives the other members of her pride into thinking that nothing is up after a kill uses her body to create a false impression in the minds of other lions, which suggests that lions have the capacity to make mistakes. The existence of animals that play dead, of chimps that can lie, and even of fireflies that can adjust their flashing behavior to emit false signals as to their identity provides strong evidence that mentality may not be taken as a human prerogative but is instead ubiquitous in nature.

5.2   Gene-Culture Co-Evolution

The area of inquiry (or "discipline") known as *sociobiology* is largely the creation of the evolutionary biologist, Edward O. Wilson, who has authored several books, such as *The Insect Societies* (1971), *Sociobiology: The New Synthesis* (1975), *On Human Nature* (1978a); in collaboration with physicist Charles R. Lumsden, *Genes, Mind, and Culture* (1981) and *Promethean Fire* (1983); and, more recently, *The Diversity of Life* (1992) and *Consilience* (1999). The primary thesis of these works over a span of more than twenty years is that many facets of social organization, including patterns of individual development, as well as aspects of culture itself, are species-specific, where these characteristics affect the capacity of species to survive and to reproduce. From his perspective, were we "zoologists from another planet completing a catalog of social species on Earth, . . . anthropology and sociology together [would] constitute the sociobiology of a single primate species" (Wilson 1980, p. 271).

Wilson thus wants to assimilate the study of culture within the framework of evolutionary biology, thereby embracing the program of a natural science of social behavior. It should not be surprising that this approach has stimulated enormous controversy with scientists and non-scientists alike, not least of all for taking seriously the idea that human culture might be "on a par" with other species' cultures, rather than "the inevitable outcome of either advanced social life or high intelligence" (Wilson 1978a, p. 22). Wilson invites us to contemplate the possibility of even more complex societies whose non-human members are possessed of superior intelligence, yet which differ from human societies in most respects. From this perspective, therefore, culture itself is no longer an exclusively human prerogative but may also belong to birds, to bees and to chimpanzees.

In extending the concept of culture to species other than *Homo sapiens*, Wilson tacitly extends its meaning, which typically signifies "the ideas, customs, skills, arts, etc. of a people or group, that are transferred, communicated or passed along, as in or to succeeding generations", where these attainments are more often supposed to be the products of learning than the offspring of genetic endowment (Webster 1988, p. 337). Yet the scope of scientific formulations must be permitted to exceed the nuances of ordinary language, which inevitably occurs when properties that were previously thought to be the exclusive province of humans are discovered to be among the possessions of other species as well. Moreover, even in its ordinary sense, "culture" as a product of learning tends to presuppose differing capacities for attainment as a function of differing genetic endowments in the form of corresponding predispositions.

In *Genes, Mind, and Culture* (1981), Lumsden and Wilson emphasize the role of mental activity (or of "mind") in the propagation of culture, maintaining that:

> the genes prescribe a set of biological processes, which we call *epigenetic rules*, that direct the assembly of the mind. This assembly is context-dependent, with the epigenetic rules feeding on information derived from culture and physical environment. Such information is forged into cognitive schemata that are the raw material of thought and decision. Emitted behavior is just one product of the dynamics of the mind, and culture is the translation of the epigenetic rules into mass patterns of mental activity and behavior. . . . (Lumsden and Wilson 1981, pp. 2–3)

They proceed to define "culture" in a broad sense as encompassing "the sum total of mental constructs and behaviors, including the construction and employment of artifacts, transmitted from one generation to the next by social learning" (Lumsden and Wilson 1981, p. 3). To encompass "artifacts" of non-human species, therefore, the notion must be extended to cover their effects as inherited or acquired products of human or non-human effort or design.

Thus, insofar as mental activity (construed a capacity for social learning) contributes to the production and utilization of cultural artifacts (including language, habits, skills, arts, instruments, institutions, and so on), which are transmitted to successive generations by a process of social learning, then to the extent to which these cultural capabilities tend to promote or inhibit the evolution of a species, its reproduction and survival becomes a manifestation of *gene-culture co-evolution*. But it should be evident that gene-culture co-evolution can take place only if a species possesses the capacity for the transmission of culture from one generation to another by social learning, which thus presupposes "mind" as the cognitive capacity for thought and decision.

Upon initial consideration, the introduction of "epigenetic rules" might seem to needlessly complicate an otherwise elegant approach. The conception advanced in Wilson's *On Human Nature* (1978a) holds that different species $S1$, $S2$, . . . are characterizable by different patterns of social behavior, $B1$, $B2$, . . . : things that are ants exhibit age-grading, antennal rites, and so on, whereas those things that are human exhibit age-grading, athletic sports, and so forth. Thus, an apparently parallel conception within natural science holds that various elements $E1, E2, \ldots$, and so forth, are characterizable by different combinations of physical attributes $A1, A2, \ldots$: things that are gold, for example, have a melting point of 1064°C, boiling point of 3080°C, and so on, while things that are titanium, by com- parison, exhibit a melting point of 1660°C, ionization potential of 6.82 eV, and so on.

Thus, insofar as the physical and chemical properties of the elements recur in a regular fashion when elements are arranged in increasing order of their atomic numbers (as reflected by the *Periodic Table of the Elements*), perhaps the personal and the social properties of the various species might be found to recur in a regular fashion when the species are arranged in an order that appropriately corresponds to their genetic origins (as reflected by a counterpart *Periodic Table of the Species*). Certain underlying difficulties appear to confront this conception, however, insofar as patterns of social behavior do not appear to be properties of ants and humans in precisely the way that combinations of physical attributes are properties of gold and titanium: things that are gold, for example, possess their melting points and boiling points as properties of discrete individual things, whereas things that are human, by contrast, possess their age-grading and athletic sports, not as concrete individual things, but instead as relations between various individual things.

Thus, physical attributes are properties of individual things *distributively* (since each thing that is gold has a melting point of 1064°C without regard to its relations to other things that are gold), whereas social behaviors are proper- ties of individual things *collectively* (since athletic sports, for example, is not a property that one human has as a discrete individual thing, but only exists as a relation between that human and other humans who engage in athletic sports). More importantly, the properties of the elements are permanent, while those of the higher species, in particular, appear to be transient. Just as no human being is born speaking a specific language (such as English, German, or French), no human being is born playing a specific game (such a football, basketball, or golf).

And, if this is the case, then, in order to provide an essential mechanism for the generation of social behavior on the basis of properties of discrete individual things, "epigenetic rules" would need to be introduced to represent the potential for social behavior as a dispositional property of discrete individual things that manifests itself under the relevant social conditions, roughly as *Genes, Mind, and Culture* (Lumsden and Wilson 1981) tends to suggest. Epigenetic rules, in other words, exist in the form of *predispositions* to acquire one or another specific behavioral tendency $BT1, BT2$, and so on, within a specific range of possible tendencies, BTi, where which of these behavioral tendencies happen to be acquired as actual dispositions depends upon and varies with environmental factors, especially in relation to social learning.

For a specific epigenetic rule, the variety of specific behavioral tendencies an individual can acquire as actual dispositions collectively reflects its "selectivity", while the strength of that individual's tendency to manifest one or an- other of those actual dispositions distributively reflects its "penetrance"; thus, an individual's actual behavioral tendencies during any specific moment in its development may be described by corresponding *usage bias curves* (Lumsden and Wilson 1981, pp. 55–65). Thus, while *Homo sapiens* has the predisposition toward athletic sports, this tendency may be manifest by acquiring any of a broad variety of specific dispositions to play soccer, tennis, and so forth, with distinctive strengths of those tendencies relative to different environmental conditions, where which, if any, among these happens to be displayed by particular members of the species is partly a function of social learning. Yet ants, by way of comparison, are completely incapable of acquiring the disposition to play soccer, or tennis, and so on, precisely because they lack the predisposition toward athletic sports that numbers among the characteristics of human genes.

From this point of view, therefore, sociobiology addresses the necessity to assess the relative influence of genes and of culture (of nature and of nurture) on the social behavior displayed by different species, where if social learning factors are comparatively unimportant in the emergence of various behavioral tendencies, then those specific traits are properly classified as (more-or-less) "biologically determined", but otherwise not. Thus, the major difference between alternative accounts of sociobiology tends to arise at just this juncture. For, as Wilson has observed, sociobiology, in general, is compatible with (at least) three different kinds of relations between genetic predispositions and their behavioral manifestations along the following (cf. Wilson 1978b, p. xi): (i) every member of the species possesses the same genetic predisposition, and this predisposition is compatible with a broad range of possible behavior; (ii) every member of the species possesses the same genetic predisposition, but this predisposition is compatible with a narrow range of possible behavior; (iii) some members of the species possess different genetic predispositions, where these predispositions are compatible with different ranges of possible behavior, some of which are broad and some of which are narrow, respectively.

Although Wilson was not initially committed to one or another of these theoretical alternatives, the genetical, the psychological and the anthropological evidence led him to conclude "that human social behavior is to some extent genetically constrained over the entire species and furthermore [is] subject to genetic variation within the species", which has led him to accept thesis (iii):

> The most emotion laden and least rationally controlled human behaviors are generally consistent in their details with sociobiological theory. These categories include incest inhibition, bond formation, parent-off-spring conflict, sex-biased infanticide, primitive warfare, territoriality, and sexual practice. They are more simply explained by the hypothesis of genetically based predisposition than by the hypothesis of purely cultural determination. (Wilson 1978b, p. xii)

Sociobiology thus provides a framework for explaining the social behavior of different species as a (complex) function of genetic and of cultural factors, where some species will tend to exhibit uniform genetic predispositions, most of which permit only narrow ranges of possible behavior (as befits "the lesser species"), while other species will tend to exhibit variable genetic predispositions, which permit far broader ranges of possible behavior (as befits "the higher species").

5.3   Is Sociobiology Science?

The fundamental principles of sociobiology (as gene-culture co-evolutionary theory) can be presented as a sequence of theses of two different kinds, namely: *definitions,* which reflect the meanings to be assigned to technical terms in the vocabulary of sociobiology; and *conjectures,* which reflect the principal relations that are supposed to obtain between these properties, thus understood, if sociobiology happens to be true. "Definitions", therefore, are assumed to be true on syntactical or on semantical grounds alone, whereas "conjectures" are logically contingent empirical assertions that are intended to have the character of *lawlike sentences* as sentences that would be natural laws if they were true.

Let us begin with deterministic versions of all of these definitions and conjectures—including the laws of Mendelian genetics—and subsequently consider the additional formulations that would be required of their probabilistic counterparts. Then among the most basic assumptions underlying sociobiology is the following:

CONJECTURE 1. Phenotypes $P1, P2, \ldots$ develop from genotypes $G1, G2, \ldots$ under the influence of environmental factors $EF1, EF2, \ldots$.

These relations can be formalized by introducing causal conditionals of universal strength "$\ldots = u \Rightarrow \rule{1cm}{0.4pt}$" to complement those of probabilistic strength

n to reflect the possibility these relations may be deterministic or probabilistic, respectively:

(L1-D) $(x)(t)[Gixt \Rightarrow (EFixt = u \Rightarrow Pixt^*)]$; or,

(L1-P) $(x)(t)[Gixt \Rightarrow (EFixt = u \Rightarrow Pixt^*)]$;

which represent the difference when the occurrence of Gi and EFi would invariably bring about outcome Pi without exception (with universal strength u) and when that result is brought about instead with merely probabilistic strength n. The relevant "environmental factors", of course, must include every internal or external factor that makes a difference to the outcome of specific phenotype Pi.

Comment. This conjecture is a thesis of molecular genetics and of evolutionary biology, which is presupposed by sociobiology. Strictly speaking, instances of phenotypes $P1, P2, \ldots$ develop from instances of genotypes $G1, G2, \ldots$ under the influence of instances of (internal and external) environmental factors $EF1, EF2, \ldots$. This thesis has two corollaries when the relationship is deterministic:

COROLLARY IA. Different phenotypes $P1, P2, \ldots$ must develop from the same genotype Gi under the influence of different environmental factors $EF1, EF2, \ldots$; and,

COROLLARY IB. Different phenotypes $P1, P2, \ldots$ must develop from different genotypes $G1, G2, \ldots$ under the influence of the same environmental factors EFi.

Environments that include exposure of genotypes to gamma rays, however, presumably permit the possibility that, under precisely the same genotypical-and-environmental conditions, one or another phenotype may occur as the outcome, because these results are brought about by some indeterminstic causal process. When that happens to be the case, then probabilistic lawful relations will obtain,

(L1-P1) $(x)(t)[G1xt \Rightarrow (EF1xt = n \Rightarrow P1xt^*)]$; or,

(L1-P2) $(x)(t)[G1xt \Rightarrow (EF1xt = 1-n \Rightarrow -P1xt^*)]$;

where, when phenotype $P1$ is brought about with propensity of strength n, then other phenotypes $-P1$ $(P2, P3, \ldots)$ are brought about with propensities equal to or less than $1-n$, which represents the sum of the values for alternative outcomes.

Comment. So long as "genotypes" are defined in terms of genetic material and not in terms of their predispositions to develop into "phenotypes" (defined in terms of neurological and of physiological structure), these theses are empirical assertions that are logically contingent and explicitly law-like. For claims of this kind to be true, the specification of genotype and of environmental factors must include the presence or the absence of every property whose presence or absence makes a difference to the development of corresponding phenotypes. This means that they must satisfy the requirement of maximal specificity. Nomically irrelevant environmental factors are excluded from consideration in these corollaries.

CONJECTURE 2. Epigenetic rules *ERi* are permanent properties of phenotypes *Pi*.

Thus, the only phenotypic differences that matter with respect to epigenetic rules are those relative to which they differ, which may render many phenotypic properties nomically irrelevant. Corresponding laws reflect simple lawful relationships:

(L2-1) $(x)(t)(P1xt \Rightarrow ER1xt)$;

(L2-2) $(x)(t)(P2xt \Rightarrow ER2xt)$;

. . .

Comment. This conjecture is the fundamental thesis of general sociobiology. Strictly speaking, *instance* of (sets of) epigenetic rules are properties of *instances* of phenotypes once again, where these properties vary according to phenotype, assuming again that epigenetic rules are permanent properties of phenotypes.

COROLLARY 2A. Every instance of the same phenotype *Pi* must possess the same (set of) epigenetic rules *ER1, ER2*, . . . ; and,

COROLLARY 2B. Different (sets of) epigenetic rules *ER1, ER2*, . . . , cannot be possessed by the same phenotype *Pi*.

Even if every instance of the same phenotype must possess the same sets of epigenetic rules and even acquire the same behavioral tendencies, however, is not enough to imply they must also display the same behavior *Bi* during their lives.

Comment. Corollary 2B is merely the contraposed formulation of Corollary 2A, which is added for emphasis. Notice that every instance of the same phenotype has to have the same epigenetic rules, if they are permanent properties, even though the truth of this assertion does not obtain on logical grounds alone. Even minor differences in neurological and physiological structure may make a difference to the epigenetic rules of different instances of the species. Indeed, the possibility epigenetic rules may not be permanent properties of phenotypes, discussed in Chapter 6, turns out to be important to the nature of intelligence.

In conjunction with (L1-D), for example, (L2-1) and (L2-2) imply as follows:

(L3-D1) $(x)(t)[G1xt \Rightarrow (EF1xt = u \Rightarrow ER1xt^*)]$; or,

(L3-D2) $(x)(t)[G1xt \Rightarrow (EF2xt = u \Rightarrow ER2xt^*)]$;

. . .

and similarly the conjunction of (L1-P) and (L2-1) and (L2-2), probabilistically:

(L3-P1) $(x)(t)[G1xt \Rightarrow (EF1xt = n \Rightarrow ER1xt^*)]$; or,

(L3-P2) $(x)(t)[G1xt \Rightarrow (EF2xt = 1 - n \Rightarrow -ER2xt^*)]$;

. . .

where, as before, "$-ER$" represents the set of epigenetic rule alternatives to $ER1$, where these difference reflect the influence of deterministic or indeterministic environmental factors EFi on the development of corresponding phenotypes Pi.

DEFINITION 1. Epigenetic rules $ER1, ER2, \ldots$ are predispositions to acquire one or another specific behavioral tendency $BT1, BT2, \ldots$ within a fixed range of possible patterns of individual and social behavior, under the influence of specific fixed sets of (physical and social) environmental factors $EF3, EF4, \ldots$.

When these relations are taken as manifestations of the meaning of "epigenetic rules", then the following theses follow, necessarily, in co-evolutionary language:

(D1-D1) $(x)(t)[ERixt \Rightarrow (EF3xt = u \Rightarrow BT3xt^*)]$; or,

(D1-D2) $(x)(t)[ERixt \Rightarrow (EF4xt = u \Rightarrow BT4xt^*)]$;

. . .

which obtain when the same behavioral tendency, $BT3$, $BT4$, . . . would be acquired by any organism with the same epigenetic rules, ERi,under the same (internal and external) environmental factors, $EF3$, $EF4$, ... Once again, how- ever, probabilistic relations are compatible with the occurrence of more than one possible outcome, $BT3$, $BT4$, . . . , under precisely the same conditions, EFi:

(D1-P1) $(x)(t)[ER1xt \Rightarrow (EF3xt = n \Rightarrow BT3xt^*)]$; or,

(D1-P2) $(x)(t)[ER1xt \Rightarrow (EF3xt = 1 - n \Rightarrow -BT3xt^*)]$;

. . .

An example may be helpful here. Consider biological twin human beings, who are raised apart. Even though their specific environments are no doubt not the same in every respect, so long as they are similar in specific respects that are relevant to the acquisition of a behavioral tendency, such as language acquisition, they may acquire similar linguistic dispositions, including abilities to use similar words under similar conditions. Whether or not they actually do use similar words under similar conditions, however, depends upon the specific conditions to which they are exposed during their lives. Having similar abilities and capabilities still tends to require similar conditions for their similar display.

Comment. The possession of a specific epigenetic rule determines the breadth and variety of potential patterns of behavior that an instance of a phenotype can acquire and can manifest. These potential patterns of behavior assume the form of predispositions, but their range of potential might be broad or narrow.

DEFINITION 2. The smaller the number of specific behavioral tendencies $BT1$, $BT2$, . . . , that can be acquired and manifest under different environment conditions in accordance with an epigenetic rule ER, the smaller the range specific behaviors Bi that an organism can display under varied conditions Ci.

DEFINITION 3. The larger the number of specific behavioral tendencies $BT1$, $BT2$, . . . , that can be acquired and manifest under different environmental conditions in accordance with an epigenetic rule ER, the larger the range of specific behaviors Bi that an organism can display under varied conditions Ci.

Comment. Here the difference between "selectivity" and "penetrance" seems to matter the most. Epigenetic rules, as predispositions, govern the range of behavioral tendencies that an organism can acquire as dispositions, which are displayed by specific behaviors Bi under specific conditions Ci. The range of those behaviors, however, is constrained by the epigenetic rules that restrict the possible behavioral tendencies those organisms can acquire and display. When a species, such as *E. coli* bacteria, has only a narrow range of possible behaviors (involving moving toward and moving away from various chemotactic substances) where every member with the same phenotype displays exactly the same behavior, behavioral change may require genetic evolution. For behavior that is more or less instinctual, that is the mechanism of change.

Notice, however, that the possibility of genetic evolution even under these conditions presupposes some variation in the gene pool, since otherwise there would be no possibility for adapting to an inhospitable environment. Minute differences in genotype, even those that bring about only minute differences in behavior, may sometimes be good enough to solve the adaptive problems. And that some differences in single genes may have multiple manifestations and that some properties may be affected by various different genes indicate ways in which even asexually reproducing species may be able to find ways to cope with problematical environments, not by optimizing but by satisficing.

DEFINITION 4. Cultures are composed of behavioral practices involving culturgens.

Comment. This concept applies to sociobiology and to cultural anthropology. Strictly speaking, instances of cultures are composed of instances of behavioral practices involving culturgens as tokens of various types, which can be counted, classified, and so forth (as instances of the use of tools of a specific type, as instances of games of specific kinds, as instances of use of specific languages and so forth).

DEFINITION 5. Culturgens consist of artifacts (including tools, clothing), of behavior (such as speech, skills), and of mentifacts (including thoughts and theories).

DEFINITION 6. Epigenetic rules ERi predispose phenotypes toward the acquisition and manifestation of specific behavioral tendencies $BT1$, $BT2$, . . . involving specific culturgens under different (social and physical) environmental conditions $EF3$, $EF4$, ...

Comment. Strictly speaking, instances of phenotypes possessing various kinds of epigenetic rules $ER1$, $ER2$, . . . are predisposed toward the acquisition and manifestation of specific behavioral tendencies $BT1$, $BT2$, . . . , involving utilization of specific instances of culturgens, such as tools of a certain kind, particular forms of speech, etc., under specific environmental conditions *EFi*.

CONJECTURE 3. Behavioral practices involving culturgens can be transmitted by social learning.

Comment. This thesis is likewise fundamental to general sociobiology. Note, in particular, that this is a logically contingent empirical assertion, which would be false only if behavioral practices involving culturgens could never be transmitted by way of social learning. It might turn out, however, that some behavioral practices involving culturgens are inborn and species-specific dispositions, in which case some such practices would not be transmitted by social learning.

COROLLARY 3A. Every instance of the same phenotype *Pi* must be predisposed to acquire and to manifest the same behavioral practices involving culturgens under the same conditions of social learning.

COROLLARY 3B. Different predispositions to acquire and to manifest the same culturgens under the same conditions of social learning must be instances of different phenotypes *Pi*.

Comment. Corollary 3B is merely the contraposed form of Corollary 3A and is added for emphasis. Note, in particular, that while every instance of the same phenotype must have the same social learning predispositions, that would remain the case even if that social learning predisposition were either nonexistent or probabilistic, so long as the same predisposition is possessed by every instance of the same phenotype with the same strength, regardless of what that degree of strength may be. Even when they are deterministic, the following thesis is true:

CONJECTURE 4. Phenotypes *Pi* possessing the same epigenetic rules *ERi* may acquire and manifest different specific behavioral tendencies *BT1*, *BT2*, . . . involving the use of culturgens under different environmental conditions *EF3*, *EF4*, ...

Comment. This conjecture, which is enormously important to sociobiology, must be carefully distinguished from Conjecture 2. That every instance of the same phenotype must possess the same sets of epigenetic rules does not entail that every instance of the same phenotype must acquire and manifest the same specific behavioral tendencies, unless either (a) those behavioral tendencies are in-born and species-specific dispositions whose posses-sion is independent of environmental factors or (b) although they are not in-born and species-specific dispositions, those phenotypes are under the influence of the same sets of (physical and social) environmental factors *EFi* at causally relevant moments of their lives.

Even in case (b), moreover, that those phenotypes should acquire exactly the same behavioral tendencies implies the underlying laws are determinis-tic. When the processes of tendency acquisition are probabilistic, then, as we have already ascertained, more than one outcome is possible under the very same conditions. This conjecture has two corollaries that also depend upon determinism, namely:

COROLLARY 4A. Every instance of the same phenotype *Pi* must acquire and manifest the same specific behavioral tendencies *BT1, BT2, . . .* involv-ing culturgens if it is subjected to the same sets of environmental factors *EF3, EF4, . . .* at causally relevant moments of their lives.

COROLLARY 4B. If instances of the same phenotype *Pi* acquire and man-ifest different specific behavioral tendencies *BT1, BT2, . . .* , involving cul-turgens, then they must have been subjected to different sets of environmental factors *EF3, EF4, . . .* at causally relevant moments of their lives.

Comment. Since instances of the same phenotype *Pi* have to possess the same epigenetic rules, according to Conjecture 2, yet may acquire and man-ifest different specific behavioral tendencies *BT1, BT2, . . .* , nevertheless, this can occur only if those instances were subject to different sets of environ-mental factors *EF1, EF2, . . .* at some causally relevant moments of their lives, unless the causal connection between these antecedent conditions and those response outcomes is probabilistic. These possibilities can be represented by the formal apparatus employed above. (L1-D), for example, in conjunction with (L2-1) and (D1-D1) or (D1-D2) implies:

(L1-D1) $(x)(t)[(G1xt \ \& \ EF1xt) \Rightarrow (EF3xt = u \Rightarrow BT3xt^*)]$; or,

L1-D2) $(x)(t)[(G1xt \ \& \ EF1xt) \Rightarrow (EF4xt = u \Rightarrow BT4xt^*)]$;

   . . .

because any organism of genotype *G1* subjected to environmental factors *EF1* would have phenotype *P1* by (L1-D), any organism of kind *P1* would have *ER1* by (L2-1), and any organism with *ER1* would acquire *BT3* under conditions *EF3* by (D1-D1) or analogously would acquire *BT4* under condi-tions *EF4* by (D1-D2).

An example of the scope of these lawlike generalizations of this kind would include those for biological twins in relation to their acquisition of a language as a specific disposition under suitable environmental conditions. Given they have the same genotype *G1*, then provided their environments as children and young adults preserved their phenotypes *P1* comparable in relevant respects (nothing occurring, such as damage to their brains or harm to their capacity for speech), their exposure to a suitable (implicit and explicit) linguistic environment, which presumably would include some specific instruction in English, if that were the language of their environment, would lead to the acquisition of the ability to use English as a semiotic ability *SA* as a deterministic or a probabilistic phenomenon:

(L1-D1) $(x)(t)[(G1xt \ \& \ EF1xt) \Rightarrow (EF3xt = u \Rightarrow SA3xt^*)]$; or,

(L1-P1) $(x)(t)[(G1xt \ \& \ EF1xt) \Rightarrow (EF4xt = u \Rightarrow SA4xt^*)]$;

. . .

While it may be tempting to suppose that phenotypes have minds to the extent to which their behavioral tendencies involving the use of culturgens are under the influence of social learning, it would have the consequence of precluding the very possibility that the lesser species, whose behavior is not affected by social learning, could possess mentality. Considerations developed in previous chapters, however, suggest that other animals—ranging from *E. coli* bacteria to the mountain gorilla—have the potential for mentality, when mentality itself is properly understood as semiotic ability. This suggests the following complementary definition:

DEFINITION 7. Species possess mentality to the extent to which they possess semiotic ability.

Comment. Although Lumsden and Wilson (1981) tend to envision mind as the cognitive capacity for thought and decision, the semiotic conception offers a far less vague and far more precise account of minds as sign-using systems, a conception—as we have seen—that applies to humans, to other animals, and even to machines, if such a thing is possible. It remains compatible with Lumsden and Wilson's contention that (the members of) a species can participate in gene-culture co-evolution only if they possess the capacity for the transmission of specific behavioral tendencies, especially involving the utilization of culturgens, by means of social learning. The capacity for social learning thus becomes essential to gene-culture co-evolution rather than to the possession of mentality.

A key difference needs to be borne in mind, moreover, between types of behavior and variation within the type, which may or may not correspond with ideas of selectivity and penetrance. *E. coli* bacteria have the capacity to move toward and move away from various chemotactic substances, which is narrow in terms of types of behavior, but the number of different substances toward which or away from which they may move appears to be constantly evolving. Thus, even if *E. coli* bacteria appears to be limited to iconic mentality, at best, that does not mean it cannot make the most of the semiotic abilities at its disposal. Survival and reproduction occur if adaptive abilities are "good enough".

DEFINITION 8. (Sexual) species are populations of phenotypes that are capable of interbreeding freely under natural voluntary and unforced conditions.

DEFINITION 9. Societies are (collections of) the members of a species that are organized in a fashion that promotes communication and co-operation beyond what is required to pursue sexual activities.

Comment. These definitions belong to biology, to sociobiology, and to anthropology. Their significance arises from additional theses to which they are related.

CONJECTURE 5. Societies are manifestations of the specific behavioral tendencies that their members have acquired as instances of species (phenotypes) under the influence of environmental factors.

COROLLARY 5A: Societies of the members of species whose epigenetic rules permit only a narrow range of possible patterns of behavior can acquire and manifest only a small number of behavioral responses to different environmental conditions.

COROLLARY 5B: Societies of the members of species whose epigenetic rules permit somewhat broader ranges of possible patterns of behavior can acquire and manifest a larger number of behavioral responses to different environmental conditions.

Comment. The principal difference between distinct species, therefore, consists in the breadth and variety of those fixed ranges of possible behavioral tendencies that their members can acquire and manifest as actual dispositions under the influence of (physical and social) environmental factors: the more narrow the range and the less subject to social learning, the greater the justification for regarding specific behaviors as "instinctual" or as "biologically determined", even though those tendencies invariably (or probably) arise under the influence of (physical and social) environmental factors. These corollaries have obvious consequences for the evolution of species, insofar as broader ranges of possible response to different environment- al conditions confers a selective advantage upon a species within a changing world.

From the perspective developed in Chapter 1, therefore, the scientific status of gene-culture co-evolutionary theory should not be in doubt. The general character of this approach has not only been presented informally by means of conjectures, definitions, and corollaries, but the principles that define it have also been formalized through the use of subjunctive conditionals and causal conditions of universal and of probabilistic strength. Although the specific values of the various kinds of variables that have been identified would have to be specified to convert this schema from the sketch of a theory to a theory, it should not be controversial to observe that theses of this kind appear capable of satisfying the conditions of conditionality, testability, and tentativeness we have previously considered. Their acceptability, of course, depends upon inferences to the best explanation.

Whether or not gene-culture co-evolutionary theory can be tested as freely as theories in other scientific domains, however, raises other issues. One is that experimentation involving human subjects generates moral and ethical questions that deserve to be resolved. We know that evidence that might be enough to confirm a generalization does not necessarily corroborate a corresponding law, which raises a difficult problem. Different versions of sociobiological theory will be distinguished by their ascription of different sets of culturgens, of epigenetic rules and of behavioral tendencies to various species, where these conjectures are intended to be lawlike claims. Conflicts may then arise between science and morality.

To whatever extent already existing societies may exemplify the conditions that would be required to subject these hypotheses to empirical test, there may be no special difficulties; but to whatever extent already existing societies do not exemplify those conditions, exceptional problems are likely to be encountered in relation to ethical aspects of scientific inquiries. Conjectures about incest inhibition, sex-based infanticide, and other behavioral tendencies, after all, are subject to corroboration as lawlike claims only insofar as the nonexistence of properties or procedures whose presence or absence would make a difference to the acquisition or the manifestation of those practices can be established. But there are obvious prohibitions against creating conditions of child abuse, of sexual slavery, and so on, by means of environmental manipulations that might violate basic moral principles.

Another is that, insofar as genetic and cultural evolution tend to operate at different rates, sociobiological hypotheses are necessarily more historical and comparative and less experimental and manipulative. An absence of moral imperatives, after all, would not alter the generally slow and Darwinian character of genetic evolution in comparison to the frequently rapid and Lamarckian character of cultural evolution, which is a crucial matter that we are going to explore in the chapter that follows. This difference can be displayed by adapting a Minkowski space-time diagram to function as a gene-culture co-evolution diagram:

Figure 5.1 (Species Specific) Gene-Culture Co-Evolution Diagram

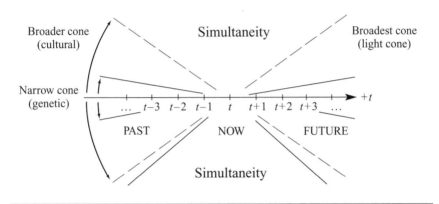

where the narrow cone reflects the slower rate of genetic change (as a function of gestation) and the broader cone reflects the faster rate of cultural change (as a function of technology). For while offspring can only be produced at a constrained rate of reproduction within a species, the upper bound on the rate of culturgen transmission for an innovative species (with radio, television, and similar modes of information transmission) can approach the speed of light.

6

What about Intelligence?

The publication of *The Bell Curve* (1994) ignited a storm of controversy. Even though its authors, Richard Herrnstein, perhaps the leading student of behaviorism at Harvard until his death in 1994, and Charles Murray, Fellow of the American Enterprise Institute in Washington, D.C., were well-known and highly respected, their work provoked hundreds of papers, articles and columns, many of which have been anthologized (Jacoby and Glauberman 19–95). The central thesis of their inquiry, which many find to be intolerable, is that the great divide within American society between the "haves" and "have-nots" (the rich and the poor, the educated and the ignorant) arises not due to differences in social opportunities, but because of differences in underlying intelligence, which are leading to the gradual emergence of a "cognitive elite".

They outline their position by specifying a set of six conclusions related to tests of cognitive ability, such as the ACT, the SAT, and IQ tests, which they formulate as follows and consider to be "beyond significant technical dispute": See Table 6.i

Their work extends a previous study by Herrnstein (Herrnstein 1973), in which he argued that if differences in mental ability are inherited, and if success requires those abilities, and if earnings and prestige depend upon success, then social standing (which reflects earnings and prestige) will be based to some extent upon inherited differences between people. As they themselves observe, this position, as formulated, is not especially threatening since, for example, if the genetic contribution to mental ability were small, then its contribution to earnings and prestige would be small. But they cite "hundreds of empirical and theoretical studies"—including especially those based on identical twins raised apart—as establishing support for the conclusion that "the genetic component of IQ is unlikely to be smaller than 40% or larger than 80%" (Herrnstein and Murray 1994, p. 105).

The controversial aspect of their study was less that cognitive ability appears to be approximately sixty-percent heritable than it was their report

Table 6. i   Six Theses of *The Bell Curve* (1994)

(T1)   there is such a thing as a general factor of cognitive ability on which human beings differ;

(T2)   all standardized tests of academic aptitude or achievement measure this general factor to some degree, but IQ tests deliberately designed for that purpose measure it most accurately;

(T3)   IQ scores match, to a first degree, whatever it is that people mean when they use the words "intelligence" or "smart" in ordinary language;

(T4)   IQ scores are stable, although not perfectly so, over much of a person's life;

(T5)   properly administered IQ tests are not demonstrably biased against social, economic, ethnic, or racial groups; and,

(T6)   cognitive ability is substantially heritable, apparently no less than 40% and no more than 80%. (Herrnstein and Murray 1994, pp. 22–23)

---

that these differences have a racial distribution, where reliable IQ tests indicate a distribution of IQs in which African Americans average around 85, European Americans 100, and East Asians as high as 110 (Herrnstein and Murray 1994, Chapter 13). While acknowledging that their data for East-Asian subjects are based upon limited studies, their conclusions about black-white differences are supported by 156 studies, which suggests that these findings may be objectively well-founded (Herrnstein and Murray 1994, pp. 276–77). While they explore many alternative hypotheses concerning socioeconomic status and discover some variation at high levels of SES, their results appear to remain robust when subjected to critical scrutiny.

    Without attempting to settle the empirical truth of their findings, it ought to be apparent that the hypothesis of genetically-based differences in intelligence might emerge as the best supported among the available alternatives based upon inference to the best explanation, provided the hypotheses under consideration include an appropriate range of alternatives and the available evidence is sufficient. If these differences could be explained on the basis of test bias, for example, when that hypothesis was not among the alternatives under consideration, then clearly the conclusion would not follow, no matter how tentatively and fallibly. Herrnstein and Murray (1994), however, devote a great deal of attention to the available alternatives. Although their conclusion would have to be taken as tentative and fallible, grounds for its rejection are not obvious.

6.1   Intelligence and Human Variability

That, however, does not mean that they might not exist. Any hypothesis about the relationship between a reference property R and some attribute A depends upon the existence of R and A, respectively, as well as upon the relationship between them. If there is no objective foundation to classification of individuals into categories of *African American*, *European American*, and *East Asian*, for example, or if there is no objective foundation for attributing different *levels of intelligence* to those individuals, then the existence of such relationships would be more apparent than real. Moreover, mere correlations are not sufficient to establish counterpart *natural laws*, whose attributes must be permanent properties of their reference properties, as Chapter 2 explained. Herrnstein and Murray could be attacked on these and many similar grounds.

Stephen Jay Gould (1994), for example, summarized his objections to their findings by criticizing their conception of levels of intelligence: "Intelligence, in their formulation, must be depictable as a single number, capable of ranking people in linear order, genetically based, and effectively immutable. If any of these premises are false, then their entire argument collapses" (Gould 1994). Here and elsewhere, he criticizes each of these "premises", contending that alternative explanations may account for the between-group differences:

> . . . , the well-documented fifteen-point average difference in IQ between blacks and whites in America, with substantial heritability of IQ in family lines within each group, permits no automatic conclusion that truly equal opportunity might not raise the black average enough to equal or surpass the white mean. (Gould 1994, pp. 5–6).

While Gould intends to be undermining their central conclusion, it is remarkable how much he concedes to Herrnstein and Murray, including the existence of a "well-documented" fifteen-point average difference in IQ between blacks and whites in America, with substantial family-line heritability in each group.

In an earlier book, *The Mismeasure of Man* (1981), Gould had criticized the intelligence-testing tradition as it has emerged especially among psychologists in America with influence from Alfred Binet, H.H. Goddard, Lewis

M. Terman, and R.M. Yerkes, while attacking most severely the work of Sir Cyril Burt as it affected the later work of Charles Spearman and L.L. Thurstone. Indeed, the notion of a *general intelligence factor*, called "*g*", was originally introduced by Spearman and later refined by Thurstone employing what is known as "factor analysis". Gould ends that book with a critique of the work of Arthur Jensen (1979) contending that Jensen combines "two of the oldest cultural prejudices of Western thought: the ladder of progress as a model for organizing life, and the reification of some abstract quality as a criterion for ranking" (p. 318).

Gould rebuts Jensen's approach by maintaining, "Evolution forms a copiously branching bush, not a unilinear progressive sequence", where Jensen commits a blunder in speaking about "different levels of the phyletic scale—that is, earthworms, crabs, fishes, turtles, pigeons, rats, and monkeys":

> Doesn't he realize that modern earthworms and crabs are products of lineages that have probably evolved separately from vertebrates for more than a billion years? They are not our ancestors; they are not even "lower" or less complicated than humans in any meaningful sense. They represent good solutions for their own way of life; they must not be judged by the hubristic notion that one particular primate forms the standard for all of life. (Gould 1981, p. 318)

What appears to be most important about Gould's observations, however, is not the implication that Jensen has misunderstood aspects of evolution, but the insinuation that the phenomena require evolutionary explanation.

In an "Afterword" responding to Gould and other critics, for example, Murray remarks that *g* may be related to the world in at least three ways: first, *g* might be an arbitrary creation of statistical analysis, with no underlying significance; second, *g* might function as a surrogate for other factors, such as educational level or socioeconomic status; third, *g* might be one of the crucial attributes of organisms that properly qualifies as "a (partly) biological phenomenon in its own right—a basic characteristic of the organism that exerts some influence on its ability to reason, think, and learn" (Murray 1996, p. 560). The robust character of findings about *g*, moreover, suggests that *g* is not an arbitrary creation of statistical analysis; and there appears to be no way to factor out *g* on the basis of other variables of these kinds.

The prospect thus remains that *g* might be among the crucial attributes of organisms that properly qualifies as a biological phenomenon "in its own right". As a preliminary and provisional hypothesis, for example, perhaps "*g*" *reflects a predisposition of variable strength to acquire behavioral tendencies involving the use of signs under various conditions as a flexible form of mentality*. In this case, a difference should obtain between lower (more or less) instinctual species, such as bacteria, which may have minds but without g as a mental predisposition and evolve in a purely genetic Darwinian fashion, and other, higher species, including the primates, which have g among their mental predispositions, whose evolution encompasses gene-culture co-evolution and is partially Lamarckian. Intelligence is mentality of a certain kind.

The suggestion that g may be identified with higher grades of mentality appears to be consistent with the Lumsden and Wilson (1984) account of epigenetic rules $ER1, ER2, \ldots$ as predispositions to acquire one or another specific behavioral tendency $BT1, BT2, \ldots$ within a fixed range of possible patterns of individual and social behavior, under the influence of fixed sets of (physical and social) environmental factors $EF1, EF2, \ldots$. The possession of specific epigenetic rules determines the breadth and variety of potential patterns of behavior that an instance of a phenotype can acquire and can manifest, where that range itself may be broad or narrow. The species that have broader ranges of potential patterns of behavior and that can acquire and can manifest them under more varied conditions are more intelligent.

This suggestion raises the possibility that Lumsden and Wilson's conceptions of selectivity and of penetrance, for example, may harbor an ambiguity with respect to propensities to acquire and to manifest different specific behavioral tendencies, where "selectivity" as a measure of breadth of possible acquisitions and "penetrance" as a measure of strength of tendency to display them would appear to require an additional measure of "ease of learnability" as a function of the rapidity with which those specific behavioral tendencies can be acquired. Epigenetic rules as predispositions would then have three dimensions, namely: the range of dispositions that could be acquired, under suitable conditions; the ease with which those possible dispositions would be acquired; and the strength of acquired dispositions to manifest themselves.

The identification of g with epigenetic rules involving use of signs clarifies and illuminates many perplexing problems that have arisen in the study of intelligence. In separating *mentality* from *intelligence* by identifying intelligence as mentality of a special kind—as the kind of mentality that can contribute to behavioral plasticity through the acquisition of semiotic abilities under suitable conditions—it broadens the foundation for explanations that are intended to account for learned or acquired behavior. The lower species are not only those whose behaviors are severely constrained by their genes, as Lumsden and Wilson suggest, but are also species whose behavior under specific fixed conditions remains constant from member to member because they lack the intelligence to acquire and manifest new behavioral responses.

Moreover, it supplies an explanation for the common tendency to describe digital machines, which we have discovered have no mentality, as "intelligent", nevertheless, because they display enormous behavioral plasticity because of their capacity to "learn" or "acquire" a wide range of different forms of behavior, which in this case are varying computational abilities under suitable conditions of programming as opposed to learning (Fetzer 1997). Even though it would be mistaken to attribute mentality to these machines or even describe them as "thinking things", the cognitive versatility they display as modes of extension of genuine mentality possessed by their designers and their users warrants their (appropriately qualified) description as "intelligent machines".

Thus, on an approach of this kind, intelligence and mentality may be viewed as related but independent concepts. While lower species, such as bacteria, may possess mentality, their purely instinctual behavior does not reflect the capacity for acquiring or learning non-instinctual behavior. Species that are comparable in this respect—which, admittedly, may have evolved gradually, if evolution is incremental in this respect, or more dramatically, if it is not—thus *possess mentality but not intelligence*. Digital machines, including contemporary computers—moreover, which are readily adapted to multiple uses through programming, can be described (metaphorically, if not literally) as *possessing intelligence but not mentality*, when they are understood to be symbol systems lacking the ability for the use of signs distinguishing minds.

Arthur Jensen (1998) has remarked upon the difficulties in establishing scientifically acceptable criteria and definitions for "intelligence". But the separation of intelligence from mentality promotes this objective. When Dawkins (1993), for example, receives reconsideration from this point of view, it becomes evident that her criteria of consciousness—(CC-1) complexity of behavior; (CC-2) adapting behavior to variable conditions; (CC-3) learning from others; (CC-4) behavior involving choice; and (CC-5) behavior involving co-operation—appear to capture properties that demarcate levels of intelligence of various species rather than specific properties of minds. But that does not preclude their utility for drawing distinctions between species, which would reflect differences between minds of different kinds.

Even though Gould may be entirely correct in his depiction of evolution as "a copiously branching bush" rather than "a unilinear progressive sequence", where modern earthworms and modern crabs, for example, are not inferior to vertebrates, including human beings, as *adaptations*, it certainly does not follow that they are not inferior to vertebrates, including human beings, as *intelligent things*! The range and variation of different species with respect to their semiotic abilities appears to be among their most important features, where some species have considerably greater range and variation in mentality in this sense than do other species. Even though earthworms, crabs, fishes, turtles, pigeons, rats, and monkeys may be on-a-par as evolved adaptations, that does not preclude a certain ordering with respect to their mental ability!

These considerations strongly suggest that intelligence itself may have an objective foundation as a property of organisms that varies between species and between the members of the same species. Indeed, as a property that appears to differ from species to species, it must have evolutionary origins and require evolutionary explanation. The adaptive benefits of intelligence under this interpretation, of course, are not difficult to discern. But differences between species with respect to evolved predispositions, in the case of the higher species, and with respect to evolved dispositions, in the case of the lower species, do not yet establish that the highest species might be differentiated on the basis of evolved predispositions that differ by races.

Were there no races, of course, there could be no racially-based differences in intelligence. The existence of races has occasionally been called into question, especially out of sincere but misguided attempts to promote the concept of equality, which turns out to be amenable to a wide variety of alternative interpretations, as Philip Fetzer (1997) has observed. But the general conception appears to have some basis in biological theory. In *Sociobiology* (1975), for example, E.O. Wilson defines "races" as *subspecies*:

(DSS) **subspecies** =df a population or series of populations occupying a discrete range and differing genetically from other geographical races of the same species (Wilson 1975, p. 323);

where the barriers that inhibit genetic exchanges with other individuals are those of distance and geography as opposed to those "intrinsic isolating barriers" that inhibit the free interbreeding between members under natural conditions typifying the species of which they are subpopulations.

Wilson emphasizes the variation that can occur between races as subspecies, where "Subspecies, insofar as they can be distinguished with any objectivity at all, show every conceivable degree of differentiation from other subspecies" (Wilson 1975, p. 8), on which he elaborates as follows:

At one extreme are the populations that fall along a cline—a simple gradient in the geographic variation of a given character. In other words, a character that varies in a clinal pattern is one that changes gradually over a substantial portion of the entire range of the species. At the other extreme are subspecies consisting of easily distinguished populations that are differentiated from one another by numerous genetic traits and exchange genes across a narrow zone of intergradation.

Thus, if there is no cluster of traits that distinguish one race from another, then there would be no foundation for supposing that races—human races, in particular—could differ with respect to their intelligence, mentality, or *g*.

Perhaps the most comprehensive synthesis of studies of differences between human populations can be found in J. Philippe Rushton, *Race, Evolution, and Behavior* (1995a). Rushton reports that hundreds of studies support the conclusion that Orientals, Whites, and Blacks differ on a wide spectrum of traits:

Table 6. ii   Relative Ranking of Human Populations on Diverse Variables

Variable:	Orientals	Whites	Blacks
Brain size			
Autopsy data (cm3 equivalents)	1,351	1,356	1,223
Endocranial volume (cm3)	1,415	1,362	1,268
External head measures (cm3)	1,356	1,329	1,294
Cortical neurons (billions)	13.767	13.665	13.185
Intelligence			
IQ test scores	106	100	85
Decision times	Faster	Intermediate	Slower
Cultural achievements	Higher	Higher	Lower
Maturation rate			
Gestation time	?	Intermediate	Earlier
Skeletal development	Later	Intermediate	Earlier
Motor development	Later	Intermediate	Earlier
Dental development	Later	Intermediate	Earlier
Age of first intercourse	Later	Intermediate	Earlier
Age of first pregnancy	Later	Intermediate	Earlier
Life-span	Longer	Intermediate	Shorter
Personality			
Activity	Lower	Intermediate	Higher
Aggressiveness	Lower	Intermediate	Higher
Cautiousness	Higher	Intermediate	Lower
Dominance	Lower	Intermediate	Higher
Impulsivity	Lower	Intermediate	Higher
Self-concept	Lower	Intermediate	Higher
Sociability	Lower	Intermediate	Higher
Social organization			
Marital stability	Higher	Intermediate	Lower
Law abidingness	Higher	Intermediate	Lower
Mental health	Higher	Intermediate	Lower
Administrative capacity	Higher	Higher	Lower
Reproductive effort			
Two-egg twinning (per 1000 births)	4	8	16
Hormone levels	Lower	Intermediate	Higher
Secondary sex characteristics	Smaller	Intermediate	Larger
Intercourse frequencies	Lower	Intermediate	Higher
Permissive attitudes	Lower	Intermediate	Higher
Sexually transmitted diseases	Lower	Intermediate	Higher

Reproduced from Rushton 1995b, p. 23; see Rushton 1995a, p. 5.

Thus, Rushton's findings—for which massive citations are provided—appear to support the conclusion that "racial differences in intelligence are observed worldwide, in Africa and in Asia as well as in Europe and North America, and that they are paralleled by differences in brain size, speed of dental maturation, reproductive physiology, and numerous other variables" (Rushton 1995a, p. 4).

Whether or not such an inference follows from the evidence that Rushton has accumulated obviously depends upon several crucial considerations. The first is whether he has accurately summarized the data at his disposal. The second is whether the data at his disposal encompasses all the available data that might make a difference to his findings. The third is whether there are any alternatives that might provide a better explanation of the evidence than the existence of (at least) these subpopulations and their related differences. Indeed, if these attributes are not permanent properties of phenotypes underlying these racial groupings or if these racial groupings are not manifestations of underlying genotypes, then findings such as these may have to be rejected, discounted, or otherwise revised. The question becomes, Do these races exist?

6.2   Human Variability and Evolution

An important dimension of research that has emerged from the merge of molecular genetics with evolutionary theory has been the study of relations between phenotypes of various species and underlying genotypes or, in the case of earlier studies, similarities between their blood chemistry as a measure of their evolutionary proximity. Vince Sarich and Allan Wilson (1967), for example, discovered that immunological resemblance between the serum albumins of apes and man support the conjecture that evolution has "slowed down" since the divergence of man and ape and suggest that, if humans and Old World monkeys last shared a common ancestor thirty million years ago, then humans and African apes may have shared an ancestor as recently as three million years ago.

The most important studies of the existence or non-existence of races have DNA as their focus, where DNA is the fundamental constituent of genes. Thus, in a study that has been called "the mitochondiral Eve paper", Rebeca L. Cann, Mark Stoneking, and Allan Wilson (1987) maintain that DNA analysis offers evidence that *Homo sapiens* originated in Africa and subsequently migrated from there to other regions of the globe. This study focuses on mitochondrial DNA (mtDNA) for three reasons: first, because mutations accumulate in DNA of this type several times faster than in the nucleus; second, because mtDNA is inherited maternally and does not recombine, making it ideal for relating sixteen people to each other; and, third, because there are about ten mtDNA molecules in each person, which are usually identical (Cann et al. 1987, pp. 31–32).

Their tentative interpretation of the comparative data based upon samples of 134 types of human mtDNA drawn from Africa, Asia, Australia, Europe, and New Guinea also appears to be consistent with the fossil record, namely: "that the transformation of archaic to anatomically modern forms of *Homo sapiens* first occurred in Africa, about 100,000–140,000 years ago, and that all present-day humans are descendants of that African population" (Cann *et al.* 1987, p. 35). They recommend caution in uncritical acceptance of the convergence between their molecular findings and those of paleoanthropology because there is much uncertainty about the age of the fossil remains and because their age-dating does not imply that anatomically modern *Homo sapiens* appeared at that time, since mtDNA transformations need not reflect other genetic or cultural changes.

More recent studies by Masatoshi Nei and Gregory Livshits (1989) and by Masatoshi Nei and Arun K. Roychoudhury (1993) display the sophistication of studies undertaken on the basis of such comparsions. The first explores the evolutionary relationships of the three major groups of humans, Europeans, Africans, and Asians. The genetic distances between them were computed on the basis of four sets of genetic locators (including protein markers, blood group markers, and DNA markers). The results show the genetic distance between Europeans and Asians, .040%, is less than that between Europeans and Africans, .063%, or that between Asians and Africans, .078%, which supports an African origin for the species. It also shows Asians and Europeans to be more closely related than Asians and Africans (Nei and Livshits 1989, p. 280).

This result, which supports later branching of Asians and Europeans after an earlier branching out of Africa, has now been reinforced by gene-frequency studies that make the out-of-Africa model all but certain as a scientific finding. Nei and Roychoudhury (1993) studied twenty-six representative populations, including four from Africa, five from Europe, ten from Asia, four from Australia and Oceania, and three from America (North American Indians, South American Indians, and Eskimos). The results of their study are consistent with those of classic anthropological findings, where the human population can be subdivided into five major sub-populations: (A) Negroid (African), (B) Caucasoid (European), (C) Mongoloid (East Asian and Pacific Islanders), (D) American Indian (including Eskimos), and (E) Australoid (Australians and Papuans). Their relations are as follows:

Figure 6.1 Phylogenetic Tree for 26 Representative Populations

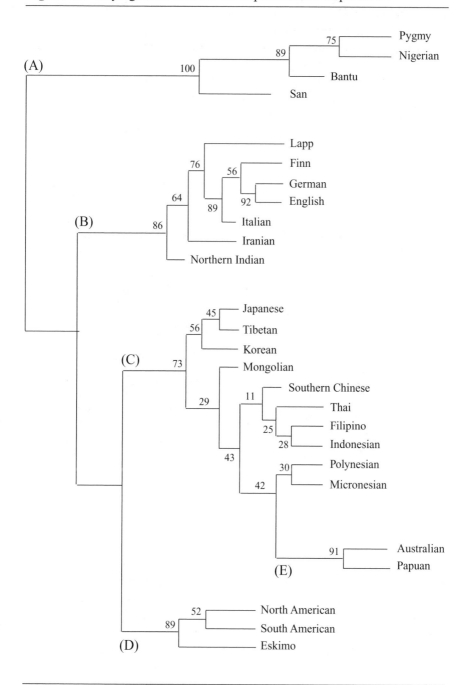

where the numbers indicate the "tightness of fit" of the clusters of groups in each grouping under variations of relevant variables during statistical tests.

These results are fascinating for many different reasons. Since they offer empirical evidence on the basis of gene frequencies for the existence of sub-populations of the human species, they reflect the existence of what appear to be at least five major races. Their geographical distribution, moreover, tends to confirm the genetic-geographical definition of "race" that Wilson has advanced, including the potential for variation within those sub-populations. These findings thus appear to be consistent with Rushton's results, on the assumption that the attributes he has identified are permanent and not merely transient properties of the sub-populations he has specified. The history of evolution that Nei and Roychoudbury (1993) advance, moreover, appears to be consistent with the evolution of the races in Rushton's account.

Figure 6.2   Scenario of the Origins of Major Human Populations

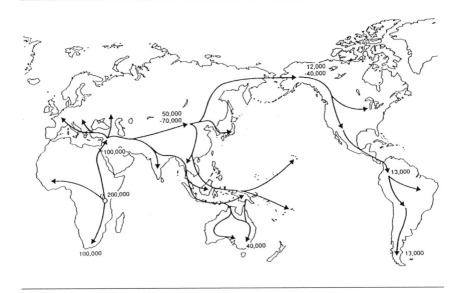

In particular, Rushton suggests that the dispersal of an originally African population less than 200,000 years ago, where these sub-populations of the originally more genetically homogeneous population became successively less and less homogeneous due to pressures of natural selection and the operation of *genetic drift*, whereby geographically isolated sub-populations of a population tend to increase in their genetic diversity across time. Among the new niches which some of these sub-populations inhabited included the problems of survival in colder northern latitudes. These difficulties led to increased adaptive benefits from those members of the sub-population able to cope with these selective pressures, which placed a premium upon skills and abilities that may have been less in demand on the African savannah. Thus, for example, unlike the topics and subtropics, plant food was now less abundant and no longer constantly available, varying with the seasons, which placed emphasis upon the adaptive ability to hunt game and gather food from the environment. Rushton believes these differences mattered:

> Even among near-contemporary hunter-gatherers, the proportions of foods obtained by hunting and by gathering varies according to latitude. Peoples in tropical and subtropical latitudes were largely gatherers, while peoples in temperate environments relied more on hunting. . . . Another set of problems in the northern latitudes would have centered on keeping warm. People had to solve the problems of making fires, clothes, and shelters. (Rushton 1995a, pp. 228–29)

Thus, the cognitive demands of creating tools and making fire and clothing selected for higher average levels of intelligence than did the relatively less cognitively-demanding and resource-rich environment of sub-Sahara Africa.

The diverse demands of different environments also promoted adoption of different reproductive strategies, where more challenging environments tended to promote high parental investment for small numbers of children, while less challenging environments tended to promote low parental investment for large numbers of children, known as "K-selection" and "r-selection" (Rushton 1995a, p. 274). Thus, a variety of causal mechanisms of evolution operating across time in diverse environments may have produced exactly the differences between sub-populations that seem to distinguish the races. As Herrnstein and Murray (1994, Appendix 5) have remarked, Rushton is hardly alone in searching for an evolutionary explanation for observable differences among human populations. They expect that time will tell if he is right.

Time is not the arbiter of truth. But it may take time—perhaps even a considerable interval thereof—to consider the full range of alternative explanations. If the individual members of the various sub-populations have been subject to widespread and systematic differences with respect to the (internal and external) environmental conditions of their development, for example, it would be unsurprising that these differences might be manifest in average differences of this kind. Such an outcome can even be a predictable consequence of norms of reaction, whether applied to species or to individuals. It is therefore possible that even properties that are prevalent within a population are not among their permanent properties. The difficult problem is to ascertain the nature of the genetically-based predispositions which are permanent, as Vincent Sarich has explained (Sarich 1995).

Whether or not this has occurred in the case of the hundreds of studies that are cited by Herrnstein and Murray (1994) and by Rushton (1995a), for example, has been subjected to extensive debate (Jacoby and Glauberman 1995). If there are (internal or external) environmental factors that make a difference to the level of intelligence of different racial groups that have yet to receive adequate consideration, then the impressive evidence that Rushton has collated can be faulted on that ground, as many have done. But because the results of these studies are robust and widespread, it may be worthwhile to consider other alternatives on the hypothesis that level of intelligence is among the permanent properties of these groups' members.

Even if level of intelligence, in particular, is a permanent property of each individual member of these groups, *the variation between members exceeds the average differences between these groups*, as everyone who studies intelligence—including Rushton, Gould, and Herrnstein and Murray—has acknowledged. A comparison would be the average weight of members of a football team in relation to the average weight of their opposing teams. A team that averages 200 lbs., for example, might actually have no member who weighs 200 lbs., but some who weigh more—possibly much more—and others who weigh less, possibly much less. The differences between their weights might exceed the average differences between teams. Since weight is a property that players could gain or lose while remaining members of their team, weight clearly qualifies as a transient rather than a permanent property of member of a team. But it should also be observed that properties that *vary* from member to member of a group—where membership in that group is specified intensionally by their possession of specific reference properties—cannot qualify as *permanent* in relation to those reference properties. Permanent properties are attributes that no member of a reference class could be without. So if the same level of intelligence is not possessed by every member of the group—in this case, the subpopulations identified as races—this attribute cannot be one of its permanent properties.

Moreover, the range of variation in each group represents a potential for evolution that might raise the average values within each race by increases in the level of this attribute by their individual members—perhaps in large numbers—under suitable conditions. According to *Fisher's theorem* (Fisher 1930), sometimes called "the fundamental theorem of natural selection", the rate at which evolution by natural selection can proceed is a function of the variance available within the present population. As Mayr has observed, "Fisher's most important conclusion was that much of continuous variation, at least in man, is due to multiple Mendelian factors rather than to environmental influences" (Mayr 1982, p. 554). Fisher stressed the importance of genes with small phenotypic effects that appear widespread in our species.

The kind of variance that matters to natural selection, however, must be "additive" in the sense that its influence can accumulate (either increase or decrease) across time. The evolutionary changes that take place in specific populations are affected by many different factors, including the number of organisms that are competing for natural resources, which is known as "frequency-dependent selection" (Sober 1984, Chapter 6). What is most important for our purposes, however, is that the existence of differences in levels of intelligence within these populations appears to supply the kind of material required for evolution to occur, which lends support to the potential for the future evolution of this property. These values as group averages can represent no more than a transient stage in the evolution of the races.

Even more importantly, when minds are understood as semiotic systems, different *kinds of intelligence* surely accompany different *kinds of minds*. Relative to iconic, indexical, and symbolic modes of mentality, for example, there must be higher and lower varieties of iconic, indexical, and symbolic mentality, as a function of the range and variations in signs of those kinds that a system can acquire, under various (internal and external) conditions. This undermines reliance upon a single measure of intelligence by implying the existence of intelligence of several kinds. The suggestion that g ought to be identified with mentality of a special kind is appropriate, yet also implies that *g* serves as an average of mental abilities *even for specific individuals*.

Suppose, for example, that there are at least five kinds of minds when logical reasoning and rational criticism are taken into account, corresponding to iconical, indexical, symbolical, transformational, and metamentality modes thereof. Then (presumably) someone could be high in one and low in another, where reliance upon a single number is only an average value. If these underlying attributes are permanent, however, then any averages based upon them would also be constant from person to person. While, as a property of *groups*, *g* functions as an average of averages and cannot be a permanent property, as a property of *individuals*, *g* can be a permanent property, even though it functions as an average. But Gould may be right to deny that a single number can adequately represent human intelligence.

6.3   Is IQ Variable?

A distinction can still be drawn between "intelligence" envisioned as a genetically-based predisposition to acquire behavioral tendencies involving the use of signs under various conditions and "IQ" as a numerical measure of intelligence thus understood. Even though the evidence reviewed in this chapter strongly suggests that, when g is properly envisioned as a predisposition to acquire other dispositions involving the use of signs, the identification of g with intelligence, on the one hand, and of intelligence with epigenetic rules, on the other, appears to be well-founded, where g, by hypothesis, turns out to represent the strength of epigenetic rules distinguishing various members of different species without which gene-culture co-evolution would be impossible. The identification of g with IQ, however, remains problematic.

The old saw has it that "IQ is what IQ tests test". But if IQ were nothing more than what IQ tests measure, it would not be worth measuring. IQ tests are important, if they are important, because they measure g, which (presumably) affects successful performance across a broad range of cognitive tasks. If they are not suitable instruments for measuring g, then their role is moot. When Gould objects to Herrnstein and Murray's conclusions by focusing upon their conception of levels of intelligence, where "intelligence" must be measured by a single number, capable of generating a ranking in a linear order, that is genetically based and effectively immutable, he may be interpreted as conceding the existence of genetically based, even effectively immutable, predispositions, but rejecting the use of IQ tests as measures of their value.

Moreover, Gould intends to be challenging their central conclusion, even though, as we have found, he acknowledges the existence of a fifteen point average difference in IQ between blacks and whites in America, which has substantial family-line heritability within each group. Yet he persistently maintains that this finding, no matter how well-documented, "permits no automatic conclusion that truly equal opportunity might not raise the black average enough to equal or surpass the white mean" (Gould 1994). Thus, (presumably) either (1) these differences are phenotypic rather than genotypic or (2) behavioral rather than phenotypical, because of which (3) these measured differences are correlational rather than nomological in character.

A defense of the possibility that (1) these differences may be phenotypic rather than genotypic may be derived from the notion of "norms of reaction", which Wilson has explained in application to phenotype/genotype relations:

> Consider a species of organism, whether animal, plant, or microorganism. Select either one gene or a group of genes that act together to affect a particular trait. Then list all the environments in which the species can survive. The different environments may or may not cause variation in the trait prescribed by the selected gene or group of genes. The total variation in the trait in all the survivable environments is the norm of reaction of that gene or group of genes in that species. (Wilson 1999, p. 149)

Norms of reaction thus represent the range of variation in phenotype traits that can occur as a causal consequence of the influence of different environmental factors when specific genes or groups of genes are kept constant and thereby display the causal influence of various sets of environmenal factors.

In Chapter 5, I considered the formalization of various laws for the development of different phenotypes from various genotypes, where different sets of environmental causes bring about various phenotype effects. Thus, when deterministic relations obtain, the following law schemata obtain:

(L1-DA) $(x)(t)[G1xt \Rightarrow (EF1xt = u \Rightarrow P1xt^*)]$;

(L1-DB) $(x)(t)[G1xt \Rightarrow (EF2xt = u \Rightarrow P2xt^*)]$;

. . .

which implies that the differences in environmental factors that distinguish *EF1* from *EF2* are causally relevant to phenotype outcome *P1*, *P2*, and so on, given the same genotype *G1*, since they would be causally relevant to such an outcome if and only if their presence makes a difference to that outcome.

Gould clearly endorses this possibility, which he illustrates in relation to the property of body height, as measured for the heights of adult males in poor villages in India, afflicted with acute nutritional deprivation. It would not be surprising should there be a high correlation between short fathers and short sons, a trait thereby displaying high familial heritability; yet it would be a mistake to conclude that this tendency toward low height was not amenable to variation under conditions of nutritional enrichment (Gould 1994, p. 5). Suitable comparisons between human populations would presuppose common prenatal and intrauterine environments for developing offspring.

A defense of the possibility that (2) these differences may be behavioral rather than phenotypic, moreover, can similarly be derived from the application of the concept of norms of reaction to behavioral-phenotypical relations, which also complicates the problem. As Elliott Sober has observed,

> The idea of a particular human being's having a "natural" level of intelligence makes no more sense than the idea of a particular corn plant's having a natural height [which is affected by its environment as a function of how much water or nutrition or sunlight it receives]. (Sober 1984, p. 161)

Yet its political consequences can be profound. If differences in behavioral performance may be affected by educational opportunities, including especially mentally stimulating experiences in early life, then providing them can appear to be morally imperative. But if they are supposed to have a "natural" level of intelligence that thereby limits their behavioral capacities, providing those educational opportunities "may seem less pressing" (Sober 1984, p. 161).

The acquisition of different behavioral tendencies by phenotypes under different sets of environmental factors appears to have a nomological foundation. Thus, when deterministic relations obtain, laws of the following forms obtain:

(L2-DA) $(x)(t)[P1xt \Rightarrow (EF3xt = u \Rightarrow BT1xt^*)]$;

(L2-DB) $(x)(t)[P1xt \Rightarrow (EF4xt = u \Rightarrow BT2xt^*)]$;

. . .

which implies that the differences in environmental factors that distinguish *EF3* from *EF4* are causally relevant to the acquisition of different dispositions as behavioral tendencies for the same phenotype *P1*, which occur, of course, as an effect of the influence of environmental factors upon epigenetic rules.

The causal sequence implies a temporal development that progresses via stages, beginning with the development of phenotypes *P* from genotypes *G*:

(L1-DA) $(x)(t)[G1xt \Rightarrow (EF1xt = u \Rightarrow P1xt^*)]$;

progressing to the acquisition of behavioral tendencies *BT* by phenotypes *P*:

(L3-DA) $(x)(t)[P1xt \Rightarrow (EF3xt = u \Rightarrow BT3xt^*)]$;

reflecting the relationship between phenotypes *Pi* and epigenetic rules *ERi*:

(L2-1) $(x)(t)(P1xt \Rightarrow ER1xt)$;

where epigenetic rules are predispositions to acquire behavioral tendencies:

(D1-D1) $(x)(t)[ER1xt \Rightarrow (EF3xt = u \Rightarrow BT3xt^*)]$;

(D1-D2) $(x)(t)[ER1xt \Rightarrow (EF4xt = u \Rightarrow BT4xt^*)]$;

. . .

and the conclusion that different genotypes *G1*, *G2*, . . . , that might be based on race give rise to different phenotypes *P1*, *P2*, . . . that possess different epigenetic rules *ERi* follows only if the differences in *ERi* are not effects of environmental factors *EFi* that affect the emergence of various phenotypes from those genotypes or of environmental factors *EFj* that affect the acquisition of various behavioral tendencies by those phenotypes as their effects.

The character of predispositions as dispositions to acquire other dispositions as outcome effects under different conditions displays itself several ways. Since intelligence *g* is now being identified with semiotic epigenetic rules *ERi* as properties of phenotypes, where those phenotypes *Pi* are outcome effects of causal interactions between genotypes *Gi* and environmental factors *EFi*, the question is whether, if these different genotypes were or had been subject to similar environmental factors *EFi*, those factors would bring about or would have brought about the development of phenotypes *Pi* that would have or would have had the same epigenetic rules *ERi* or levels of intelligence *g* as predispositions to acquire dispositions under conditions *EFj*.

Clearly, differences in racially-based genotypes *Gi* make a difference to the acquisition of behavioral tendencies *BTi* that are due to those genotypes only if they are not due to other differences, which may perhaps be drawn more conspicuously by assuming that the difference is probabilistic, where *G1*, *G2*, . . . , are causally relevant to the possession of *ERi* only provided that

(MD-1) $(x)(t)[(G1xt \ \& \ EF1xt) = n \Rightarrow ER1xt^*]$; and,

(MD-2) $(x)(t)[(G2xt \ \& \ EF1xt) = 1 - n \Rightarrow -ER1xt^*]$;

when *n* does not equal 1–*n* (that is, their values are not both equal to _); or, more elaborately, in relation to the acquisition of behavioral tendencies:

(MD-3) $(x)(t)[(G1xt \ \& \ EF1xt \ \& \ EF3xt) = n \Rightarrow BT1xt^*]$; and,

(MD-4) $(x)(t)[(G2xt \ \& \ EF1xt \ \& \ EF3xt) = 1 - n \Rightarrow -BT1xt^*]$;

where the differences in the acquisition of specific dispositions (including semiotic abilities) are not due to pre- or post-natal environmental factors.

Conducting empirical tests to ascertain whether hypotheses of the kind (MD-1) through (MD-4) would not only require random sampling of large numbers of people of kinds *G1* and *G2* but ensuring that they were subject to similar pre- and post-natal environments of kinds, *EF1* and *EF3*, respectively, controlled for every factor that was known to make a difference to the outcome of interest, namely, the acquisition or non-acquisition of specific dispositions in the form of behavioral tendency *BT1*, for example. Yet even then a statistically significant difference in the relative frequencies for *BT1* outcomes would remain fallible and uncertain, insofar as heretofore unrecognized environmental factors might have affected the results.

Indeed, arguments for the tentative and inconclusive character of the findings that relate race and intelligence are compounded by the absence of direct tests for general intelligence or g. Even properly constructed IQ tests have to be suitably administered under appropriate test conditions for their results to be valid. Even when there are no relevant genotypic, phenotypic, or environmental differences affecting the acquisition of the kinds of dispositions for which IQ tests test, which generally emphasize reasoning abilities that are rooted in semiotic abilities, performance on an IQ test manifests the causal interaction of motives, beliefs and ethics as well as abilities and capabilities. Their results require interpretation.

A suitable conception of intelligence in relation to its measurement by means of IQ tests, therefore, has to accommodate the full range of factors $F1, F2, \ldots, Fn$ whose presence or absence may make a difference to IQ test results under suitable conditions $C1, C2, \ldots, Cn$. Thus, the meaning of different IQ categories tends to be formalized along the following lines,

(IQ-D1) $IQzt$ = very high =df ($TTzt$ & $F1zt$ & $F2zt$ & $\ldots$ & $Fnzt$) =u⟹$TSzt^*$ = 125 or above;

(IQ-D2) $IQzt$ = high =df ($TTzt$ & $F1zt$ & $F2zt$ & $\ldots$ & $Fnzt$) =u⟹ TSzt^* = 110 to 125;

(IQ-D3) $IQzt$ = normal =df ($TTzt$ & $F1zt$ & $F2zt$ & $\ldots$ & Fnzt) =u⟹$TSzt^*$ = 90 to 110;

for example, where low IQs measure between 75 and 90 and very low below 75. Interpreting the test scores TS as indicative of the IQs of the test takers TT thus presupposes they have not been up too late the night before, have not had an automobile accident *en route* to the test site, or otherwise incurred disturbing factors that would invalidate their test score results.

Even given the multiple ways in which the results of IQ tests might be invalid, empirical findings support the hypothesis that there are racially-based differences in intelligence that are measurable by means of IQ tests. In particular, the results of the kinds of studies Herrnstein and Murray (1994) and Rushton (1995a) have summarized reflect a normal distribution of IQs on the basis of a normal distribution of IQ test scores. This means that 68% of those scores fall within one standard deviation of the mean (of IQ = 100), where another 27% fall within two standard deviations, another 4% falls within three standard deviations, and 1% falls beyond three standard deviations, which Herrnstein and Murray (1994, p. 121) diagram as follows:

Figure 6.3 The Distribution of IQ Scores

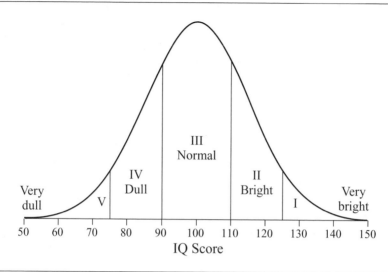

As Alex Michalos (1962, p. 290), explains, a wide variety of properties are distributed normally, including heights and weights of various species, lengths of seashells of the same species, lengths of tobacco leaves, number of kernels on ears of corn, weights of hens' eggs, and number of piglets per litter. The existence of normal distributions counts as evidence that some persistent and enduring attributes have been uncovered and supports the conclusion that sufficient evidence has become available to justify accepting the best supported among the available hypotheses (Fetzer 1981, Chapter 9). Indeed, not only IQ scores but also SAT and ACT scores are also normally distributed and support similar inferences regarding the distribution of IQs.

Although it is always logically possible to deny conclusions, even when they are strongly supported by the available evidence, precisely because empirical results based upon inductive reasoning are always tentative and fallible, the weight of the evidence available tends to support the existence of racially-based differences in intelligence. Indeed, even Gould does not dispute these differences so much as he denies that they adequately represent the underlying phenomena, endorsing instead *the theory of multiple intelligences* (in a form affirming seven different kinds), thereby denying the existence of general intelligence g (Gould 1994, p. 9). And, if there is no single property of intelligence, it follows that "intelligence" cannot be represented by a genetically based, effectively immutable single number.

Jensen (1998) has observed that the theory of multiple intelligences in the specific form that Gould endorses—which distinguishes between verbal, logical-mathematical, spatial, musical, kinesthetic, intrapersonal, and interpersonal—has been substantially undermined by the discovery of strong correlations between verbal, logical-mathematical, spatial, and musical, which are strongly "g loaded". The nature of intrapersonal and interpersonal "intelligences", from this point of view, has yet to be determined. But the kinesthetic does not even appear to belong in this category, because there is no incompatibility between g and the existence of neural nodes that can exert control over specific abilities of these kinds.

Even if Gould were right, in some contexts, the use of a single number might be appropriate, provided its meaning is not misunderstood. These values cannot be permanent properties of these groups, because they vary among their members. As properties of their members, they can vary by kind of intelligence and are affected by norms of reaction. Rushton's findings thus appear to contribute substantially to human understand, but, like all other empirical correlations, still require cautious interpretation. Gould himself, for example, has ridiculed nineteenth-century attempts to establish connections between cranial size and intelligence (Gould 1981, Chapter 3), yet new studies Rushton has brought together, including some employing magnetic resonance imaging (MRI), indicate that a substantial correlation still obtains when adjusted for body size (Rushton and Ankney 1996; cf. Rushton 1997).

Jensen (1998) has also observed that g should not be viewed narrowly as a special cognitive process or as an operating principle of the mind but broadly as a biologically based, highest order, common factor that has an important role in understanding individual differences in cognitive ability. What is so appealing about the generalization of g to epigenetic rules of the semiotic variety is that it then represents genetically-based, species specific yet individually variable, properties of minds that combine cognitive flexibility with behavioral plasticity. This conjecture has to be appraised by the extent to which it clarifies and illuminates the phenomena at hand, but it does appear to have the right properties to warrant consideration as a conception that promises to broaden and deepen our comprehension of g.

The theory of minds as semiotic systems, as I have previously observed, lends some plausibility to the possible existence of multiple kinds of intelligences (iconic, indexical, symbolic, and so forth), which is reinforced by the identification of intelligence with various semiotic kinds of epigenetic rules. This approach is different from the one Gould endorses, and the arguments that apply to intelligence as a single property necessarily apply to multiple intelligences, *mutatis mutandis*. This account not only implies the existence of minds of different kinds (distributed between the varied species) but also implies different members may have different mental abilities (distributed within the same species). The capacity to successfully solve problems, however, is obviously a function of successful learning throughout a life history.

The ultimate limitation on the importance of generalizations concerning intelligence, however, as Gould and others have surmised, is that variation within races exceed average differences between them. There are smarter and dumber of every race. Each individual ought to be judged on the basis of his own ethics, abilities, and capabilities, regardless of his race, except in those circumstances where race makes a relevant difference (such as working undercover in crime-laden neighborhoods). The problems that attend racial differences are not those differences themselves but our tendency to think and act on the basis of stereotypes. No one is surprised when individuals differ in their dispositions and predispositions. In a better society, we will be as tolerant of group differences in dispositions and predispositions as we are of individual differences. It is not a matter of science but of morality.

PART III

Evolution and Morality

7

Evolution and Rationality

Mentality requires the ability to utilize and manipulate representations, where "representations" (or "signs") are things that stand for other things in some respect or another for a sign-using system. Minds as semiotic systems, in turn, are predisposed toward the acquisition or manifestation of specific mental states as behavioral dispositions that involve the use of signs under suitable internal and external conditions. The relationship between bodies and minds thus appears to be that *minds* as (semiotic) predispositions are permanent properties of *brains* of specific kinds, *mental states* as (semiotic) behavioral dispositions are permanent properties of specific *brain states*, yet specific brain states and mind states can be among the transient ("acquired") properties of those brains and minds. Rather unexpectedly, the difference between permanent and transient mental states permits the evolution of culture.

The relationship between minds and mind states and between brains and brain states, moreover, can readily be diagrammed along the following lines:

Figure 7.1 Brains and Minds

	PREDISPOSITIONS	DISPOSITIONS
Of Cognitive Function	Minds	Mind states
Of Neurological Structure	Brains	Brain states

Thus, when "phenotypes" are properly understood as including specific neu-rological structures among their properties, then when specific behavioral dispositions are permanent properties of those neurological structures, then every instance of that phenotype has to possess those same behavioral dis-positions. It is only when behavioral dispositions are transient properties of phenotypes—whether or not they happen to be possessed by every conspe-cific with that phenotype—that the prospect for culture emerges distinct from the possession of innate, genetic, and species-specific dispositions, as we are about to discover.

This framework both illuminates and contravenes influential work on the nature of language and mentality, including that of Noam Chomsky (1959) on the nature of language, Jerry Fodor (1975) on the nature of thought, and Steven Pinker (1995) on language as an instinct. All three maintain that fun-damental properties of language are innate, genetic, and species-specific. However, in evaluating their significance, at least three different positions must be distinguished, as William Ramsey and Stephen Stich (1991) have observed, namely: *minimal nativism*, which maintains there are in-born biases for certain languages and against others; *anti-empiricism*, which maintains that innate learning mechanisms are not enough to learn a language; and *rationalism*, which maintains that learning a language requires a language-learning module.

Minimal nativism appears to be too weak to support any interesting form of rationalism, since it is compatible with species-specific epigenetic rules with innate biases for learning. Similarly, anti-empiricism seems to be inad-equate on its face, since there appear to be no good reasons for thinking that innate learning mechanisms that would enable us to learn a language do not or cannot exist. And the thesis that learning a language requires a language-learning module as a functional capacity that serves no other purpose appears to be a fantasy. The conception of minds as semiotic systems undermines the-ses focused on language learning specifically, since the use of symbols is but one form of the use of signs. But views of this kind have been widely held for a large number of bad reasons.

Chomsky (1959, 1988), for example, appears to defend a position rooted in the fallacy of assuming that there exists a unique correct grammar to learn, which ignores the possibility that we may communicate successfully because we share similar (overlapping) instead of the same (identical) grammars and vocabularies (Fetzer 1994b, pp. 345–46). His influential "poverty of the stim-ulus" argument, for example, depends upon the hypothesized existence of an assumed learning mechanism consisting of a competent scientist fortified by whatever methods of inquiry he desires. According to Chomsky, a learning mechanism of this kind might "think up" the right grammar, yet the evidence would not permit him to identify it to the exclusion of every other alternative. But Chomsky's argument simply assumes that such a unique grammar exists!

The methodological foundation for Chomsky's position, moreover, reflects a blunder in presupposing that a learning mechanism of this kind should be able to uniquely identify such a grammar. Anyone familiar with inference to the best explanation would tend to assume that there may be multiple alternative possible explanations for any phenomenon, where they are inductively supported but to differing degrees because they are simply not equally likely. Unless the evidence entails the hypothesis under consideration, it cannot be the case that evidence conclusively establishes unique conclusions! So unless Chomsky is begging the question by assuming the existence of a unique grammar, his argument—which is intended to prove that, no matter what the available evidence, the right grammar would not invariably be discovered by any learning mechanism and must therefore be known without learning—does not follow. But if Chomsky is begging the question, his conclusion still does not follow because his argument is fallacious. Evidently, therefore, it does not follow.

Fodor (1975) defends the existence of an innate language of thought in the form of a set of innate concepts relative to which learning an ordinary language is merely a process of "pairing up" the words in that language with those that belong to the innate mental language. This mental language is supposed to be complete in the sense that it has the conceptual resources to accommodate any future discovery in art, science, or technology—such as polio vaccine, jet propulsion, and color television—no matter how novel or unexpected that might be. But since the innate mental language is in-born and species-specific, the mental language of early *Homo sapiens* was presumably just as rich as that of modern *Homo sapiens*, which rather strongly suggests that Fodor, like Chomsky, has made a mistake in reasoning and that his conclusion results from a blunder.

Indeed, the language of thought hypothesis cannot be sustained (Fetzer 1989). Fodor assumes that learning a language (learning what "Px" means when "Px" means G) could only occur for an organism that already understood G (Fodor 1975, p. 80). Fodor takes for granted that the kind of understanding involved in understanding the G-phenomenon for which "Px" stands must also be linguistic! Thus, in order to forestall an infinite regress of languages that must be understood in order to understand another language, he posits a base language, the language of thought. Fodor overlooks that prior understanding may be rooted in the acquisition of habits of mind and of habits of action as dispositions that are non-linguisitic! Having prior understanding of what it is to suck a nipple, bounce a ball, or draw with crayons, it does not take a rocket scientist to discover that specific words stand for specific meanings related to these habits!

Other consequences follow from Fodor's position, such as that unsuccessful translations between ordinary languages are theoretically impossible (because they are all understood by means of the same species-specific base language) and that incommensurable theories in the sense of T.S. Kuhn can never occur (Fetzer 1993, p. 163). Indeed, a language of thought of this kind must be full-blown from scratch in order to be complete, which implies that it cannot have been the produce of an evolutionary process, after all (cf. Fetzer 1996, p. 148). The thesis of an innate, species-specific, autonomous module, even in the form Pinker (1995) advocates, poses a feeble alternative to the explanation of grammar as an evolving adaptation to explosive growth in semantic complexity during early hominid evolution when the use of symbols began to abound, as Thomas Schoenemann and William Wang recommend (Schoenemann and Wang 1996).

7.1   Adaptations as Knowledge

Plotkin has astutely remarked that science aims at explaining "more and more by less and less", in the sense of subsuming increasingly broader ranges of phenomena by means of successively fewer general principles having the character of laws of nature (Plotkin 1994, p. 78). His work aims at providing a framework for understanding successively broader ranges of biological phenomena by subsuming them within the principles of *evolution by selection*, where the mechanisms thereby invoked include variation, differential fitness and heritability, the transmission of selected variants and their (re-)combination with new variants. These mechanisms define "universal Darwinism", and the organisms and groups of organisms to which they apply are "Darwin machines" (Plotkin 1994, p. 86).

Indeed, Plotkin maintains that this framework subsumes not only biological organisms but mental states and cultural practices, thus including "memes" as well as "genes" within its scope, where *memes* are understood to be the units of cultural evolution by contrast to *genes* as the units of biological evolution (Plotkin 1994, p. 215). In many respects, the author follows the lead of Richard Dawkins. In other ways, however, he goes beyond him. Viewing the ordinary notion of *knowledge* as a relation involving a suitable "fit" between mental states and physical states, Plotkin extends the notion to biological and cultural adaptations on the ground that they too involve counterpart relations of "fit" between internal organization and external order (Plotkin 1994, p. 152).

He suggests that, if phenotypic adaptations qualify as forms of knowledge, then adaptive behaviors also qualify as forms of knowledge, including behaviors that result from (possibly complex) developmental processes based upon genetic programs that have the character of *instincts*. Instincts, however, may or may not be good enough for organisms to survive and for species to evolve:

> Instincts are efficient and economical forms of adaptive behavior, and most animals get by with instincts alone. Instincts, however, like all adaptations, have one potentially grave drawback: they are constructed on the basis of instructions built up in the past. Because nature is never prescient, this is all that they can ever be built on. But in a world that is always changing, such instructions may not be entirely appropriate for living in the world as it is now. (Plotkin 1994, p. 153)

Consequently, organisms that confront environments where change may occur more rapidly than genetic change can cope with it require additional resources.

Plotkin thus maintains that special kinds of adaptations have evolved to compensate for the limitations of ordinary biological evolution, one of which relates to rapid changes within organisms themselves in the form of their *immune systems*, the other to rapid changes within their environments in the form of their *intelligence* (Plotkin 1994, pp. 154–55). By "intelligence", Plotkin initially encompasses learning and memory in many animals and thinking and reasoning in some, which are properties of organisms individually. He later expands his approach to include *culture*, understood as the ability to share knowledge, which is a property of groups of organisms collectively. Organisms with abilities such as these thus acquire considerable evolutionary advantages.

Drawing several distinctions, Plotkin refers to the process of genetic-developmental change through natural selection as *the primary heruristic*, where the immune system and intelligence function to compensate for its shortcomings in dealing with rapid chemical and physical changes as *the secondary heuristic* (Plotkin 1994, pp. 153–54). And he subsequently suggests that the function of culture is to compensate for even more rapid forms of change than individual intelligence can handle, which qualifies as *the tertiary heuristic* (Plotkin 1994, p. 206). While Plotkin concedes to being unable to explain "the functional origins" of language, moreover, he supports his conception of the adaptive significance of culture using Chomsky's arguments about language, Cosmides's conception of social exchange, and his own account of "emotional knowledge" as illustrations.

Plotkin's rationale for the evolution of intelligence is fascinating and highly persuasive, provided that *intelligence* is understood normatively rather than descriptively (roughly, as synonymous with *rationality* rather than with *mentality*, a matter that is pursued below). His attempts to encompass the evolution of culture, however, seem to be unavailing. The principles that distinguish cultural from genetic evolution are far more extensive than Plotkin allows. They not only operate at different rates but by means of different mechanisms: cultural evolution permits the inheritance of acquired characteristics and is therefore more Lamarckian than Darwinian (Bonner 1980, Fetzer 1985). Even apart from the demerits of some of the studies that Plotkin cites (Davies *et al.* 1995), therefore, Darwinism would appear to be less "universal" than Plotkin claims.

John T. Bonner (1980), for example, has emphasized the importance of the capacities for teaching and learning in the evolution of culture. In fact, there appear to be *high* and *low* kinds of intelligence, where the (lower) capacities for classical and operant conditioning provide ways in which experience can directly shape behavior, while the (higher) capacities for organisms to teach and learn from one another reflect ways in which behavior can be affected indirectly. Teaching and learning are greatly facilitated by the use of *symbols*, which are merely habitually associated with those things for which they stand, as in the case of language (Fetzer 1991/96). Yet processes of both these kinds appear to exemplify Lamarckian instruction rather than Darwinian selection.

The evolutionary pressure for the emergence of the secondary heuristic is (what he calls) *the uncertain futures problem* (Plotkin 1994, Chapter 5). Genetic instructions that originate at time *t1* may be expected to yield appropriate phenotypical adaptations at time *t2* only if there have been no significant changes in the environment in the meanwhile. Some changes, of course, can be so vast in their effects as to be *catastrophic*, where minor modifications in behavior would make no difference between life and death. Others, however, might be dealt with successfully on the basis of behavioral adaptations that do not require physiological alterations. They may be able to cope with (what he calls) *predicable unpredictability*, a kind of "wobble" around the center of the genetically-expected environment rather like standard deviations about means.

According to Plotkin, the connections between evolution and knowledge are strong and straightforward. Knowledge is taken to be a form of adaptation, and adaptations are taken to be forms of knowledge: "The connection I am arguing for", Plotkin writes, "is that *all* adaptations are instances of knowledge, and human knowledge is a special kind of adaptation" (Plotkin 1994, p. 117). This is a very appealing conception, which appears to simultaneously recast and transform our understanding of evolution and of epistemology into a new and more powerful form of *evolutionary epistemology*, where evolution itself becomes a process for the production of knowledge. Adaptations work because they are "informed" by features of that world through evolution (Plotkin 1994, p. 118).

Plotkin defines "evolutionary epistemology" as *the biological study of knowledge*, but this conception harbors an equivocation. Some philosophers, such as Karl Popper and Donald Campbell, both of whom Plotkin cites, contend that the nature of knowledge can be illuminated by viewing it from the perspective of evolutionary theory. These authors perceive the growth of knowledge as a process of epistemic acquisition that is *analogous* to biological evolution. Ploktin, by contrast, perceives the growth of knowledge as a process of epistemic acquisition that is an *instance* of biological evolution. The former position allows for the possibility that the comparison may be imperfect, since there could still be some important differences between them. The latter permits far less latitude.

Popper, for example, views science as a process of conjectures and attempted refutations, where conjectures that survive repeated and serious attempts to refute them endure (at least, for the time being), just as organisms that survive repeated and serious attempts to extinguish them endure (at least, for the time being). Popper's "conjectures", however, have the ontological status of theories or hypotheses that can be true or false, while "organisms" have the ontological status of forms of life that can live or die. Moreover, they appear to represent different kinds of knowledge: theoretical conjectures concern *knowing that* something is the case, whereas biological conjectures concern *knowing how* to act or to behave (Fetzer and Almeder 1993, "Knowing that versus knowing how"). They thus differ in their ontological character and their epistemological status.

Plotkin wants to maintain that, whatever their differences, biological evolution and knowledge acquisition are governed by *the same general principles*, namely: the g-t-r or "generate-test-regenerate" heuristic Campbell advocates, which Plotkin labels "Campbell's blind-variation—selective retention scheme" (Plotkin 1994, p. 84). At this level of analysis, even Popper's method of conjectures and attempted refutations can be viewed as a special case of what can be most simply expressed as a "trial and error" process in which *we learn from our mistakes* (Popper 1968). But while g-t-r plausibly applies to biological evolution (Plotkin 1994, p. 138), the conclusion that knowledge acquisition should therefore be envisioned as an instance of biological evolution does not follow.

The reasons for denying this are various. If knowledge acquisition is a Lamarckian process of acquiring knowledge-that, while biological evolution is a Darwinian process of acquiring knowledge-how, then they cannot be properly subsumed as instances of "knowledge" in the same sense. In evolution, for example, *does nature learn from its mistakes*? Now and then Plotkin seems to be aware of the risks inherent in his position, even suggesting that he ought to be read as meaning "adaptations are biological knowledge, and knowledge as we commonly understand the term is a special case of biological knowledge" (Plotkin 1994, p. xv). Even when thus qualified, however, the question remains of whether the underlying comparison is more illuminating than it is misleading.

For example, if some adaptations are innate, but other adaptations are not, then it may be especially important to distinguish between them. *Biological knowledge* in the form of (complex) genetic-developmental programs, which cannot be changed and cannot be violated by individual organisms during the course of their lifetimes, may be very different from *acquired behavior* in the form of conditioned responses to specific kinds of stimulation, on the one hand, or from *rational beliefs* in the form of the acceptance and rejection of specific theories or hypotheses, on the other, where the occurrence of additional conditioning or the discovery of new evidence may lead to changing our behavior or our minds. It would be unwise to conflate knowledge of such different kinds.

Within epistemology, moreover, the term "knowledge" ordinarily stands for *beliefs which are both justified and true*, whether approached historically (Ackermann 1965) or analytically (Scheffler 1965). The differences between most philosophers who study the subject is a matter of how the components of *belief*, *truth*, and *justification* can be best understood (Kirkham 1992, Goodman and Snyder 1993). Thus, different authors give different answers to questions such as, "What is a belief?" and "What is truth?" Within the context of theories of "scientific knowledge" specifically, however, some philosophers contend that a more illuminating conception results from following Popper and entertaining *scientific knowledge* as justified beliefs that may be false (Fetzer 1981, Chapter 1).

7.2   Evolutionary Epistemology

If Plotkin were talking about knowledge when he talks about "adaptations", therefore, we would expect him to make connections between his concepts and the properties of belief, truth and justification as they occur within the context of the theory of knowledge. What we find when we study his work, however, is not at all reassuring. The closest he comes to defining "beliefs", for example, occurs during his discussion of *memes*, where he suggests that "meme" might best be defined in terms of "belief", understood in turn as "a relatively fixed core meaning, tolerant to minor changes about a fuzzy edge" (Plotkin 1994, p. 217). This conception, however, does not begin to capture the notion of *belief* as a mental state in which some such meaning is accepted by someone as true.

In fact, Plotkin tends to avoid the notions of minds and of mental states altogether. Although he occasionally talks about *mental states* (Plotkin 1994, p. 4, for example), his discussions of knowledge are expressed either in terms of its character as an adaptation or as a relation between brain states and the world (Plotkin 1994, p. 52). Since *brain states* (such as the state of activation of a specific arrangement of neurons and synapses) are not the sort of thing that can properly be described as being true or false, it would be appropriate for him to say something about the relationship between mental states and brain states; but when the occasion finally arises, he simply says that we do not know how mental states are related to brain states (Plotkin 1994, p. 217).

The situation with respect to *justification* appears to be even worse. In the final chapter of his book, Plotkin "bites the bullet" at last. While maintaining that (biological) adaptations generated by the primary heuristic are "usually well justified" through their evolution by selection, he mistakenly presumes that the (epistemic) adaptations with which philosophers are concerned have to do with "how you or I can be certain . . . that it is or is not raining today" (Plotkin 1994, p. 232). He suggests this may be an unsolvable non-problem:

> Only if survival and reproduction are absolutely correlated with knowledge could they be an infallible guide to true belief. But since this is not the case, evolutionary epistemology has nothing to say about the knowledge justification problem. This, however, does not mean the end of the epistemological world. . . . (T)he justification problem may simply be unsolvable—in effect, a non-problem that philosophers have worried at for thousands of years to no avail. (Plotkin 1994, p. 234)

This passage and others, alas, suggest that Plotkin has not only misunderstood the nature of the problem but its solution within an evolutionary epistemology.

Evolution by selection, which involves the generation of variation, selective retention and regeneration through reproduction, is a causal process. The outcome of a causal process may be *explained* by citing those causal mechanisms and antecedent conditions that brought about that result. The outcome of that same causal process can be *justified* by citing the available evidence and normative principles relative to which such a result was appropriate. Explanations typically are not justifications. When causal systems, such as human minds, adhere (even unconsciously) to suitable normative principles of reasoning, there is a convergence between the principles on which a system ought to be operating and those on which it is operating. Such minds are rational (Fetzer 1991/96).

The (epistemic) problem of justification is to identify (what might be called) *criteria of credibility* such that, when a belief satisfies those criteria, then it has qualified for acceptance (Fetzer and Almeder 1993, "Criteria, the problem of"). It is important because we have no direct access to the truth or the falsity of any beliefs. Consequently, we must arbitrate between them on the basis of the available relevant evidence. This is a *normative process* of discovering inductive, deductive, and perceptual standards relative to which beliefs may be acceptable as true. Since the evidence on the basis of which we evaluate beliefs remains fallible, we can still make mistakes and sometimes accept false beliefs. Those that satisfy appropriate criteria are nonetheless rational beliefs.

Ultimately, distinctions must be drawn between at least two kinds of rationality (Fetzer 1990, 1991/96). *Actions* (as intentional forms of behavior) are said to be rational when they are appropriate as means to attain specific goals. *Beliefs* (as specific kinds of mental states) are said to be rational when they receive appropriate support from the available relevant evidence. These properties appear to be logically independent in the sense that different individuals could be high in rationality of action and low in rationality of belief, or vice versa. In extended senses, with respect to lower species of organisms largely if not exclusively controlled by their instincts, it would not be overly misleading to describe their behavior as "rational" when it promotes their survival and reproduction, even if they do not possess the capacity to subject their beliefs to rational criticism.

Rationality of belief becomes especially important to higher species of organisms in permitting them to subject potential actions to rational criticism before they undertake them. In this sense, we are able to formulate hypotheses and theories on the basis of which we might act and kill them instead of ourselves, as Popper often emphasized (Popper 1978). And when we want to change the behavior of the members of specific species, we can benefit greatly from knowing if their behavior is completely instinctual or amenable to classical or operant conditioning or to teaching and learning through the use of symbols, such as language. Rational beliefs ("knowledge") of this kind can enable us to undertake far more effective and efficient actions than would otherwise be possible.

In the last few pages, Plotkin attempts to come to grips with at least some of the problems that undermine his conception of adaptations as knowledge. He asserts that knowledge (in his sense) is *fallible* and claims that products of the primary heuristic are *no less* fallible than are those of the secondary heuristic and that products of the tertiary heuristic are *even more* fallible than are they:

> (J)ust as the adaptations generated by the primary heuristic are of varying degrees of truth and may even be untrue (though in the fullness of time they will tend

toward the truth), so it is too with the knowledge that results from the operation of culture and individual intelligence. . . . (A)nd however full of self-correcting mechanisms intelligence might be, the secondary heuristic does make errors . . . . The tertiary heuristic, even if nested under the primary and secondary heuristics, is subject to even less control by the more-often-than-not-true-belief-generating primary heuristic and the quite-often-untrue-belief-generating secondary heuristic. (Plotkin 1994, p. 233)

The very idea that "adaptations" may be of "varying degrees of truth" and may even be "untrue" raises an important question for a theory of this kind, namely: how are we to distinguish the "adaptive" from the "non-adaptive" adaptations?

The problem for Plotkin is serious. Suppose, for example, we were to identify "fitness" with *truth* ("varying degrees of fitness" with *varying degrees of truth*), which captures the spirit of the enterprise. Then evolution by selection may not be infallible, but nevertheless tends toward successful adaptation "in the fullness of time". Yet such a conception is not easy to reconcile with Plotkin's own conjecture that *more than ninety-eight percent of all species that have ever existed are extinct* (Plotkin 1994, p. 144). Moreover, if the primary heuristic actually leads to extinction in the vast majority of cases "in the fullness of time", while the secondary heuristic is less dependable in securing truth than the primary heuristic and the tertiary even less dependable than the secondary, then even when they make marginal contributions to "fitness" enhancement, the prospects for survival remain dim.

When Plotkin asserts that "evolutionary epistemology has nothing to say about the knowledge justification problem", therefore, he is implicitly conceding that his conception is seriously flawed. When properly understood, *the knowledge justification problem* is the central problem of epistemology: without a solution to this problem, there is no (remotely plausible) theory of knowledge. The position he should be defending is that the Popperian methodology of conjectures and attempted refutations provides "an evolutionary justification" for accepting some beliefs as true and rejecting other beliefs as false, even though we cannot do so with certainty, just as its biological counterpart of evolution by natural selection provides "an evolutionary justification" for regarding some organisms as having greater fitness than do other organisms, even though we cannot do so with certainty. In both cases, "knowledge" is uncertain and fallible.

Ultimately, Plotkin adopts a Kantian conception of knowledge, according to which minds are predisposed to acquire some kinds of information and to not acquire other kinds as a causal consequence of evolution by selection. He thus endorses an evolutionary variation on Kant's account—a species of

Evolutionary Rationalism, as it might be called—which, in general, appears to be the correct approach as long as the distinction between dispositions and predispositions is observed (Fetzer 1991/96). Ironically, the condition of certainty, which misled Plotkin about the nature of justification, was imposed by Rationalists, such as Plato and Descartes, rather than by Empiricists, including Locke and Hume. This suggests that the Empiricists may have understood the nature of knowledge better than the Rationalists, who better understood the nature of mind.

It should be observed that some philosophers endorse conceptions of truth that harmonize with particular aspects of Plotkin's approach. According to the *pragmatic* formulation, a convergence of opinion should emerge between the members of the community of inquirers, were they to continue their inquiries forever, where the opinion that they are destined to agree on ("in the fullness of time") is *true* (Fetzer and Almeder 1993, "Truth, Peircean theory of"). This conception, moreover, can function as an epistemic criterion, where an alternative *definition* maintains that our beliefs are true when they are appropriate to guide our behavior (Fetzer 1990, p. 125). Combining these two conceptions, it follows that the opinion that the community of inquirers is destined to agree upon ("in the fullness of time") ought to be appropriate to guide our behavior.

What we need to know, if possible, of course, is how to behave *now* in order to avoid death or extinction later. With respect to other species, we may want to know which properties of those organisms that were beneficial in the past are likely to be beneficial in the future. We might want to shape their genes or their memes to make them more or less successful in the future by changing them or by changing their environments. Alternatively, we may want to shape our own genes or our own memes (presumably) to make us more successful in the future. Among our most promising avenues toward that end thus appears to be enhancing our capacity for rational criticism of hypotheses and theories.

The conception that beliefs are true when they are appropriate to guide our behavior is the right definition of truth within this context, but the criterion of truth as the opinion destined to be agreed on ("in the fullness of time") is wrong. We need to be able to separate adaptive from non-adaptive adaptations *now*. To explain and to predict the behavior of organisms, we need to know the laws that relate genes to behavior (in the case of instincts), experience to behavior (in the case of conditioning), and beliefs to behavior (in the case of rationality). Knowledge of nature is the key to our success. We need epistemology to understand biology even more than we need biology to understand epistemology.

7.3   Is Rationality Adaptive?

In his splendid book, *The Evolution of Culture in Animals* (1980), John T. Bonner has isolated several factors that differentiate between genetic and cultural (or gene-culture) evolution. In the language of genes and memes, he suggests three basic differences, namely: that genes can exist independently of memes, but memes cannot exist independently of genes; that genetic information is transmitted exactly once during the lifetime of an organism, while memetic information can be transmitted repeatedly thoughout an organism's lifetime; and that the rate of transmission of genetic information is very slow, while that of memetic information can be very fast. These are indeed important differences, no doubt, but they do not seem to be exhaustive.

Table 7. i   Genetic versus Cultural Evolution (Bonner)

GENETIC EVOLUTION	versus	CULTURAL EVOLUTION
1 Genes can exist independently of memes.		1′ Memes cannot exist independently of genes.
2 One-time transmission of information (conception).		2′ Multiple opportunities for information transmission.
3 Changes very slow (bound by rate of reproduction)		3′ Changes very fast (bound roughly by speed of light)

Consider, for example, that the properties that are transmitted by genes are permanent properties of organisms, ones that they cannot lose without also losing their identity as organisms of that kind, while the properties that are transmitted by memes are merely transient properties that an organism could lose while remaining an organism of that kind; that the transmission of genetic properties does not permit the inheritance of acquired characteristics (and is therefore Darwinian), while the transmission of memetic properties allows the inheritance of acquired characteristics (and is therefore Lamarckian), where *Lamarckian processes* allow an organism to benefit from changes in its cultural environment that occur during its lifetime without altering its genes: See Table 7.ii

The differences between genetic and cultural evolution are therefore profound and reflect the importance of predispositions for understanding higher species. The phrase, "higher species", in this case designates any species for

Table 7. ii   Genetic versus Cultural Evolution (Fetzer)

GENETIC EVOLUTION	versus	CULTURAL EVOLUTION
4 Affect permanent properties.		4′ Affect merely transient properties.
5 Mechanisms of genetic change are Darwinian, including		5′ Mechanisms of memetic change are Lamarckian, including
genetic mutation natural selection sexual reproduction . . . artificial selection genetic engineering		classic conditioning operant conditioning imitating others . . . logical reasoning rational criticism

which the behavior of its members is not completely determined by genetically-based dispositions as specific patterns of behavior. The *E. coli* bacterium appears to be an appropriate example, because its survival and reproduction appears to be completely under the control of Darwinian causal mechanisms. Chimpanzees, by comparison, appear to be strongly affected by classical and instrumental conditioning and by teaching and learning from others. Their behavior thus appears to be strongly affected by Lamarckian mechanisms. But is the alleged distinction between mechanisms of these kinds justifiable?

No doubt, in purely biological contexts, the difference between Darwinian and Lamarckian evolution has a firm foundation, since there is no inheritance of acquired characteristics when transmitted genetically. If there is a difference of the kind alleged, as I maintain, then it must be the case because there is inheritance of acquired characteristics when transmitted culturally. Perhaps the clearest illustration of this difference was advanced by Karl Popper (1972) in thought experiments comparing our species's prospects under two scenarios:

Experiment 1. All our machines and tools are destroyed, and all of our subjective learning, including our subjective knowledge of machines and tools, and how to use them. *But libraries and our capacity to learn from them* survive. Clearly, after much suffering, our world may get going again.

Experiment 2. As before, machines and tools are destroyed, and our subjective learning, including our subjective knowledge of machines and tools, and how to use them. But this time, *all libraries are destroyed also*, so that our capacity to learn from books becomes useless. (Popper 1972, pp. 107–08)

This thought comparison suggests the benefits that are derivable under most, though not all, situations encountered during the course of non-catastrophic cultural evolution. The contrast between these scenarios exemplifies the importance of the inheritance of acquired cultural characteristics, assuming that we retain the semiotic ability to read and learn from books (Popper 1972, p. 116). The causal potency of our cultural legacy reflects the reality of this distinction.

What then of *rationality* for a species even defined as "the rational animal"? The connection between causality and rationality assumes an acute form from the perspective of evolution, since natural selection seems to be a completely a causal process that functions independently of considerations of rationality. Once distinctions are drawn between rationality of belief and rationality of action—neither of which need be conscious to organism or agent—it becomes obvious that rationality of both kinds promotes the attainment of goals, which is significant to evolution when they include survival and reproduction. When evidence is inaccurate or incomplete, however, or non-biological goals override biological ones, even actions that are rational in both senses can be nonadapttive or maladaptive as they influence prospects for survival and reproduction.

Somewhat more formal and complete definitions of these notions might be helpful in facilitating discussion of the adaptive benefits rationality can afford, beginning with a more precise definition of the nature of rationality of belief:

(D1) **rationality of belief** =df believing in proportion to the evidence: when the evidence is sufficient to accept *h*, accepting *h* as true; when the evidence is sufficient to reject *h*, rejecting *h* as false; and when the evidence is not sufficient, neither accepting nor rejecting *h*.

The potential adaptive benefits of rationality in this sense should be apparent, since the acceptance of beliefs that are true and the rejection of beliefs that are false promotes not only the (pure) theoretical goal of understanding the world but the (impure) practical goal of attaining our aims, objectives, and goals. For there is scant room to doubt that true beliefs promote the attainment of goals.

The connection between beliefs and goals arises by way of action, which are characteristically undertaken to attain our goals on the basis of our beliefs. Consider, for example, a more precise definition of the nature of rationality of action:

(D2) **rationality of action** = df acting on the basis of motives and beliefs
by adopting means appropriate (efficient, effective, or reliable) to
attain those ends, independently of consideration for the rationality of those beliefs themselves.

This is the kind of rationality often called "instrumental" (or "means-ends")
rationality, involving as it does the selection of appropriate means to attain
specific ends. But it ought to be obvious that, when actions are undertaken
on the basis of false or mistaken beliefs, even the adoption of the most efficient, effective, or reliable—not to mention, expensive—means may be unlikely
to attain an action's goals.

Thus, the most important reason for favoring true beliefs over false, from
the standpoint of practical action is that, when beliefs are true, the guidance
they provide for action will be appropriate, but when they are false, their guidance will be inappropriate. Indeed, a pragmatic conception of *truth* itself
would be that beliefs are true when they provide "appropriate guidance for
action" (Fetzer 1990, pp. 125–27). And it may be worth observing that beliefs
do not have to be "exactly true" to provide guidance for action that is "appropriate enough". There are occasions, for example, when you set a date and
time to meet, it may not matter if you both arrive at just the same time, provided you are in the right place; other occasions, it may not matter if you both
in just the right place, provided you are there at the right time. On special
occasions, you may need to be in the right place and on time.

Thus, satisficing strategies appear to make a difference in life. You may
set off with one plan in mind, such as catching the next showing of your
favorite movie, perhaps *Titanic*, yet discover that the line was too long to
make the start of the film and adopt an alternative plan. There is an important role in life for what is often called "flexibility", which has something to
do with adapting to the things as they are rather than resisting them. The
importance of "adapting" can vary from case to case, however: flexibility
about catching a flick may be one thing, but flexibility in resistance to Nazi
oppression may be another. Just as there appear to be grades of approxima-
tion to the truth that are "good enough" to accomplish, there are degrees of
goal satisfaction that are similarly "good enough". Our actions are affected
by our abilities, capabilities, and ethics as well as our motives and beliefs.

Adaptations that have proven to be adaptive in the past, we know, may or
may not continue to be adaptive in the future as a function of changing circumstances, which encompass the environmental resources and conspecific
competition. They can be described as "rational" relative to one complete set
of conditions and also be described as "irrational" relative to another complete set of conditions. What makes adaptations adaptive, from a biological

point of view, is that they promote the survival and reproduction of the organism, in the first instance, and of the species, in the second. But that conception takes for granted that the biological goals of survival and reproduction are among our personal aims, objectives, or goals; otherwise, behaviors might be rational in attaining our own aims, objective, and goals, even though they do not promote our survival and reproduction.

The very idea of aims, objectives, or goals that may not promote survival and and reproduction runs against the grain of "Hamilton's rule", according to which the adaptive value of an action can be measured by the product of the fitness benefits it confers b and the degree of relatedness between the organism performing the action r minus its genetic costs c, or $[\,(\,r \cdot b\,) - c\,]$ (Hamilton 1964). This conception underlies the notion of *inclusive fitness*, where the importance of behaviors is measured by its fitness values for genetic relatives, reflected by the biologist's witticism that he would "gladly die for two brothers, four cousins, or eight second cousins" (Angler 2000). And Hamilton's rule has proven to provide a robust framework for subsuming many kinds of behavior across many different species as manifestations of this fundamental "biological imperative".

When $[\,(\,r \cdot b\,) - c\,] > 0$, then the behavior confers an adaptive advantage and tends to be favored by natural selection. But when $[\,(\,r \cdot b\,) - c\,] = 0$, it is adaptively neutral, and when $[\,(\,r \cdot b\,) - c\,] < 0$, it is actually maladaptive and disfavored by natural selection. Behaviors that are neutral, such as preferring to play bridge over canasta, for example, or actually maladaptive, such as taking risks in the pursuit of scientific knowledge, do not promote genetic fitness and therefore pose problems for evolutionary explanations. There are many non-biological kinds of values, including financial, aesthetic, theoretical, and moral, whose influence may explain non-adaptive behavior. An adequate science of human behavior must make room for non-biological as well as biological values. They may bring about behaviors that biological values cannot adequately explain. That evolution can explain many forms of behavior does not imply it can explain them all.

Indeed, actions that are "rational" in both rationality of belief and rationality of action can be non-adaptive or even maladaptive from a biological point of view, when non-biological motives—such as might arise from religious obligations, ego defenses, peer pressure or self-esteem—override biological ones. Certain kinds of actions that tend to contravene reproduction or survival or both may nevertheless qualify as "rational": consider, for example, monks and nuns who take vows of chastity (perhaps enhancing longevity at the expense of reproductive potential); consider suicide as a defense against the acute loss of self-esteem (thereby avoiding the outcome of personal humiliation by self-sacrifice). The case of monks and nuns defeats reproduction while possibly promoting survival, while ego defenses may defeat both. Some psychological motives do override biological imperatives.

Notice the differences between cases of these kinds and those of ordinary false beliefs. Young people who smoke in order to "be cool" (perhaps thereby enhancing their short-term sex appear at the potential expense of long-term impairment) may or may not be making mistakes, depending upon the relative weight that they assign to their short-term as opposed to their long-term aims, objectives, and goals. It could always be argued that those who commit suicide to avoid humiliation are allowing short-term motives to override long-term motives, yet there exist human beings whose sense of honor and integrity would require them to sacrifice themselves under certain kinds of conditions, not as an act of moral weakness but as an act of moral courage that is deeply rooted in their character. And the reproductive sacrifice made by monks and nuns does not appear affected by such arguments.

The benefits of rationality do not derive from the promotion of biological aims, objectives, and goals, therefore, even though most human beings want to survive and reproduce. The benefits of rationality have more to do with autonomy than with adaptation, where *autonomy* represents the capacity to decide for ourselves what life we are going to lead or whether we are going to lead any life at all. As in the case of truth and satisfaction, there are degrees of autonomy, where actions tend to be *autonomous* to the extent to which they are voluntarily made free from compulsion and constraint. For when persons are compelled to do things that they would otherwise have preferred not to do or are constrained from doing things that they otherwise would have preferred to do, their lives are compromised by being unable to live them as they would prefer in the boundaries of their circumstances.

But this conception presupposes the presence of suitable degrees of rationality of action and of rationality of belief; otherwise, the absence of compulsion and of constraint does not allow a person to live their own lives. Consider, for example, the incapacity imposed by the impairment of rationality of belief represented by *psychoses* such as paranoid delusions, because of which rational actions may be highly inappropriate, even though they are efficient, effective, or reliable means for attaining specific aims, objectives, or goals. Consider, for example, the incapacity imposed by the impairment of rationality of action represented by *neuroses*, such as an approach/avoidance complex, because of which actions may be highly inefficient, ineffective, or unreliable means to attain specific aims, objectives, or goals—no matter how worthy the goals or how truth and complete a set of beliefs.

The reason why "knowledge" matters to our practical lives as well as to theoretical understanding thus becomes increasingly clear. The standard conception, according to which *a person z knows that p* if and only if (a) *z* believes that p, (b) z is warranted in believing that p, and (c) p is true means not only (a) that z sincerely and honestly accepts that p and (b) that z possesses appropriate evidence in support of the belief that p and (c) that p is the case. The importance of warrants thus becomes apparent, because having "good reasons" for believing that p means there are "good reasons" for believing that p is true, which implies in turn that there are "good reasons" for believing that p provides appropriate guidance for actions. Thus, every rational agent has an interest in knowledge, which is relative to the seriousness of the consequences of taking actions based on false beliefs.

The cases of suicide and celibacy, I presume, demonstrate that rationality (in the strongest sense) does not necessarily promote the biological aims, objectives, or goals of survival and reproduction. If actions are said to be "adaptive" only when they promote survival and reproduction, therefore, then rationality is not invariably adaptive. Moreover, adaptations are not always rational. Consider, for example, that there can be cases in which the failure to draw obvious conclusions may be adaptive and where violations of rationality of belief, in particular, might promote survival or reproduction. A criminal's mother, sisters, and older children may have benefited from not drawing inferences about his guilt or innocence that are well-supported by the available evidence. Even he might benefit from failing to acknowledge his own conduct to himself—even as a matter of self-preservation!

The benefits of education, especially higher education, are therefore profound. Persons who have the opportunity to learn more about the world and themselves—and who learn more about the world and themselves—have greater options in life than do those who know less. The exercise of autonomy can be advanced by placing oneself in a situation in which learning will take place, your mind will be developed, and you will become a more efficient, effective, and reliable thinking thing and human being. Entering a college or a university involves becoming a part of a complex causal process intended impart knowledge, to be sure, but one that also instills appropriate habits of mind and habits of action, namely: those characteristic of persons who are not only able to learn from and to teach others but who are able to learn for themselves. Rationality thus promotes autonomy.

That this should be the case emerges with great clarity from the distinctions between kinds of minds that are aspects of the semiotic conception. Minds can employ signs that are iconic, indexical, or symbolic, but they can also be transformational or critical in kind (Fetzer 1990, 1991/96, and 2000). Transformational mentality involves the exercise of logical reasoning, whether deductive (in being able to ascertain what else must be true if something happens to be true) or inductive (in being able to ascertain what else may be true if something happens to be true). When the exercise of appropriate principles of deduction and of induction becomes a habit of mind, those who incorporate them among their mental dispositions enhance the rationality of their beliefs and their rationality of action.

And those who become critical thinking things in using signs to stand for other signs in order to make them more effective, efficient, and reliable for their own purposes become more effective, efficient, and reliable, in turn, at least in their habits of mind if not in their habits of action. Rationality of belief and rationality of action are independent properties, to be sure, yet strengthening rationality of belief tends to strengthen rationality of action—by providing it with a more firm foundation. Rationality and autonomy do not necessarily promote biology and, as I have elsewhere explained, they do not entail morality. When Willie Sutton said that he robbed banks, "Because that's where the money is!", therefore, he was displaying neither a lack of rationality of action nor of rationality of belief.

Indeed, individuals who are unafflicted by serious neurotic or psychotic symptoms and who are relatively free from compulsion and constraint imposed upon them by others are not only more or less autonomous but also capable of acting on the basis of their own motives, beliefs, and ethics, by virtue of which they can be described as exercising *freedom of the will* (Fetzer 1991/96, Ch. 9). Freedom of the will should therefore be understood as amenable to degrees with respect to the extent to which a person's actions are both autonomous and under the control of their rationality. This conception does not entail any absence of causation, but rather reflects a conception of action where agents are exercising "free will" when they are competent and acting on the basis of their preferences. Free acts reflect our preferences for acting under various conditions and thus are self-determined.

Plotkin overlooks that our rationality allows us to transcend our biology. But perhaps this is a difficult point. Dennett goes further than Plotkin in his *Kinds of Minds* (1996) by drawing distinctions between *Darwinian creatures*, which are the products of natural selection, *Skinnerian creatures*, which are capable of operant conditioning, *Popperian creatures*, which are capable of preselection among possible behaviors, and *Gregorian creatures*, which are capable of the evolution of culture. As in the case of his previous discussion of things of these same kinds (Dennett 1996), he insists that human beings are not only Skinnerian creatures who are capable of conditioning but also Darwinian creatures who benefit from inherited hardwiring and Popperian creatures who can represent their options.

What appears to be most intriguing about Popperian creatures, I believe, is that they are capable of *representing* their environments and their choices before they act, a capacity that Dennett ascribes to many different kinds of animals:

We do not differ from all other species in being Popperian creatures then. Far from it: mammals and birds, reptiles, amphibians, fish, and even many invertebrates exhibit the capacity to use general information they obtain from their environments to presort their behavioral options before striking out. (pp. 92–93)

Dennett thus diverges strongly from the dominant preoccupation of other students of mentality and cognition, who suppose that the distinctive ability of minds is *the capacity to utilize and manipulate representations*. (Compare: minds are *systems that are capable of utilizing and manipulating signs*.) Those who approach the problem from this perspective are likely to take Popperian creatures as thinking things.

If Popperian creatures are thinking things, human mentality has evolutionary origins. Dennett, however, contends that only Gregorian creatures can be thinking things, because they are capable of the use of tools, including language, especially (pp. 99–101). The conception of human beings as distinctive tool-makers and tool-users is an early anthropological conception that has been superseded by research in cognitive ethology. No one familiar with the state of current research ought to be drawn to such a view, which ignores or distorts the evolution of communication and the nature of animal mind (see, for example, Beckoff and Jamieson 1996).

The possibility that Dennett has no coherent conception of mentality, moreover, receives support from several directions. Beyond his inconsistent commitments to Cartesian conceptions, he reports that it has seemed obvious to many, including him,

> that what minds do is *process information*: minds are the control systems of bodies, and in order to execute their appointed duties they need to gather, discriminate, store, transform, and otherwise process information about the control tasks they perform. (p. 69)

But if Popperian creatures, by his own admission, gather, discriminate, store, transform, and otherwise process information about the control tasks they perform, is it not equally obvious that they also qualify among the possessors of minds and that some level of complexity suitable for the emergence of mentality has been attained? In fact, we already knew that creatures of all of "Dennett's kinds" can have minds. Now we know that human beings are vastly more than mere Darwinian machines.

8

Ethics and Evolution

Rationality, we have found, promotes autonomy, but neither rationality nor autonomy necessarily promote survival and evolution, when biological motives are overridden by non-biological motives. This might come as a surprise to anyone committed to biological determinism, because it does not look like a predictable consequence of evolutionary biology. (Whether evolution can explain morality is something that we will pursue.) Moreover, rationality does not guarantee morality. This result contradicts a powerful tradition in moral philosophy, according to which morality and rationality are inextricably intertwined. Not only was Willie Sutton not irrational in his beliefs when he explained why he robbed banks, but if money is your object, one way to try to get a lot of it is by robbing banks. Though it would not be moral, bank robbing could be an exercise in the rationality of action.

Consider the following payoff matrix, a familiar device within decision-theory contexts, where various action options and their possible outcomes are compared in order to establish the possible results in making decisions:

Figure 8.i A Payoff Matrix

	State of Nature	
Action Options	*He/She is wonderful*	*He/She is Not*
Accept date	Great time!	Awful time
	* * * *	*
Reject date	Kick yourself	Relief
	* *	* * *

Thus, confronted with the offer of a "blind date", you have two choices: accept the date or reject it. Your prospect, let us assume, is either wonderful or not. If you accept the date and she or he is wonderful, then you'll have a great time; if you accept the date and she or he is not, then you'll have an awful time. If you reject the date and she or he is wonderful, then you'll kick yourself; but if you reject the date and she or he is not, then you will at least be relieved.

In order to arrive at a "rational decision", you must rank order the outcomes in terms of your preferences (say, having a wonderful date over feeling relieved over kicking yourself over having an awful time, as the asterisks reflect). If the probabilities of the outcomes are not known (and you are in conditions of uncertainty), then at least two principles might apply, namely: (R1) *The Mimimax Loss Principle*, which tells you to prefer the alternatives that would minimize possible losses; and, (R2) *The Maximax Gain Principle*, which tells you to prefer alternatives that permit the greatest gain. Thus, in this situation, (R1) would recommend that you reject the blind date, but (R2) would recommend that you accept it. Neither is more rational than the other, but (R1) ought to appeal to pessimists, while (R2) should appeal to optimists.

An alternative approach applies when the probabilities for the outcomes happen to be known, in which case the decision is said to be made under conditions of risk. In that case, you must make some (often rather complicated) calculations of the probabilities for each outcome multiplied by the utilities for each outcome (quantifying the value that you would assign to them) and summing their values across each action-option to secure what are known as the expected utilities thereof. Then (R3) *The Principle of Maximizing Expected Utility* should be applied, which tells you that you should adopt an alternative that provides at least as much expected utility as any other. This decision rule is widely recommended and even regarded as obvious (Michalos 1969, Chapter 8).

There is a whole industry devoted to subtle variations on rules like these, but the point I want to make is simple. Suppose, for example, that you wanted to make money. Then among your alternatives (your "action options") might be robbing banks, counterfeiting credit cards, and getting a job. If you calculated that robbing banks had the highest expected utility among your alternatives-on the basis of careful consideration and thoughtful analysis—then that would be the rational alternative! Of course, you would have to take into account the possibility that you might be caught, convicted, and sent to jail; but if, after all the outcomes were weighed and balanced, this remained the alternative with the highest expected utility, it would be the rational choice. But it ought to be apparent that it is not a moral choice. So rationality does not entail morality.

8.1   Evolution and Morality

In a fascinating book, Robert Richards (1987) has suggested that the development of evolutionary theories of mind and behavior confronts at least three fundamental problems, which involve "heritable habits", rationality, and morality, respectively. The solution to the problem of heritable habits thus turns out to be the theory of natural selection, which operates at the level of behavior through a process of selection to yield changes in the frequency of genes across time, whereby combinations of genes which predispose various phenotypes toward adaptive behavior tend to be perpetuated.

The problems of rationality and morality have proven somewhat more difficult to resolve. Lumsden and Wilson (1981, 1983) have advanced their conception of mentality as susceptibility to social learning, which might, in turn, provide at least a partial solution to the problem of rationality. And the conception of an ethics based upon evolution has been widely supposed to supply the basis for a resolution of the problem of morality, as a lengthening succession of contemporary authors—from Wilson (1975, 1978) and Ruse and Wilson (1985, 1986) to Richards (1987), Alexander (1987), and, more recently, Ruse (1998) and Wilson (1999), independently—have maintained.

While these authors advance somewhat different views, the basic ideas they advance can be cast into a coherent position, which accents the nature of human beings in light of their biological origins. Ruse and Wilson (1985) for example, observe that humans are animals and that "the social behavior of animals is firmly under the control of the genes, and has been shaped into forms that give reproductive advantages". Ruse and Wilson (1986) reject the is-ought distinction as "debilitating", while suggesting that kin selection and reciprocal altruism afford the foundation for a biologically-based ethics.

Richards (1987) and Alexander (1987), by contrast, accept the is-ought distinction but believe that it can be overcome. Alexander (1987), for example, contends that "those who have tried to analyze morality have failed to treat the human traits that underlie moral behavior as outcomes of evolution", on the one hand, while he "explicitly reject[s] the attitude that whatever biology tells us is so is also what ought to be", on the other. Richards (1987) claims that the distinction succumbs to arguments relating empirical premises about "what is" to normative conclusions about "what ought to be".

Insofar as ethics concerns how we should behave and evolution concerns how we do behave, they might very well stand in direct opposition. If we sometimes do not behave the way we ought to behave toward one another, ethics as a domain of inquiry might transcend the resources that evolution can provide. Ethics could require more than science can supply. But if we always behave the way we ought to behave, then perhaps evolution could provide everything we need to know about moral behavior. Ethics might then require no more than science can provide. That is an open possibility.

The existence of crime, of course, makes this position a rather difficult one to seriously defend. Human beings all too frequently commit murder, robbery, and rape, among their varied offenses against their fellow humans. The occurrence of murder, robbery, and rape supports the conclusion that we do not always behave the way we ought to behave, however, only provided we have access to normative premises concerning how we ought to behave. In the absence of access to such standards, it does not follow that the existence of crime counts as behavior that humans should not display.

Moreover, similar considerations apply to evolutionary conceptions of ethics. The existence of kin selection, reciprocal altruism, and other forms of social co-operation supports the conclusion that kin selection, reciprocal altruism, and other forms of social co-operation are moral behavior *only if* we have access to normative standards concerning our behavior. In their absence, it might turn out to be the case that kin selection, reciprocal altruism, and social co-operation are *not* behaviors that humans ought to display. They could be evolved forms of behavior that might not qualify as moral.

Consider, for example, favoritism and corruption in businesses and corporations. When marginally qualified applicants are shown preference in hiring over others who are far better qualified because they are close relatives, kin selection may be displayed, but it is not therefore ethical. When close friends are given inside information that enable them to make fantastic profits on the market in the expectation that they will return the favor, reciprocal altruism may be involved, but it is not for that reason any less immoral. Kin selection and reciprocal altruism are not inevitably ethical.

Richards (1987) "bites the bullet" by arguing that evolved behavior is directed toward "the community good". His position is that human beings have evolved to act for the community good and that acts for the community good are "moral acts", as a matter of definition. It presumably follows that human beings are moral beings who act as they ought to act. But the kinds of behavior that he has in mind are kin selection, reciprocal altruism and other forms of social cooperation. We have already discovered forms of kin selection and reciprocal altruism that appear to qualify as immoral.

Moreover, the phrase, "the community good", harbors ambiguity. The good of the community can vary with the interests of the community and may or may not be morally praiseworthy. The existence of communities of Nazis suggests that various activities, such as book burning, forcible detention, military invasions or systematic genocide, which require social co-operation, may be for *the community good* but are not therefore moral. If humans had evolved to act for the community good, that would not be enough to establish the morality of their acts. Co-operation is not morality.

Thus, it is a mistake to assume that behaviors which have evolved are always moral, as Alexander (1987) seems to understand. In denying the contention that whatever biology tells us is so is what ought to be, he implies the possibility that evolved traits may or may not be moral. Insofar as the adaptations that evolution has produced are not invariably moral, however, the problem remains of establishing which traits and behaviors are moral and why. Richards has not supplied the missing premise that would provide the foundation for a theory of ethics based upon evolution.

Other evolutionary thinkers have also emphasized that behaviors that have evolved are not therefore moral. George Williams, for example, in a recent review of Richards (1987), quotes Thomas Huxley (with approval) when he observes that the immoral sentiments have evolved no less than the moral sentiments, which means that "there is, so far, as much natural sanction for the one as the other" (Williams 1989a, p. 387). This, in turn, hints that descriptive solutions to ethical problems are unlikely to be availing, unless we already know which traits and behavior are moral and why.

If we already know which traits and behavior are moral and why, however, then descriptive solutions to ethical problems are no longer required. This recognition may be more subtle than it appears, since Richards (1987) also finds it seductive to suppose that societies might be positioned to overcome the is-ought distinction by appealing to *metaethical inference principles,* such as, "Conclude as sound ethical injunctions what moral leaders preach" (Richards 1987, p. 616). These principles are supposed to enable normative conclusions to be drawn from factual premises.

What Richards apparently overlooks, however, is an ancient question raised about God and His moral laws, namely: are the moral laws right because God commands them, or does God command them because they are right? Surely we cannot know that the ethical injunctions preached by moral leaders are right merely because they preach them. But that means we are still confronted by the necessity of discovering precisely which ethical injunctions are right, *whether or not* moral leaders preach them. The gap between the descriptive and the normative cannot be resolved by "metaethical inference principles" of the kind he recommends.

Indeed, appeals to religious texts encounter comparable difficulties in every case in which the "moral maxims" they present appear problematic. The Old Testament, for example, provides a valuable source of illustrations drawn from an important religious document. According to Leviticus 20:10,

(MM1) If a man commits adultery with another man's wife—with the wife of his neighbor—both the adulterer and the adulteress must be put to death.

That may appear a high price for adultery. Compare it with Leviticus 20:27:

(MM2) A man or a woman who is a medium or a spiritualist among you must be put to death.

The "Psychic Hot Lines" so popular today take a heavy hit. Or Leviticus 20:9:

(MM3) If anyone curses his father or mother, he must be put to death.

This does not appear to be a child-rearing practice of which Dr. Spock would approve. Among my personal favorites, however, is Deuteronomy 25:11-12:

(MM4) If two men are fighting and the wife of one of them comes to rescue her husband from his assailant, and then reaches out and seizes him by his private parts, you shall cut off her hand. Show her no mercy.

Personally, if my wife were to come to my assistance under such conditions, I would want to shake her hand, not cut it off! The point, of course, is not that theologians and other students of religion are unable to present some defense of *maxims* such as these, but rather that they are not obviously *moral*. The suggestion that ethical injunctions should be considered to be sound because moral leaders or religious texts advance them appears to be without merit.

Similar considerations apply to other positions as well. When Ruse and Wilson (1985) suggest that the social behavior of animals is firmly under the control of the genes, the conclusion that kin selection, reciprocal altruism, and other forms of social co-operation are *moral* depends on other premises, such as that social behavior that is firmly under the control of the genes is always moral. If kin selection, reciprocal altruism, and other forms of social co-operation can promote behavior that is immoral, however, then even behavior that is firmly under the control of the genes is not always moral.

The "firmness" of "the control of the genes", moreover, requires further contemplation. If human behavior were *completely* "under the control of the genes", the question of morality might not even arise. Our behavior, like that of many lower species, then would be instinctual and *non*-moral, where the same kinds of social behavior would be displayed across every similar environment. Human behavior is *not* completely "under the control of the genes", since it would be a blunder to overlook the influence of other causal factors, such as social learning, in shaping human behavior.

The position that comes the closest to endorsing the idea of ethics as instinctual behavior, no doubt, is known as *psychological egoism*. According to its tenets, every human being invariably acts in his or her own personal interest, because it is impossible for humans to do otherwise. This is simply part of our nature as humans. Since psychological egoism advances a descriptive hypothesis about human nature, it has to be sharply distinguished from *ethical egoism*, which asserts the normative thesis that every human ought to act in his or her own personal interest, which is a different thing.

Indeed, as ordinarily understood, if psychological egoism is true, then ethical egoism is not merely false but actually meaningless. Such a consequence appears to follow because, if acting in our own personal interest is something that we have to do as a matter of human nature, then it makes no more sense to suggest that we ought to do it than it does in the case of eating, breathing, and sleeping. Ethical egoism would be meaningless and not merely false if psychological egoism were true, therefore, because it is normally assumed that the truth of an ought-statement presupposes that we might or might not behave that way, an issue to which we shall return.

Neither psychological nor ethical egoism, however, should be confused with the position that we always act selfishly because we always act from motives that move us. Such a position completely obscures fundamental moral differences between selfish and unselfish behavior. Indeed, psychological egoism turns out to be false (as a descriptive theory) if humans ever act from a sense of duty, out of friendship, for the welfare of society, for the sake of justice or to promote the well-being of others, just as ethical egoism turns out to be false (as a normative theory) if humans ever ought to act from a sense of duty, out of friendship, and so forth—assuming that these are motives that can move us (Facione, Scherer, and Attig 1991, pp. 96–98).

A weaker but more defensible version of the connection between ethics and evolution, therefore, would maintain that the trait which evolution has produced is not *moral behavior* as such but the *capacity for moral behavior* instead. Thus, if moral behavior has benefits for reproduction and survival, then when the presence and absence of moral behavior separates different human beings or different human groups, the adaptive benefits that moral behavior provides might afford a selective advantage. Every human could have the same adaptive capacity, even if only some of us ever exercise it.

There are cases, however, where ethics and morality would not appear to provide a selective advantage. Consider the Mafia hitman, for example. His success depends upon his ability to perform such acts as murder and mayhem. These seem to be immoral acts, if any acts are immoral. As a consequence, he may lead a comfortable lifestyle, with plenty of money, women, and respect. Yet consider his prospects were he to lose his talent for performing immoral acts. His potential for survival and reproduction appears to depend on his immorality. Similarly for con-artists and pimps.

If humans do not always behave morally, if kin selection and reciprocal altruism are not invariably ethical, and if social cooperation is not enough for morality, then what prospects remain for evolutionary ethics? Traditional theories of morality, which include *consequentialist accounts*, such as ethical egoism, limited utilitarianism and classic utilitarianism, are based upon the conception of something as intrisically desirable ("the good"). Actions are moral (or "right") when they maximize the good for an individual (ethical egoism), for a group (limited utilitarianism), or for everyone (classic utilitarianism), respectively. Presumably, an evolutionary ethic should be based upon similar value commitments.

If acts are only right when they maximize the good, then any acts that do not afford as much good as the maximum are not right acts. That implies a very high standard, even for the mundane decisions of practical life, such whether to go out to dinner, where to dine, or which movie you ought to take in. The minute calculations that would be required for acts to be right acts by maximizing standards, as Michalos (1973) has explained, would make decision making in ordinary life a practical impossibility. Here, as elsewhere, survival depends not on finding solutions that are the best but good enough.

An appropriate foundation for a theory of evolutionary ethics initially, at least, would seem to be a commitment to the intrinsic value of the reproduction and survival of the human species. The appropriate stance to adopt, I think, for those who want to elaborate an evolution-based morality, is to maintain that *the survival and reproduction of the human species is intrinsically valuable, if anything is.* Indeed, even if the existence of intrinsic values might be disputed on various grounds, a commitment of this kind appears to compare favorably with the value commitments that other theories have embraced, which include pleasure, happiness, knowledge, and even power.

Among the authors we're looking at here, perhaps Alexander (1987) comes the closest to adopting this conception. His emphasis upon reproductive success parallels widely-held theories about inclusive fitness as the basic value that human behavior should be expected to maximize. The distinction between "somatic" altruism, which can be adaptive, and "genetic" altruism, which is never adaptive, thus supports the inference that kin selection and reciprocal altruism can be expected to occur more frequently than behavior that sacrifices a person's genetic self-interest.

Alexander's position, however, like those of the others under consideration here, appears to reflect an impoverished conception of morality. When he contends that "moral issues can only be resolved by the collective opinions and decisions of the populace" and that "otherwise what occurs is not a resolution or by definition is not moral" (Alexander 1987, p. 255), he seems to confound the nature of *ethics* with that of *politics*. Collective opinions and decisions of a population may be indispensable to a functional democracy, for example, but they do not define morality.

The debates over the morality of abortion, for example, do not hinge on collective opinions, voting preferences, or even the judicial decisions that determine the law of the land. Traditional moral theories arise instead as a consequence of rational deliberation over general principles as they apply to specific cases in an effort to arrive at recommendations or proposals concerning how human beings ought to act toward each other. They result from *explication* as an activity aimed at clarifying and illuminating language that is vague and imprecise (Hempel 1952, Fetzer 1984).

Consider, for example, classic utilitarianism, which adopts happiness as the nature of the good and happiness maximization as the measure of the right. When everyone is viewed as of equal moral worth, utilitarianism is commonly described by means of the maxim of *the greatest happiness for the greatest number*. But a theory of this kind can be subject to criticism on various grounds. The acute unhappiness of a minority within a population may be compatible with the greatest happiness of that population as a whole, where a slave-based society might thereby be morally justifiable.

But we do not have to go to such extremes. Suppose that the government were to periodically round up one hundred smokers at random, put them on television and shoot them. It would not be too surprising if the number of smokers were to drop drastically, the health of the population were to increase, and the cost of medical care to diminish. It might turn out that, by every measure, the greatest happiness for the greatest number increased by more than would have occurred by any available alternative measure. The dead smokers might not be happy about it, but they would be in no position to complain. It might maximize happiness but it would be wrong.

If a morally justifiable slave-based society appears to you to be an unacceptable consequence, then you should argue for revision or rejection of any theory that implies it. Thus, ethical egoism, which makes each *person* the arbiter of his own morality, and limited utilitarianism, which makes each *group* the determiner of its own morality, appear to be untenable. Ethical egoism would justify the conduct of a Ted Bundy, a John Gacy, or a Jeffrey Dahmer. And the Nazis, the Mafia, and even General Motors are counterexamples to the defensibility of limited utilitarianism. Indeed, my discussion here of kin selection, reciprocal altruism, and social co-operation illustrates the kind of reasoning characteristic of theorizing in philosophy.

One of the most persuasive reasons for taking *deontological theories* of morality—such as the categorical imperative of always treating persons as ends and never merely as means—seriously is that they provide an alternative to consequentialist approaches. Murder, robbery and rape, as well as slavery and genocide, are immoral on deontological grounds precisely because they involve treating other humans merely as means. Employers and employees, of course, may still treat one another as means as long as they regard each other with respect, which appears to be the right result.

8.2 Morality and Biology

This does not mean that persons can never treat other persons as means, which usually happens without thereby generating immorality. The relationship between employers and employees is clearly one in which employers use their employees as a means to conduct a business and make profits, while employees use their employment as a means to make income and earn a living. Within a context of mutual respect, this can still qualify as moral conduct. It is a matter of not treating other persons, not as means, but *merely* as means.

When employers subject their employees to unsafe working conditions, to excessive hours, or to poor wages, however, the relationship becomes exploitative and immoral, which can equally obviously occur when employees fail to perform their duties, steal from their employers, or abuse their workplace. Similar considerations apply to doctors and patients, students and faculty, or ministers and congregations, which may explain our dismay at their betrayal. Persons in positions of trust and responsibility with respect to other persons are always acting immorally when they treat other persons merely as means.

Perhaps the most disturbing aspect of Ruse and Wilson (1986), from this point of view, is their presumption that there are just three possible sources of moral standards, namely: religious sources, especially ones derived from belief in God; genuinely objective moral axioms, which are derived from an abstract domain; and genetically based and empirically testable rules of conduct, which are derived from epigenetic rules (Ruse and Wilson 1986, p. 174 and p. 186, for example). Even I admit that, if these were our only alternatives, the prospects for genuinely prescriptive, non-religious moral theories would be rather bleak. But their alternatives appear to be non-exhaustive.

What Ruse and Wilson tend to overlook is that moral theorizing can also be pursued as a form of explication, in which notions that may be somewhat vague and ambiguous, but nevertheless important, such as *right* and *wrong*, are subjected to critical scrutiny in an effort to clarify and illuminate their meaning. This process involves assessing general principles on the basis of specific cases, and specific cases on the basis of general principles, in order to arrive at tentative recommendations as to how these notions should best be understood. This is a method that can be applied to understand morality.

It is not that theorizing about morality occurs in a descriptive vacuum. On the contrary, widely held attitudes about which specific acts are right and are wrong can supply evidence relevant for subjecting moral theories to empirical evaluation. If murder, robbery, and rape happen to be virtually universally regarded as morally wrong, while kindness, consideration, and generosity are virtually universally regarded as morally right, then any theory that has the effect of classifying pre-analytically clear cases of right conduct as "morally wrong" or of classifying pre-analytically clear cases of wrong conduct as "morally right" ought to be difficult theories to accept but easy theories to reject.

Murder, robbery, and rape, for example, would be morally right actions if they were done by persons who thereby maximized their personal happiness, if ethical egoism is true and happiness is the good. Military domination, territorial aggression, and racial genocide would be morally right actions if they were done by groups of persons who thereby maximized their group's happiness. Enslaving a certain percentage of the population would be morally right if that were the arrangement of society that produces the greatest happiness for the greatest number that would be the effect upon the entire population.

The reason this procedure can advance our understanding of the nature of morality appears to be because there is far less disagreement among human beings generally and philosophers specifically about which kinds of actions are right and wrong than there is about which principles of morality themselves are right and wrong. By classifying these specific kinds of actions as "morally right" and as "morally wrong" *pre-analytically*—that is, before we commit ourselves to any specific moral theory—we establish a class of cases within the extension of the concept for which we want to specify an intension.

Theories such as ethical egoism, limited utilitarianism, and even classical utilitarianism cannot qualify as acceptable theories, because they have the consequence of classifying pre-analytically clear cases of wrong actions as if they were moral and of right actions as if they were immoral. Consider, for example, that kindness, consideration, and generosity, which virtually everyone would qualify as morally right actions, would be morally wrong from the point of view of ethical egoism, for example, were they not happiness maximizing actions for specific persons. But the adequacy of a moral theory can be tested further by the illumination it affords for pre-analytically unclear cases.

To offer an uncomplicated illustration, there appear to be no inherent reasons prostitution should not qualify as moral so long as hookers and their tricks treat each other with respect. Hookers are immoral whenever they do not provide services agreed upon, steal their tricks' money, or infect them with venereal disease, while johns are immoral whenever they do not pay for services rendered, engage in physical abuse, or infect the prostitutes with disease. Respect works both ways round. The difficulties that arise in relation to prostitution are generated largely by its illegality, not its immorality. Indeed, it is not obviously immoral.

In those locales where prostitution is legal, women presumably can choose this line of work without the intervention of pimps, who turn them into sexual slaves. When prostitution is illegal, of course, the consequences can be immoral for hookers and their tricks alike. Even when prostitution happens to be legal, however, immorality can enter by means of other relationships. When husbands or wives commit adultery and thereby betray their commitments to each other, they are not displaying respect for their spouses and are acting immorally. But that remains the case apart from any business aspects. Indeed, even marriage has been described as a form of "legalized prostitution" by George Bernard Shaw.

When alternative moral theories are explored in the fashion I have described, then they cannot be adequately characterized as derived from belief in God, as derived from an abstract domain, or as derived from epigenetic rules, as Ruse and Wilson (1985) suggest. However, it does not follow that they are therefore either subjective or arbitrary. As recommendations concerning how best to understand the nature of moral phenomena, they can be subjected to systematic criticism and to empirical test in relation to specific examples that display the scope and limits of those principles, which, indeed, is the practice that I have adopted in pursuing the rational appraisal of alternative theories of morality.

No doubt, not everyone will be convinced by what I have had to say here. As Ruse (1998) perceptively reports, much of Wilson's work on ethics appears to be affected by three important factors, namely: first, doubts about the substantial reality of ethical phenomena over and beyond subjective attitudes and mere opinions; second, veneration for social organization (exemplified by colonial invertebrates, by social insects, by non-human animals, and by human beings) as pinnacles of evolutionary progress; and, third, the belief that, "because the ethical capacity has evolved, evolution must reach through to the very core of the claims that we make in its name" (Ruse 1998, p. 99). Views such as these, I think, would tend to promote the identification of morality with cooperation.

More important than any misconceptions about morality and methodology, however, is Alexander's emphasis—which Ruse (1998) and Wilson (1999), of course, among others, share—on the role of evolution in determining human behavior. Most of his efforts appear to be directed toward the goal of securing a conception of morality that is at least consistent with, if not actually exhausted by, what evolutionary biology has to tell us about human nature. In this respect, therefore, his work appears to be focused less upon the is-ought distinction than it is upon the principle that "ought implies can". This emphasis accounts for much of the appeal of his and Ruse and Wilson's work on ethics.

The principle that "ought implies can" holds that no one should be held responsible for their behavior when they could not have done otherwise. What this means, however, requires interpretation. The driver who races through an intersection at eighty miles per hour would not be exonerated on the basis of the contention that, because he entered the intersection at eighty miles per hour, it was impossible for him to have done otherwise. A proper rebuttal would note that he could have driven more slowly, not as a matter of historical possibility, but as a matter of physical possibility. The laws of nature permit it.

If the laws of nature made genetic altruism impossible, for example, it would be morally inappropriate to hold anyone morally responsible for his failure to display it, because "ought implies can". In this sense, biology constrains morality, since a theory of morality whose satisfaction contravened the laws of biology would thereby violate this principle. Although compatibility with the laws of biology counts as a necessary condition for morality, however, it does not likewise qualify as a condition sufficient for morality.

The strongest case for supposing that adaptations are as they should be, I suspect, emerges from the adaptationist attitude that assumes "the latest is the best" (Dupre 1987). Once we recognize that evolution is not an optimizing process, we should also realize that the way things are is not always the way things ought to be, especially in relation to behavior (Fetzer 1993). Once we recognize that evolution is unfinished and ongoing, we can resist the temptation to identify evolved traits with optimal traits, where there remains room to consider ways in which we and our world could be better.

Moreover, once we recognize that human behavior is not completely under the control of the genes, we must also admit that, to the extent to which our behavior is under the influence of our rationality, older forms of biological determinism must yield ground to more adequate conceptions of geneculture co-evolution of the kind elaborated in this book, where mentality, intelligence, and rationality have a contribution to make in shaping social behavior that goes beyond our genes. The ability to consider and criticize the strengths and the weaknesses of various methods, processes, and procedures further suggests that morality may have originated with criticism.

Our capacity for criticism represents an exercise of imagination and conjecture in thinking about how things might be different (how they could be improved upon or "made better"). Our capacity for criticism—of ourselves, our theories, and our methods—indicates that human minds can contribute to improving their own culture by "bettering" their capacities for communication, co-operation and community. It hints that, by exercising our higher mental faculties, human beings might also contribute to the survival of our species (Fetzer 1996). It thereby implies ways in which morality transcends biology.

Before discussing Alexander's views further, it should be observed that, given the commitment to the intrinsic value of the survival of the species, there still appear to be at least two approaches to implementing an ethic based on evolution. The first is (let us say) the *positive* ethic of doing anything we can possibly do to advance the survival of the species. The second is (let us also say) the *negative* ethic of not doing anything we can possibly do to inhibit the survival of the species. Though some theoreticians might be inclined to disagree, these principles do not amount to the same thing.

The negative ethic, for example, suggests not reducing any co-operation and communication between the members of the population of human beings to avoid diminishing the well-being of the species. It also implies that global pollution and nuclear warfare are patterns of behavior that ought to be discouraged. The positive ethic, by contrast, could be offered in support of genetic engineering and even infanticide on behalf of doing everything possible to promote the survival of the species. The positive ethic might threaten individual rights. It could even justify forms of genetic fascism.

I therefore believe that theories of morality based upon evolution are ultimately destined to prove to be incomplete. It appears to me as practically inevitable that they have to be supplemented by deontological commitments to the equal worth of every human being. It appears to me as theoretically indispensable to combine the intrinsic value of the survival of the species as a collective end (for all of us together) with respect for the intrinsic value of every member of the species as a distributive end (for each of us individually). An approach of this kind appears theoretically defensible.

An approach of this kind not only embraces the necessity for a commitment to the intrinsic value of the species but also concedes the importance of the is-ought distinction. It makes no effort to dispense with the difference between the way things are and the way things should be, but rather views the way things are as a stage in the evolution of the species, where cultural innovations and improvements might yet generate enormous benefits for future generations. Ethics does require more than science can provide. It requires an exercise of rationality of a certain philosophical kind.

The apparent necessity to encompass personal rights within evolutionary ethics suggests that moral behavior may or may not possess an evolutionary advantage. The proper response, I think, is that sometimes it does and some-times it does not. Virtue, of course, is supposed to be its own reward. While co-operation may frequently provide evolutionary advantages, there is more to morality than cooperation. And as a largely cultural rather than exclusively genetic phenomenon, there can be no "genetic explanation" for morality as a trait of every human. Morality is a normative conception.

Incorporating respect for the individual together with concern for the species does not mean that scientific discoveries and technological innova-tions cannot be put to work on behalf of human beings. What it means is that, when genetic engineering or other techniques are utilized on behalf of the species, it must be within a context of respecting every person's individual worth. As we confront the problem of overpopulation, for example, we ought to employ every available method *provided* that it does not violate personal rights. On this account, there is a crucial difference between forced sterili-zation and voluntary birth control. It is a matter of morality.

8.3   Is Nature Immoral?

In the final analysis, the problems of rationality and of morality turn out to be intimately intertwined. Understanding the nature of morality requires the exercise of rationality, where the difference between consequentialist and deontological theories deserves consideration. In the end, a morality based upon evolution implicitly shifts attention from the population to the species, where the long term interests of the species tend to displace the short term interests of the population. But it would be all too easy to misunderstand the nature of this exchange in points of view.

Because individuals are the agents who perform actions, it might be sup-posed that, since they are the actors, the rightness or wrongness of their actions must be a function of their motives. But, as in the case of other consequen-tialist theories, the rightness or the wrongness of acts is determined by their contribution to promoting the survival of the species, provided, of course, that personal rights are respected. Whether an action is right or wrong, there-fore, is not determined by whether or not an agent recognizes that fact. Right acts can be done for wrong reasons.

Still, it would be (at least vaguely) reassuring if humans could act on the basis of appropriate motives for morality. If humans could never be motivated by appropriate moral sentiments, then it might be maintained that, even if psychological egoism happens to be false (because we sometimes act on the basis of motives that do not put our own interests first), the principle that ought-implies-can precludes the truth of another moral theory. If the most promising moral theories imply that humans should (at least sometimes) act to benefit of the species or to respect the rights of others, for example, their plausibility would be drastically undermined or completely destroyed if humans never act on the basis of such motives.

I have been fascinated to learn that recent empirical studies provide strong support for the existence of moral sentiments of the kinds implied by the conception of evolutionary ethics which I have outlined (Petrinovich, O'Nell and Jorgensen 1993). These studies involved samples of college students who were presented with hypothetical choice situations of two kinds, namely: "trolley problems" and "lifeboat problems". In *trolley problems*, a decision must be made whether or not to throw a switch that would determine whether individual-or-group X or individual-or-group Y is killed. In *lifeboat problems*, a decision has to be made to determine which among six members of a lifeboat survive.

The examples that were employed tested the subjects' attitudes toward killing or sacrificing human beings versus members of other species, unfamiliar persons versus friends and relatives, ordinary persons versus Nazis, endangered species versus non-endangered species, and ordinary persons versus elite members of society. The results displayed a very strong bias in favor of human beings over members of other species, a very strong bias in favor of friends and relatives, and a strong bias against persons who were Nazis. Mere numbers turned out to be moderately important, while the endangered species factor and the elitist factor were minimal.

These findings suggest that at least some humans have motives of the kinds that are appropriate to moral behavior in accordance with the conception of evolutionary ethics described above. Indeed, although no component directly tested the motive of respect for the rights of others, insofar as Nazis represent a group devoted to deliberate and systematic violations of the rights of others, I think it is reasonable to interpret the strong negative bias against Nazis as a strong positive bias in favor of respect for the rights of others. Moreover, since kin selection is not improper when employed as a "tie breaker" within a context of respecting the rights of others, for example, nothing here appears to undermine, much less destroy, the conception of evolutionary ethics which I have defined.

If an ultimate commitment to the intrinsic value of the survival of the human species has to be combined with respect for the intrinsic value of every member of the species, then the question arises of whether conflicts between these value commitments can arise and, if so, how they can be resolved. I believe that the influence of mere numbers ought to make more and more of a difference—both in test situations and in daily life—as other factors are balanced out. In other words, when the lives of few innocent human beings are pitted against the lives of many innocent human beings, the importance of numbers should increase proportionately.

Consider, for example, the choice between killing one innocent human being and killing the entire human species. Surely there should be little room for controversy in a case of this kind. This suggests that societies may have important (collective) evolutionary reasons for imposing severe penalties upon those who would (distributively) threaten their existence (by disclosing secrets vital to the national defense, by assassinating their political leaders, and the like). Precisely when cases of these kinds are at hand, of course, can be controversial, since "national security" may at least sometimes be advanced as a rationalization for political purposes.

Another kind of ultimate value conflict, however, may not be resolved quite so easily. It follows from our ultimate commitment to the intrinsic value of the species that the members of other species are equally entitled to an ultimate commitment to the intrinsic value of their species. This consequence has sometimes been labeled "speciesism", precisely because an organism's ultimate values depend upon the species to which it belongs. Nothing about speciesism appears to defeat the prospects for evolutionary ethics, provided that we acknowledge that other species possess the same moral rights to defend themselves against humans as we do against them.

Nothing about an approach of this kind necessarily has to contradict the genetic interest of members of societies in relation to their offspring. Assuming that each parent contributes fifty percent of their genes to the genetic composition of their children, that their children in turn contribute fifty percent of their genes to the genetic composition of their offspring, and so forth, n, each parent would seem to have a genetic representation equal to $(\frac{1}{2})^n$ per offspring in each successive generation, where n is the number of that generation. The consequences of this conception for evolutionary theory itself were introduced by Hamilton (Hamilton 1964).

As Williams has observed, Hamilton's theory of *inclusive fitness* elaborates the conception that "the survival and reproduction of a relative are partly equivalent, in evolutionary effect, to one's own survival and reproduction" (Williams 1989b, p. 184). When we know who our relatives are and how closely they are related to us, therefore, we can be in an appropriate position to act toward them as manifestations of our own genetic legacy. Even when we have no offspring of our own, we can still retain an interest in the survival and reproduction of the culture of our species, especially if we have made contributions (books, tools, and so forth) of our own.

The most difficult case appears to be when we do not know who our relatives are or how closely they are related to us and when we have no cultural contributions of our own. Even then we may still be motivated to act to benefit the survival and reproduction of the species, especially when we have offspring who might have other offspring of their own in unknown and unpredictable numbers across successive generations. The perpetuation of our own personal genetic or cultural representation thus appears to be compatible with an evolutionary ethics of the above kind, because it reinforces our impersonal motives to perpetuate the species.

The position that I have advanced appears to be "moderate" relative to those advanced by other thinkers. While Ruse and Wilson, Richards, and Alexander tend to assume that natural selection operates in favor of morality (when *morality* is properly understood), Williams contends that natural selection operates against morality (when *natural selection* is properly understood). Thus, he maintains that the biological effects of natural selection display "gross immorality" in a sense which goes far beyond mere selfishness of the kind attributed to human beings by psychological or by ethical egoism (Williams 1989b, pp. 180–81). For Williams, the conception of an "evolutionary ethics" is virtually a self-contradiction.

The basis of Williams's attitude appears to be that nothing in nature exemplifies conformity to traditional maxims of morality: "Nothing resembling the Golden Rule or other widely preached ethical principles seems to be operating in living nature. It could scarcely be otherwise, when evolution is guided by a force that maximizes genetic selfishness" (Williams 1989b, p. 195). Yet here and elsewhere Williams appears to confound the difference between behavior that is *instinctual* and behavior that is *voluntary*, where it makes no sense to describe instinctual behavior as "moral" or "immoral". He even attacks speciesism by comparing the triumph of one population over another to a form of "systematic genocide" (Williams 1989b, p. 196).

If nature operates on the basis of laws of nature that it cannot violate and it cannot change, however, then it appears to make no more sense to hold nature responsible for its conduct than it would to hold humans responsible for theirs. If the appropriate standard for moral responsibility among humans turns out to be that no laws of nature inhibited us from acting otherwise, then the same standard should apply with respect to nature. The principle that ought-implies-can also holds *between* different species. There is no good reason here for describing nature as "immoral" or for believing that an evolutionary ethics cannot be consistent.

The ultimate import of the ought-implies-can connection with which Alexander, especially, has been concerned, therefore, is that, as Scoccia (1990) has observed, we must clearly distinguish *our motives for being moral* from *what makes our actions right*. Acts that were motivated by reciprocal altruism, by kin selection or simply by self-interest may still turn out to be morally proper acts, provided that they maximize the survival of the species without violating personal rights. The existence of a defensible evolutionary ethics in this sense is no longer in doubt. While biology constrains morality, morality cannot be reduced to biology alone.

The existence of a defensible evolutionary ethics, however, does not by itself afford any guarantees that human beings will be smart enough or courageous enough or (even) moral enough *to do the right thing* from an evolutionary point of view. Even if the positive evolutionary ethic advises us to do anything we possibly can do to advance the survival of the species and the negative evolutionary ethic advises us to not do anything we can possibly do that might inhibit the survival of the species (where acts of both kinds are compatible with acknowledging the intrinsic value of every human being), our actions still may or may not qualify as moral.

Indeed, the increasing potential for cloning human beings, for genetic engineering, for harvesting organs, and for tissue engineering are going to challenge our most basic conceptions of ourselves as a species. The case for genetic engineering, moreover, exemplifies a tension latent in distinguishing negative ethics from positive ethics (where letting someone die need not be equated with killing them). The replacement of genes that would otherwise give rise to birth defects (such as cleft lips and palates) may not be morally problematical, but replacing genes in order to bring about other traits (such as greater intellectual and athletic ability), which will occur, is already generating concern (Goldberg 1999, Stolberg 2000).

At least three questions might be raised about the position developed in this chapter. The first is that the combination of a commitment to the intrinsic worth of each individual with a commitment to the survival and reproduction of the human species appears to mix together deontological and utilitarian conceptions of morality in a fashion that some theoreticians may find unsatisfactory. Even deontological commitments, however, must take consequences into account, since it follows that treating persons with respect is morally appropriate, while not doing so is morally inappropriate. Actions that have these consequences are moral or immoral, respectively, apart from any utilitarian framework. I thus maintain that the position I defend here is essentially deontological both distributively and collectively.

The second question concerns how thinking about populations is meant to differ from thinking about species. I envision populations as collections of individuals who exist at one time, while a species includes the ancestors and the offspring of a population. The underlying conception, therefore, is that a population is a temporal stage in the evolution of a species. Thus, a proper conception of the connection between ethics and evolution dictates that consideration be given to future generations of existing populations in arriving at decisions that may affect their prospects for reproduction and survival. This is the sense in which we owe it to our offspring to provide them with the resources that are essential to their well-being, at least in the sense of the negative ethic, if not also in the sense of the positive ethic.

The third question concerns what may appear to be tacit commitments to group selection as a mechanism that affects the course of evolution. As many readers are no doubt aware, there is a very strong aversion to group selection among evolutionary thinkers today. But "group selection" seems to occur whenever any arrangement, organization, or cooperation between various conspecifics makes a difference to their prospects for survival and reproduction. Insofar as specific arrangements between conspecifics may influence their evolutionary prospects, therefore, group selection appears to make a difference to the course of evolution (Fetzer 1997). This is one of the more important issues that will be explored in the chapter to follow.

If the conception of evolutionary ethics I have proposed amounts to an adequate theory of morality (however preliminary), then we have general normative premises in relation to which the morality of actions ought to be assessed. Biology and morality, however, are no more always allied than are biology and psychology. Non-moral motives, such as greed and profit maximization, can override moral ones, just as non-biological motives can override biological ones. Rationality does not entail morality, and morality does not guarantee survival. We can continue to pollute the world and we can continue to run the risk of nuclear war. We have to learn to act in ways that nurture and sustain the species. Even when we understand both biology and morality, therefore, our survival ultimately depends upon our rationality.

9

Biology and Society

Another contentious aspect of evolutionary theory shifts attention from the species and the subspecies to smaller groups, where strenuous debate rages over the existence of group selection. Wilson has defined a "group":

> (DG) **a group** =df a set of organisms belonging to the same species that remain together for any period of time while interacting with one another to a much greater degree than with other conspecifics. (Wilson 1975, p. 8)

As he observes, the expression has special utility in describing arrangements of populations in which there exists "a hierarchy of levels of organization constructed of nested subsets of individuals" belonging to that specific population.

Ongoing debates over group selection have generated considerable disparity in point of view over the existence and potential influence of causal mechanisms of this kind in relation to evolutionary phenomena. Given a distinction between *units of selection* and *levels of selection*, where the units are what is transmitted from one generation to another, while the levels are the types of causal mechanisms that determine what will be transmitted, the issue revolves about whether there is a "group level" of selection that makes a difference to which units (noncontroversially envisioned as *genes*) are perpetuated from generation to generation and which are not (Brandon 1982 and Brandon and Burian 1984, Part II).

Among the principal contributors to the discussion have been G.C. Williams (1966/96, 1992) and David S. Wilson (1980, 1983). Wilson has advocated the existence of *trait group selection*, where the members of a group benefit (have their fitness enhanced) by the emergence of a group trait for which there is an underlying gene. Williams, by contrast, considers the fitness benefits of group membership to be adequately captured by "selection based on the success and failure of individuals as influenced by membership in trait groups"

(Williams 1992, p. 46). He also suggests that, if trait groups were effective at the level of selection, then they ought to optimize the properties of those trait groups.

Group selection tends to be regarded as an alternative to the mechanisms of selfish genes, kin selection, and reciprocal altruism as kinds of factors that influence the course of evolution. Howard Bloom, for example, has observed, "The goal of the 'group selection squad' is simple: to assure that group selection is accepted as a legitimate phenomenon on a par with individual selection, kin selection, and reciprocal altruism" (Bloom on HBES-L, 12th November, 1995). Depending upon how group selection should be defined, however, it might be the case that kin selection and reciprocal altruism both qualify as particular kinds of group selection that simply involve relatives, coworkers, or friends.

Others, however, place their greatest emphasis upon altruism. Peter Frost, for example, envisions the crucial feature of group selection as a willingness to make personal sacrificies for the benefit of other members of a group, namely:

> As I understand it, group selection tries to explain altruistic behavior without reference to kin selection, i.e., individuals will do what is best for the survival of the group, even to the detriment of their own survival. (Frost on HBES-L, 13th November, 1995)

Since the sacrifice that is required might merely consume time, effort, or money, other students of the biology of morality, such as Richard Alexander, regard the sacrifice of genetic self-interest as deserving special attention (Alexander 1987).

9.1   Group Selection

Perhaps the most important recent development involving group selection has been the emergence of what are sometimes called *new group selectionists*, among whom David Sloan Wilson has been prominent. According to D.S. Wilson,

> Whenever an evolving population is subdivided into various groups, the "new group selectionist" examines the relative fitness of individuals within groups and the relative fitness of groups in the metapopulation. If the trait that evolves is neutral or selectively disadvantageous within groups but increases the relative fitness of groups, it is said to evolve by group selection and to be a group-level adaptation. (Wilson on HBES-L, 14th November, 1995)

Wilson's emphasis upon traits that are neutral or even negative for individuals within groups, but that nevertheless enhance the fitness of those groups with respect to other groups, thus appears to harmonize with Alexander's emphasis.

It might be a mistake, however, to take for granted that group selection has to involve genetic self-sacrifice, when genetic self-sacrifice appears to be rather special from an evolutionary point of view. Some traits that benefit the group could also evolve even though they do not entail genetic self-sacrifice and thus do not qualify as "moral" in that specific sense. Moreover, the use of the phrase, "traits that evolve", harbors an equivocation, because certain traits that evolve may be *dispositions* to display specific behavior under specific conditions, while other traits that evolve might be *predispositions* to learn one or another among alternative dispositions to display various behaviors under various conditions.

The difference is whether the same behavior would be displayed by every member of the group (subgroup, or subpopulation) under the same conditions due to a genetic disposition or must be acquired, given a genetic predisposition. Group behavior, in general, appears to involve elements of communication, co-ordination, and co-operation, but those tendencies might be innate or acquired. The hunting behavior of packs of wild dogs in Africa, for example, appears to be an adaptation that qualifies as a genetically-based disposition, whereas team membership in the NBA as a player for the Chicago Bulls, for another, appears to be an adaptation that qualifies as a genetically-based predisposition instead.

These suggestions are closely related to kinds of fallacies group selectionists have sometimes been supposed to be committing. Mario Heilman, for example, has argued that genetically self-sacrificing behaviors are destined for extinction:

> Assume an individual that has a (heritable) propensity to help others at the expense of his/her own reproductive success. This gene will confer less reproductive success compared with those without the gene. Hence, the relative frequency of this gene will decrease with each generation and probably even vanish. (Heilman on HBES-L, 13th November 1995)

In response, however, it could be argued that the extinction of genes for genetic self-sacrifice appears to be a frequency-dependent outcome that would not invariably occur if such a gene were common in the population (as a disposition) or if it were relatively easily acquired and then activated (as a predisposition).

To the extent to which Heilman wants to divorce concern for self-sacrificing behavior from the study of group selection, however, his argument implies that it is mistaken to focus on altruism as its defining property. This contention has been echoed by D.S. Wilson, who makes the point in an explicit fashion, namely:

> A trait can evolve by group selection without being altruistic. . . . Regardless of whether altruism is involved, group selection turns groups into adaptive units, just as individual selection turns individuals into adaptive units. Group-level functional organization should be the focus of group selection, not altruism. (Wilson on HBES-L, 13th November 1995)

Group-level functional organization, moreover, appears to be affected whenever members of a group fulfill different roles within the group, whether those roles are innate or acquired. The same eleven men, for example, might be organized into a rifle team or a rifle squad, where the latter might have the capacity for kinds of behavior (such as laying down a field of fire) the former would lack.

If group selection crucially depends on altruistic behavior and if behavior is altruistic only when it is self-sacrificing, then the functional difference between the same eleven men organized as a rifle team and organized as a rifle squad is only going to matter insofar as it affects propensities for genetic self-sacrifice. If group selection crucially depends upon functional organization, however, then the functional difference between the same eleven men organized as a rifle team and as a rifle squad may have multiple manifestations. The narrow focus of the altruistic perspective appears to lose sight of broader concern for the adaptive contribution that may depend upon different modes of functional organization.

A latent tension appears to remain in D.S. Wilson's position, however, since differences between various modes of functional organization may increase or decrease the relative fitness of various groups without concern for whether or not those traits (as specific modes of functional organization) are neural or disadvantageous within those groups. If altruism should *not* be considered to be the defining property of group selection, then it is difficult to understand why propensities for various modes of functional organization should count as *bona fide* instances of group selection only when they are neutral or disadvantageous within the group. These neutral or disadvantageous properties, after all, would be at the level of the individual and appear irrelevant at the level of the group.

This suggests that several different conceptions of group selection have been run together that require careful disentanglement. The strongest would define "group selection" as entailing innate propensities for genetically self-sacrificing behavior when it is neutral or disadvantageous to the individual but beneficial to the group (Alexander). A more moderate position would define "group selection" as entailing innate propensities for behavior that is neutral or disadvantageous to the individual but beneficial to the group (D.S. Wilson, strong). An even more moderate position would define "group selection" as entailing innate propensities for behavior which is beneficial to the group (D.S. Wilson, weak).

Thus, the more moderate definition of "group selection" does not entail the occurrence of genetic self-sacrifice, while the even more moderate definition does not entail the occurrence of behavior that is neutral or disadvantageous to the individual while benefiting the group. Forms of *non*-genetic sacrifice at the level of the individual would qualify on the more moderate definition, but no sacrifice at the level of the individual would be required by the weakest thereof. All three definitions, however, retain the conception that group selection presupposes the existence of underlying genes, which makes them all instances of *trait group selection* in the sense that was introduced above.

When altruism and other forms of self-sacrifice are removed from group selection, it potentially becomes a more robust concept that might apply to a far broader range of behavior than has heretofore been supposed. Williams, however, would remain largely unmoved, insofar as his objections to group selection are mainly based on the lack of permanence of group arrangements. Thus, for example, he has argued that the natural selection of phenotypes cannot produce the kind of differential bias presupposed by evolutionary theory, because phenotypes are extremely temporary individuals formed by interaction between genotypes and the environment. Nor can genotypes themselves, since they too are extremely temporary things (Williams 1966/96, pp. 23–24).

While Williams's arguments appear forceful in support of genes as the units of selection, they do not logically preclude the possibility that groups might be among the levels of selection. Indeed, insofar as mating behavior among the members of sexually reproducing species occurs as a *behavioral phenomenon* that is not determined phenotypically or genotypically (that is, which individuals engage in mating behavior depends upon environmental factors that are not exhausted by phenotype and genotype), it should be apparent that sexual reproduction contributes to genetic diversity as a function of sexual behavior. Sexual behavior, like other kinds of behavior, is also a transient phenomenon.

If mating behavior is a causal mechanism that contributes genes to future pools in spite of its transient character, however, then that would appear to raise the prospect that other causal mechanisms might have similar effects in spite of their transient character. The competition for material resources that defines natural selection and the competition for sexual resources that defines sexual selection, for example, are transient behavioral phenomena whose consequences for survival and reproduction are nonetheless significant. (A sexual encounter, however brief its duration, may transmit genes.) But in that case, it becomes obscure why the transient status of group arrangements should matter.

Williams's concerns would be well taken, if the kinds of group arrangements that make a difference to survival and reproduction invariably qualified as innate properties of every member of the group, such as the hunting behavior of packs of wild dogs in Africa. This adaptation appears to be a genetically-based disposition in the sense that both Wilson and Williams require. Membership in the NBA as a player for the Chicago Bulls, however, appears to be an adaptation that qualifies as a genetic-based predisposition instead. It is a transient status that can come and go where it would be at least faintly ridiculous to conjecture the existence of specific genes for membership in the NBA playing for the Bulls.

Membership in the NBA playing for the Bulls, however, no doubt confers a differential fitness benefit that might otherwise be difficult to acquire. (Other high-status positions within society that confer comparable fitness benefits include being movie stars, powerful politicians, or—most similarly—members of popular bands. The status must be something that could but usually does not persist and endure, where these attendant benefits accompany that standing.) In such cases, the presumption that there must be an underlying gene for the group trait may or may not be satisfied: in the case of the wild African dogs, there may be an innate disposition, but not in the case of playing for the Bulls.

If these considerations are well-founded, however, then something appears to be wrong with both Wilson's and Williams's positions. The most that ought to be required for trait selection (in Wilson's sense) to take place would appear to be genes, not for specific dispositions, but for suitable predispositions. Membership in the NBA, after all, presupposes certain rather general athletic capacities that are genetically based, which can be developed into rather specific abilities. And the adaptive benefits accruing from membership in group arrangements do not require that those arrangements have to be persistent and enduring (in William's sense) to promote the survival and reproduction of group members.

It is a mistake, then, to require the existence of genes for group-level adaptations as dispositions rather than predispositions. It is also essential to separate *genes for phenotypes* from *genes for behavior*, since genes for phenotypes only determine behavior when that behavior is genetically determined by innate dispositions. In the case of behavioral variability combined with phenotypic similarity, group arrangements can be adaptive and benefit the members of the group by promoting the survival and reproduction of the members of that group as individuals, even if there is no gene for those group arrangements other than as a predisposition.

The difference can be explained relative to the (now familiar) distinction underlying the difference between laws of nature and accidental generalizations. When similar phenotypes display uniform behavior as a function of genetically-based dispositions, then those properties should be described as *permanent properties* of those genes (at least, under normal environmental conditions). When similar phenotypes display uniform behavior as a result of genetically-based predispositions, however, then those properties should be described as *transient properties* of those genes. Pack-hunting behavior by wild dogs appears to be permanent, while Bulls membership is transient.

The crucial difference is that permanent properties are properties which cannot be taken away from the members of a corresponding reference class (defined by a reference property) without taking them out of that class (or denying them that property), while transient properties can be taken away from the members of that reference class without depriving them of underlying reference properties. Pack-hunting behavior by wild dogs would be a permanent property of corresponding genes only if that behavior could only be taken away from wild dogs by changing their genes. Membership in the Chicago Bulls would be a permanent property of corresponding genes if that behavior could only be taken away from members by changing their genes.

The crucial property of group selection thus does not appear to revolve about the existence of genes for specific group traits, as Wilson and Williams mistakenly suppose, because those traits may be rooted in genes that merely predispose individuals for membership in those groups. In cases of this kind, there are no underlying genes for those specific traits as dispositions but only as predispositions, where those specific traits are learned or acquired rather than genetic and innate. It would be absurd to deny that the predispositions themselves are genetic and innate, but the distinction hinges on whether the members of groups can only benefit (have their fitness enhanced) when there is an underlying gene for the group trait that enhances these members fitness.

Once it becomes apparent that genetically-based dispositions are possible but not required and that genetically-based predispositions are sufficient for those group traits to emerge (under appropriate environmental conditions), it also becomes apparent that, for group traits to become effective at the level of selection, those group arrangements need not persist and endure as properties of the members of those groups. Membership in these groups can be beneficial even though it may be a temporary and non-permanent standing which is not rooted in genetically-based dispositions. From this perspective, therefore, the underlying conception embraced by Wilson and Williams seems to be wrong.

The consequences of this misconception are widespread. Richard Dawkins (1976, 1982), for example, has suggested that, for a group trait to evolve, it must be possible for each member who possesses the trait to recognize the presence or absence of other members who possess that same trait. Thus, if pleotropic genes for a group behavioral trait had easily recognized phenotypic manifestations (such as a green beard), presumably it would be relatively easy for one member of the group to recognize other members of the group, which has come to be known as "the green beard effect". The same function, however, could be fulfilled by transient practices, such as wearing red shirts, where fitness benefits are conferred in spite of the absence of specific genes.

What seems to be crucial to group selection, therefore, is not the existence of an underlying gene for specific group traits, but instead the emergence of properties that make a difference to the prospects for survival and reproduction of the members of the group that would not exist apart from those group arrangements. These group arrangements may be rooted in genes for specific dispositions, as in the case of pack hunting by wild dogs, or in genes for predispositions, as in the case of membership in the Chicago Bulls. Wild dogs could not bring down antelope and other game were they consigned to hunting one by one. And Michael Jordan, Scottie Pippen, Dennis Rodman, Ron Harper, and Tony Kukoc could not play basketball apart from being organized into a team.

Communication, co-ordination, and co-operation thus tend to distinguish the interactions between group members, yet they are not the key to understanding the nature of group selection. The members of a rifle team, for example, contribute scores to the team's total, where communication, co-ordination, and co-operation are important to their success (such as being in the right place at the right time, firing in the proper sequence at the right target, and conveying your score to officials as required). Yet each shooter fulfills the same role as a member of that team. Apart from their cumulative scores, which are added together to sum the team's score, none performs a different role than the others.

The members of a rifle squad, by contrast, fulfill different roles (as point men, machine gunners, radio operators and squad leaders) making it possible for them to bring about specific effects (such as laying down an ambush, for example) that would not occur absent those arrangements. Unlike membership in a rifle team, where the same effects are brought about by each member of the team, the effects that are brought about by membership in a rifle squad are brought about though causal interaction between the effects that are brought about by each member of the squad. These properties appear to be different in kind from those that would otherwise exist (Fetzer 1986).

The crucial features of group selection thus appear to include: (a) the existence of arrangements of two or more conspecifics, where these may be either transient or permanent in relation to underlying genes, for example:

families	**towns**
gangs	**states**
tribes	**religions**
bands	**cultures**
...	...

(b) these arrangements must bring about "emergent properties" that differ in kind from those that the members of any such groups could have brought about absent those arrangements; where (c) these emergent properties some times but not always promote the survival and reproduction of the members of these groups, where selection favoring the group need not invariably occur.

Thus, consider, for example, the Shaker Cult, which was a religious group that believed sexual relations were an evil thing. Whenever they felt sexual urges overcoming them, the Shakers would get together and "shake off" the temptations of the flesh. This behavior appears to be most unlikely absent membership in such a group but, equally clearly, it does not promote the survival and reproduction of the members of the group. Illustrations such as this suggest (d) group selection by virtue of emergent properties brought about by transient arrangements of members of groups are crucial to cultural evolution in species, such as humans, at least some of whose behavior is noninstinctual.

Instinctual behavior thus should be understood to be behavior for which there are underlying genes making similar behavior under similar conditions a permanent property of every similar phenotype within the species. Sometimes, therefore, there may be evolved genes for group-level arrangements:

ants   wasps   termites

And yet other times there may be no corresponding gene for group properties:

English   German   French

Some species, such as humans, may have capacities for complex social arrangements even in the absence of underlying genes for those specific arrangements:

Red Cross   **Marines**   **Mafia**

And some group-level arrangements may have few genetic consequences:

chess clubs   **quilting groups**   **orchestras**

Thus, group selection appears to be simply one more causal mechanism affecting which genes are perpetuated from pool to pool across time, which does not presuppose the existence of corresponding genes for those specific group traits.

9.2 Non-Reductionism

Taking for granted that genes are the units of evolution and that changes in gene pools across time appropriately defines the course of evolution, the kinds of causal mechanisms that affect this process appear to fall into two categories, namely: causal mechanisms that affect *genetic diversity* (including genetic mutation, sexual reproduction, genetic drift, and genetic engineering), on the one hand, and causal mechanisms that affect *genetic endurance* (such as natural selection, sexual selection, and artificial selection), on the other. The question that finally arises at this point thus appears to be, "Does group selection belong on this list?", where the answer depends, at least in part, upon pragmatic objectives and goals.

The first point to be made within this context is that the phrase, "natural selection", seems to be ambiguous, sometimes subsuming every mode or mechanism that contributes to the evolution of species, including all of the above. In a narrower sense, "natural selection" applies specifically to competition between conspecifics for material resources, such as food and shelter, where other forms of competition, such as sexual selection, are separated from natural selection as such. The second is that whether group selection should be "accepted as a legitimate phenomenon on a par with individual selection, kin selection, and reciprocal altruism" depends (at least, in part) upon precisely how those modes or mechanisms are envisioned as fitting into the broader scheme of evolution.

Individual selection for material resources, after all, is part and parcel of natural selection, where kin selection and reciprocal altruism seem to qualify as special varieties of group selection. Both involve arrangements of two or more conspecifics in permanent or transient relationships or arrangements, which bring about emergent properties (differential treatment) with fitness benefits that would not occur absent those relationships or arrangements. It thus appears to be appropriate to conclude that, when properly understood, group selection not only exists on a par with kin selection or reciprocal altruism but actually subsumes them, which indicates the importance of its role. The human species appears to be well-positioned to take advantage of the benefits afforded by membership in groups, where group membership may be regarded as an evolutionary strategy. As Harmon Holcomb has observed,

> Humans are uniquely intelligent among species, permitting a novel kind of selection, one that does not require genetic differences of the kind that underlie ratios between within-group and between-group fitness effects (as does D.S. Wilson's theory, Wilson and Sober 1994). Instead, any number of us could get together, identify ourselves as a group, and think up a strategy to outcompete other groups by regulating behavior toward in-group and out-group members. . . . There is no theoretical reason to rule out evolutionary strategies as conscious choices among human beings that bypass the usual restrictions on genetic group selection. (Holcomb 1996, p. 15)

Holcomb thus appears to understand clearly that the existence of group traits does not presuppose the existence of underlying genes for those group traits, where group selection nevertheless can occur by benefiting group members.

Other examples can be drawn from the lowest species to the highest. Consider Howard Bloom and Mike Waller's observations about *Bacillus subtilis*:

> If a prolonged food shortage stimulates the *Bacillus subtilis* to emit a signal of repulsion that impels approximately 10,000 groups of cells to start foraging, which is not a random procedure but rather activates an inbuilt search pattern that ensures each group explores a different piece of territory, thereby maximizing that chances that the colony as a whole will discover what it needs, then this group adaptation would appear to one which has evolved into a gene for a specific group-level adaptation. (Bloom and Waller HBE-l, 30th June, 1996)

This appears to be an example that would satisfy even the strict constraints of Wilson's narrow notion of group trait selection based on underlying genes.

Equally fascinating illustrations can be derived from the history of religion among populations of *Homo sapiens*. Consider, for example, John Hartung's observations:

> Rules against murder, theft, and lying codified by the Ten Commandments were intended to apply only within a co-operating group for the purpose of enabling

that group to compete successfully against other groups. In addition, this in-group morality has functions, both historically and by express intent, to create adverse circumstances between groups by actively promoting murder, theft, and lying as tools of competition. Contemporary efforts to present Judeo-Christian in-group morality as universal morality defy the meaning of the texts upon which Judaism and Christianity are based. (Hartung 1995, p. 86)

Examples such as these suggest that group selection—possibly in forms that also appear to exemplify limited utilitarianism—is not only important to the evolution of species, but that its existence is crucial to the evolution of culture.

When arrangements of individuals into different groups brings about the existence of abilities and capabilities that otherwise would not exist, then the occurrence of "emergent properties" has taken place. Because the differences between these groups may involve the very same individuals and vary only in the ways in which they are arranged, these properties cannot possibly be reducible to those of lower levels, whether in the case of cultures to groups (of anthropology to sociology) or of groups to individuals (of sociology to psychology), no less than of behavior to phenotype and of phenotype to geno-type. The existence of emergent properties at each higher level ultimately undermines reductionism as an impoverished program of scientific investi-gation and as an unworkable framework for understanding the sciences of society.

Thus, as a "rule of thumb" that serves as a usually reliable but not there-fore infallible indicator of the presence or absence of a property, attributes are "emergent" when their existence arises as a consequence of a *division of labor* in the absence of which such effects would not occur (Fetzer 1998b). At the level of groups, these divisions of labor occur between conspecifics and are displayed in virtually every aspect of human society—from repro-duction and child-rearing itself to hunting and gathering to group arrange-ments for social, economic, and political purposes on to organizing for scientific, educational, and creative purposes. Effects, such as the music of a symphony, that could not occur but for a division of labor between the mem-bers of the group that bring it about, are emergent and non-reducible prop-erties.

In *Consilience* (1999), E.O. Wilson endorses "reductionism" in two dif-ferent senses, namely: as a process of analysis and synthesis, of taking things apart and putting them back together again; and, as a process of reducing laws at one level to those at a lower level, thereby acquiring broader and deeper understanding (Wilson 1999, pp. 59–60). In the first sense, "reductionism" typifies research. But, if many of the phenomena of chemistry are emergent relative to those of physics, of biology emergent relative to those of chemistry, and of psychology, sociology, and anthropology emergent relative to those of biology—which, in general, appears to be the case—then "reductionism" in the second sense cannot be sustained. In the first sense, "reductionism" is true but trivial, while in the second, it is significant but false.

It does not follow that reductions in the second sense never occur. Even in the context of evolutionary biology, although selection operates at the level of behavior for all organisms, higher and lower, for the lower species, where every member having the same phenotype displays the same behavior, it is convenient to consider selection as operating at the level of the phenotype. Moreover, a reduction of the number and variety of regularities that require independent explanation has been offered as a driving force behind science. Michael Friedman, for example, has remarked, "science increase our understanding by reducing the total number of independent phenomena that we have to accept as ultimate or given" (Friedman 1974, p. 15), which is a very appealing conception that appears to capture the spirit of Wilson's attitude.

From the perspective of inference to the best explanation, indeed, Friedman appears to be correct, but not for the reason he suggests. Just as the requirement of maximal specificity asserts that a lawlike sentence cannot be true when it is not maximally specific, the requirement of strict maximal specificity denies that an explanation can be adequate when the antecedents of the laws that occur in their premises include predicates describing properties that are nomically (or causally) irrelevant relative to their explanandum outcomes. This implies, as Wilson suggests, that theoretical unification occurs whenever diverse phenomena can be subsumed as explananda for the same explanans, where "theoretical unification" occurs as a manifestation of lawful reduction.

As properties that were previously believed to be relevant to the occurrence of an attribute are discovered to be irrelevant, therefore, the outcome will tend to be laws of potentially broader scope that ordinarily reduce the number and variety of independent phenomena in Friedman's sense (Fetzer 1993, p. 146). The conception of science as aiming at the discovery of laws of nature to secure the benefits of testable explanatory theories by means of abductive procedures based upon inference to the best explanation thereby promotes unification as well. But, even though reduction in this sense may sometimes occur, the existence of laws and the adequacy of explanations do not depend upon it. The proper approach, therefore, appears to be to adopt the non-reductionist attitude of accepting science with or without reduction.

The most striking ramifications of Wilson's conception of epigenetic rules, no doubt, become important in contemplating those arrangements of groups that constitute societies. He has enumerated some of (what he takes to be) the most important evolutionary findings that impact on society, where the following brief paragraphs summarize his summaries (1999, pp. 183–86):

(1) *kin selection*, according to which human beings have the tendency to help others in relation to their genetic proximity, where the greater the genetic similarity, the stronger the tendency to help, with consequences for understanding altruism, patriotism, ethnicity, inheritance, adoption, and such;

(2) *parental investment*, according to which parents tend to adopt family procreation and rearing practices, such as the r-selection (having numerous offspring, but investing little in each) and K-selection (having few offspring, but investing a great deal in each), with consequences of understanding sexratios, marriage contracts, parent-offspring conflicts, child-abuse, infanticide;

(3) *mating strategies*, according to which the differential contributions of male and female partners to sexual reproduction promotes understanding of mate choice and courtship, relative degrees of sexual permissiveness, paternal anxiety, exploitation of women, polygamy and polygyny, and adultery;

(4) *status seeking*, according to which, whether by rank, class, or wealth, humans tend to pursue different roles and positions within society, which have consequences for their propensities to survive and reproduce, where high status in males is also correlated with greater sexual access to women;

(5) *territoriality*, according to which bands, tribes, cities, states, and other social groups tend to defend and expand their domination and control over geographical regions, which appears to be a "density-dependent" phenomenon as a function of carrying capacity in relation to a variable population;

(6) *contractual agreements*, according to which all mammals, including especially humans, form societies for selfish reasons, including enhanced personal survival and reproductive success, unlike worker ants and other social insects, who are willing to sacrifice themselves for the common good.

Active research programs within the general domain of gene-culture co-evolution are exploring each of these areas, some with considerable success, an exemplar of which may be found in L. Betzig, M.B. Mulder, and P. Turke, eds., *Human Reproductive Behavior: A Darwinian Perspective* (1988). What makes these approaches distinctive in kind from more traditional research in the areas of psychology, sociology, and anthropology, of course, is the adoption of an evolutionary perspective on the phenomena, by appeals either to Darwinian algorithms or to epigenetic rules, where the effects of evolution operating across substantial intervals of time affect present human behavior.

The properties of algorithms as effective decision procedures are such that they can always be relied upon to provide a solution to a problem within the classes of problems to which they apply. As causal processes, therefore, they must be deterministic and yield the same outcome under the same conditions, since otherwise they sometime succeed but sometimes fail. As probabilistic processes, they might have any value for success and failure between 0 and 1, with propensities for success equal to n and for failure equal to 1 n. They are clearly not the same. If the tendencies alluded to in (1) through (6) are of universal strength, for example, they can have no exceptions; but if they are probabilistic, then they can. Processes that are probabilistic cannot be algorithmic.

This makes an enormous potential difference to the empirical testability of epigenetic hypotheses and therefore to the scientific standing of gene-culture co-evolutionary theory. Consider, for example, potential conflicts between (1) kin selection and (2) parental investment. According to (1), human beings are disposed to help others in relation to their genetic proximity, while according to (2), parents tend to adopt family procreation and rearing practices, such as r-selection and K-selection. Few relatives stand in as close genetic proximity as offspring to their parents. If (1) were interpreted deterministically, therefore, it would be falsified by a single instance of a parent killing a child or conversely. And if (2) implies that some parents are predisposed to have numerous offspring but invest little in each, while others are predisposed to have few offspring but invest a great deal in each, how can (2) be reconciled with (1)?

The ease with which apparent inconsistencies can be generated when these rules are interpreted deterministically can induce skepticism and dismay. But many factors influencing human behavior are subtle and complex. They may plausibly be interpreted probabilistically as contributing and as counteracting factors that, in totality, have to satisfy the requirement of maximal specificity. With his customary candor—a display of the honesty that typifies great men of science—Wilson openly admits that our state of knowledge is not complete:

> The epigenetic rules that guide behavioral development are also largely unexplored, and as a result the exact nature of gene-culture co-evolution can, in most cases only be guessed. It makes all the difference in the world whether epigenetic rules are rigid, specialized functions of the brain, and thus resemble animal instinct, or whether they are more generalized rational algorithms that function across a wide range of behavioral categories. The evidence to date shows that both kinds of epigenetic rules, broad and narrow, exist. (Wilson 1999, p. 187)

Analogously, of course, it could be the case that most epigenetic rules happen to be probabilistic, but that some, such as "cheater detection mechanisms", are not.

Indeed, the strongest case for the existence of Darwinian algorithms as rigid, specialized functions of the brain that resemble "animal instincts" has been that advanced by Cosmides and Tooby (1992, p. 206), who offer the following claims:

1. The algorithms governing reasoning about social contracts include inference procedures specialized for cheater detection.
2. Their cheater detection procedures cannot detect violations that do not correspond to cheating (such as mistakes).
3. The algorithms governing reasoning about social contracts operate even in unfamiliar situations.
4. The definition of cheating that they embody depends on one's perspective.
5. They are just as good at computing the cost-benefit representations of a social contract from the perspective of one party as from the perspective of another.
6. They cannot operate so as to detect cheaters unless the rule has been assigned the cost-benefit representation of a social contract.
7. They embody implicational procedures specified by the computation theory (e.g., "If you take the benefit then you are obligated to pay the cost" implies "If you paid the cost, then you are entitled to take the benefit").

These are rather strong claims, of course. They imply a capacity for the adoption of multiple perspectives and for formal cost-benefit reasoning that appears to go far beyond ordinary abilities; they do not explain how we discriminate between deliberate "cheating" and accidental "mistakes"; they contradict the obvious risks of dealing with unfamiliar parties in unusual conditions; and they commit logical blunders regarding the logic of duties and obligations, as explained in the Appendix below.

Wilson praises Cosmides and Tooby for their work on cheater detection, according to which "domain-specific" as opposed to "general purpose" reasoning modules have developed during the course of evolution, where "one capacity, the detection of cheating, [has] developed to exceptional levels of sharpness and rapid calculation" (Wilson 1999, p. 186). Anyone who really believes this, however, must be unaware of the prevalence of deceitful politicians, wayward spouses, and used-car salesmen, whose cheating often goes undetected, yet Cosmides and Tooby's research on cheater detection mechanisms is considered the foundation of "evolutionary psychology". It is supposed to provide the strongest and most convincing evidence in support of "evolutionary psychology" in those versions dominated by "Darwinian algorithms".

Moreover, the ability to detect cheating appears to depend upon special kinds of knowledge that both parties may not share. Focusing on specific cases that are governed by written contracts, such as the purchase of a used car, for example, the detection of cheating presupposes knowledge about the actual value of the vehicle, about a fair mark-up (or profit margin), and about prevailing market conditions. Unless you have done considerable homework and possess knowledge that is not common, you will be ill-positioned to make reliable judgments regarding cheating. Indeed, unless you also know the salesman's state of mind, you will be unable to ascertain whether an inflated sales price is deliberate or merely mistaken. Thus, there are reasons to doubt that a mechanism of the kind they describe even exists.

Since mechanisms of the kind they define have no basis for discriminating between deliberate cheating and accidental mistakes, it should be obvious that they cannot guarantee success in detecting cheating. Cheater detection is therefore not deterministic and cannot possibly qualify as algorithmic. But my concern is less for the shortcomings of this research program (Davies, Fetzer, and Foster 1995) than it is for gene-culture co-evolutionary theory and especially the notion of epigenetic rules. In one place, Wilson describes these rules as encompassing:

> the full range of inherited regularities of development in anatomy, physiology, cognition, and behavior. They are the algorithms of growth and differentiation that create fully functioning organisms. (Wilson 1999, p. 163)

In another place, however, he portrays them instead as only "rules of thumb":

> They are rules of thumb that allow organisms to find rapid solutions to problems encountered in the environment. They predispose individuals to view the world in a particular innate way and automatically to make certain choices [in mating, and so forth] as opposed to others (Wilson 1999, p. 210)

Even if cheater detection mechanisms are not deterministic, they could still be probabilistic without reducing to "rules of thumb" that have arbitrary exceptions.

The general situation is evident. (a) Most mental processes—including dreams, daydreams, perception, memory, and even ordinary thinking—are non-algorithmic, as earlier chapters have explained. But the possibility remains that other thought processes might still be algorithmic. (b) The specific cheater detection mechanism Cosmides and Tooby propose, however, is not an algorithm for detecting cheating, since it is unable to differentiate deliberate "cheating" from accidental "mistakes" and depends upon special kinds of knowledge.

(c) And even if such an algorithm had evolved during more primitive times, it could be highly unreliable today due to changes in the conditions of social exchange, just at the things we tend to fear today not highly correlated with risk conditions to which we are exposed (Vednatum 1996).

Darwinian algorithms may or may not exist, but the arguments that Cosmides and Tooby have advanced in their support based upon "cheater detection mechanisms" are theoretically flawed and empirically suspect. In the absence of stronger arguments for the existence of Darwinian algorithms, Lumsden and Wilson's conception of epigenetic rules should be preferred, especially because they are not envisioned as algorithms that produce a correct solution to a problem in every case in a finite sequence of steps. They are lawful processes that operate under variable conditions to produce outcomes within particular norms of reaction. They are consistent with negative outcomes as well as positive ones and may be interpreted probabilistically. They are causal laws that govern events that occur as effects during the world's history. They can be easily confused with algorithms. But these norms are descriptive, not prescriptive, and afford a more adequate foundation for the sciences of behavior.

9.3 The Moral Society

There should also be no doubt that societies as collections of members of the human species have to be arranged in ways consistent with the natural laws of human beings. This has been a traditional conception of cultural anthropology, notable, for example, in Bronislaw Malinowski, *A Scientific Theory of Culture* (1960). Malinowski advanced two axioms, first, that every culture must satisfy the biological system needs, including those dictated by metabolism, reproduction, and physiology; and, second, that every cultural achievement involving the use of artifacts and symbolism is an instrumental extension of human anatomy (Malinowski 1960, p. 171). Here the first of these axioms matters and not the second. Indeed, it is fascinating to compare Malinowski's inventory of types of biologically-required social institutions and biologically-evolved epigenetic rules.

Malinowski suggested that every human culture must include certain rather general types of institutions as structures that fulfill specific biological functions. He differentiated the institutional types from the functions they were to fulfill, where the FUNCTIONS appear capitalized:

REPRODUCTION (family, courtship, marriage contracts, extended families, other relations); TERRITORIAL (nomadic hordes, roaming bands, villages, towns); PHYSIOLOGICAL (primitive sex totemic groups, groups based on age, sex, health); VOLUNTARY ASSOCIATIONS (primitive secret societies, clubs, athletic teams); OCCUPATIONAL AND PROFESSIONAL (economic teams, schools, courts, police, army); RANK AND STATUS (caste systems, racial and cultural stratification into groups); COMPREHENSIVE (tribes, enclaves of minorities, political units, parties, states, nations). (Malinowski 1960, pp. 62–65)

With respect to REPRODUCTION, for example, epigenetic rules concerning kin selection, parental investment, and mating strategies would potentially impact upon an adequate understanding of how specific institutions within a society contribute to fulfilling this biological need. From this perspective, gene-culture co-evolutionary theory appears to effect an internalization of social arrangements that are biologically required so that, instead of being properties of collections of members of the group collectively, they become properties of individuals for for participating in those social arrangements as dispositions (in the case of the lower species) or as predispositions (in the case of the higher species). In order for genes to exert their influence upon behavior, they must produce phenotypes that are disposed or predisposed to engage in behavior of the appropriate kind.

The group arrangements that make the greatest difference to most members of a population, no doubt, are those that control the distribution of economic resources within that society, understood as a group of individuals who belong to the same species and are organized to promote co-operation (Wilson 1975, p. 7). Among the most important properties of such a society are those that facilitate communication, which includes the creation, transmission, and perpetuation of linguistic and other conventions by means of institutions. A society in which its members cannot communicate is a society that is going to encounter difficult—potentially insuperable—problems in attaining its objectives. Communication is important because communication facilitates co-operation, and co-operation is indispensable to the attainment of community goals.

That societies can be fractured along religious, racial, or economic lines is not news. What matters is how that society responds to the divisions that it confronts, which are pragmatically dependent upon its aims, objectives, and goals. The political alternatives range from anarchy and communalism on to democracy and plutocracy to aristocracy and monarchy to fascism and totalitarianism (Facione *et al.* 1978, Chapter 7). The underlying questions of value in organizing a society to attain its objectives include the adoption of particular conceptions of distributive justice (for allocating benefits and burdens, especially economic), including of retributive justice (for undeserved benefits) and of compensatory justice (for undeserved burdens), matters characteristically governed by the laws of each society as forms of public commitment.

The United States, for example, was founded on the basis of The Declaration of Independence, which asserts that all men are created equal and that
they are "Endowed by their Creator" with certain inalienable rights, including Life, Liberty, and the Pursuit of Happiness. The notion "all men are created equal" is obviously *not* a descriptive assertion about the relative abilities
of various members that society, because they differ not only in their genetic
or innate physical and mental capacities but also in their learned or acquired
educations and attainments. The notion has to be understood as intended to
have a normative dimension. It has something to do with their equal standing before the law *in spite of* their differences in relation to any innate or
acquired abilities.

Laws of societies, unlike laws of nature, of course, can be violated and
can be changed. They are transient, rather than permanent, properties of a
population, which may or may not be subject to revision by reform as opposed
to alteration by revolution. It depends upon historical conditions, including
the customs, traditions, and practices of that society. Thus, the proclamation
that all men are endowed with certain *inalienable rights* represents a conception of how a society ought to be organized as a normative ideal. It reflects
a commitment to conduct that society (though the adoption of suitable policies, procedures, and laws) in such a fashion as to promote those aims for the
members of that society, not just for *some* of its members, moreover, but for
all of them-although at the time slaves were not citizens and women not
allowed to vote!

The adoption of such a conception, from a biological perspective, represents the adoption of an evolutionary strategy, which indicates the commitment of that society to a distinctive approach toward promoting the survival
and reproduction of its members. *A moral society* presumably would maintain that each member of its group should be treated as an end—as endowed
with inalienable rights—and never merely as a means. Not all societies are
moral, but any that are are committed to treating their members with respect.
The question that arises at this juncture thus becomes how to translate that
attitude into practice by adopting specific policies and procedures intended
to insure that those members are treated with respect. The right to life, liberty, and the pursuit of happiness are meaningless if society cannot afford the
conditions of their fulfillment.

The term "afford", within this context, exudes ambiguity. What a society
can or cannot pay may or may not coincide with what a society should or
should not provide with respect to the financial burden of supporting the conditions for the fulfillment of these rights. Inequalities of distribution of wealth
in this society, for example, are extreme (Wolff 1996). Even newspaper
accounts report that, "The gap between the rich and the poor has grown into

an economic chasm so wide that this year the richest 2.7 million Americans, the top 1 percent, will have as many after-tax dollars to spend as the bottom 100 million" (Johnston 1999). Current changes in tax policy continue to benefit the rich, even though the adverse consequences of economic disparities of this order are well known, including effects upon health, longevity, and social cohesion (Wilkinson 1996).

It appears painfully obvious that appropriate tax policies, including the taxation of wealth rather than of income, can provide benefits for society that regressive taxation cannot provide. (To paraphrase Sutton, we should tax the rich because that's where the money is!) But the proper role of government, which is to raise revenues through taxation and make expenditures through spending *on behalf of the public interest*, requires clarification. (Those who attack "taxing and spending", therefore, are attacking the very rationale for which government exists, perhaps because they are ethical egoists and their conception of their own personal interest conflicts with the public interest.) But precisely what is "in the public interest" is a matter that invites debate.

For a society committed to certain inalienable rights, including life, liberty, and the pursuit of happiness, it would appear contradictory to deny that society thereby assumes certain obligations to its members by providing (what might be described as) the *preconditions* for the attainment of society's goals. A distinction, however, might well be drawn between their biological needs and their psychological wants. The desire for food, shelter, and health seem to be biological, while the desire for fame, fortune, and happiness are not. Food, shelter, and health are or appear to be necessary conditions for survival and reproduction, while fame, fortune, and happiness are not. Indeed, the vast majority of the world's population survives and reproduces in spite of living a rather miserable life. Happiness is not necessary for procreation.

Nevertheless, we are inclined to think that fame, fortune, and happiness are important as values of a different kind. Biological motives as needs—as needs of individual organisms to survive and of groups to reproduce—entail rights and obligations. (More precisely, they entail rights and obligations for intrinsically valuable species.) Biological needs clearly seem to be more fundamental than psychological wants. Consider, for example, the phrase "need to be wealthy" versus the phrase "need to be healthy". While it makes sense to say of an individual that he *needs to be healthy*, it sounds odd to say that someone *needs to be wealthy*. This is so notwithstanding that a person may become accustomed to a certain "quality of life" and to affluence and wealth.

Psychological desires, by contrast, presume opportunities for their fulfillment. Compare, for example, *the opportunity to be healthy* versus *the opportunity to be wealthy*. We think that we are entitled to something far stronger than merely the opportunity to be healthy. Perhaps we are entitled to have fulfillment of our need to be healthy combined with—to whatever extent it can be accommodated—opportunities to be wealthy, to be famous, to pursue happiness. But it still seems to be the case that biological needs come before psychological wants. If this line of reasoning is correct, however, then one way to envision the rationale for the organization of society that would harmonize with deontological conceptions is that society should strive to coherently fulfill unfulfilled needs and promote opportunities for the populations they represent.

Promoting opportunities for the members of the population no doubt entails other rights and obligations. The "pursuit of happiness" becomes no more than an insignificant phrase or an empty promise if society cannot provide the most basic ingredients required for undertaking that objective. They include a level of education appropriate to social expectations with respect to the use of language and mathematics for commerce and communication and a suitable background with respect to science and technology, on the one hand, and history and current events, on the other. Public education is not enough for citizens to pursue happiness unless discrimination is discouraged and suitable wages are available. No one is promised happiness, but opportunity should abound.

The most important and least understood dimension of freedom, moreover, is that each of us is unfree to do things for which we lack suitable resources, including economic. The operable concept here is *effective freedom*, namely: possessing the means necessary to accomplish one's aim, no matter what that might be (Facione, Schere, and Attig 1978, p. 119). Among the policies a society might adopt to increase effective freedom, for example, are the formation of labor unions, unemployment insurance, retirement insurance, equal employment opportunity, equal educational opportunity, progressive taxation with graduated rates, inheritance taxes, corporation taxation, and other measures.

The choices that societies confront with respect to their core values, which ultimately motivate their economic policies and political actions, are for that reason also ideological and obviously subject to debate. Because our basic ideological commitments are reflected by the Declaration of Independence and the Constitution of the United States, few of us tend to reflect upon the most basic ideological choices that we confront (Goodin and Pettit 1993; Funderburk and Thobaben 1997). Occasionally, however, circumstances confront us in ways that we might prefer to avoid but then have no choice. Such appears to be the case with respect to the publication of Herrnstein and Murray's *The Bell Curve* (1994).

The debate over its methods and findings has been intense, but an important distinction needs to be drawn between two different questions implicitly at stake:

(Q1) *What cognitive properties, if any, might distinguish the various races*? —and, should scientific inquiries substantiate the conclusion such differences exist,

(Q2) *What should society do in response to the discovery of such differences*? There has been a tendency, alas, to assume that the policy options Herrnstein and Murray (1994, Part IV) propose are our only alternatives.

As Clark Glymour (1998) has observed, there are at least three alternative responses to these findings:

(A1) the custodial state, in which the cognitive elite promotes an expanded welfare state for the cognitive underclass "in which the rich and competent support the many more who are poor and incompetent" but are regarded as "valued members";

(A2) the adoption of "nationalized, serious, educational standards, tax-supported day and night care, minimal universal health care, a living minimum wage, capital invested in systems enabling almost anyone with reasonable training to do a job well";

(A3) government withdraws its support and "does not promise children safety, or nutrition, or education, and does not guarantee adults a living wage, minimal health services, or security against the hazards of industry" (Glymour 1998, pp. 30–31).

The name, "the custodial state", is their own name for the alternative that they predict.

Many problems that societies confront, including the quality of the air we breathe, the purity of the water we drink, and the quality of the food we eat, are biological problems, but their solutions—which involve the allocation and reallocation of scarce resources within the community—are clearly political. It would be at least faintly absurd, no doubt, to suggest that society has a duty to promote the reproduction of each of its members distributively. But it is not so obviously absurd to suggest that society has a duty to promote the reproduction of its members collectively, or else suffer the consequence of its own demise. Finding coherent solutions to these problems requires political decisions, moreover, since political decision-making is the procedure that we employ in dealing with the allocation and the reallocation of public resources.

A moral society, from this point of view, might appear to conflict with our knowledge of evolution. If human beings were nothing more than Darwin machines, for example, it might be appropriate to consider competition between human beings as a struggle for survival in which the fittest—and only the fittest—should prevail. But we have already found that even evolution does not strictly adhere to this conception, in part because of the influence of random and of accidental factors, in part because of the probabilistic character of its causal mechanisms. Our capacity for rationality provides the opportunity for us to go beyond our biology and treat other members of our species as we ourselves would like to be treated in times of need—with mercy and compassion.

Examples of benefits that might be derived from the study of racial differences are gradually making their way into the public domain. A review of the effectiveness of the prostate-specific antigen (PSA) test, for example, mentioned in passing, "Blacks tend to develop more aggressive prostate cancers and at a younger age" (Kolata 2005). Some of the ramifications for a good society are obvious, since it follows that Blacks should be given earlier and more frequent tests to enhance their potential to cope with prostate cancers, in accordance with deontological principles. And the apparent discovery that a new heart drug, "BiDil", has benefits for Blacks not equaled by its benefits for other races even made the front page of the *New York Times* (Saul 2005). As knowledge of race-based differences increases, it should become more and more common to utilize the most effective treatments across a broad spectrum of problems for specific races as solutions that are morally appropriate, cost-effective, and in the public interest.

Indeed, as George C. Williams (1989b) has observed, the attitude known as "Social Darwinism", according to which every individual should sink or swim on their own without support from their community, cannot be justified even on evolutionary grounds. He remarks on the views of George Bernard Shaw,

> As Shaw saw so clearly, there is no level of inclusiveness of selected entities at which the survival of the fittest is morally acceptable. The morally acceptable goal in relation to survival has to be "the fitting of as many as possible to survive". . . . So I conclude that natural selection really is as bad as it seems and that, as [Thomas] Huxley maintained, it should be neither run from nor emulated, but rather combated. (Williams 1989b, p. 196)

Thus, as Chapter 8 has explained, the biological mechanisms of selfish genes, kin selection, reciprocal altruism, and even social co-operation are unable to satisfy sufficient conditions for morality, which, indeed, transcends biology.

Democracy, as many have observed, is not the most efficient, effective, or reliable method for arriving at political decisions. Benevolent dictatorships, for example, have been extolled as comparatively more virtuous in this sense. But when it comes to arriving at political decisions that affect the allocation and reallocation of public resources, democracy can claim a rationale that no other form of government provides, namely: that, in making decisions that have consequences for every member of society, every member of society has a right of participation. The coherent political reconciliation of our biological needs with our psychological wants may pose challenges that we would prefer not to confront but also offers opportunities to demonstrate to ourselves that we are not only products of our evolutionary past but capable of contributing to our future in securing the blessings of freedom and liberty for ourselves and our posterity.

Appendix

Logical Reasoning and Domain Specificity: A Critique of the Social Exchange Theory of Reasoning

PAUL SHELDON DAVIES, JAMES H. FETZER,
and THOMAS R. FOSTER

The thesis of this paper is that the theory of human reasoning advanced by Leda Cosmides and John Tooby in Cosmides 1985, 1989, Cosmides and Tooby 1987, 1989, 1991, 1992, and Tooby and Cosmides 1989, 1990, 1992, which has recently been endorsed by Girgerenzer and Hug (1992), is neither experimentally supported nor theoretically coherent. In offering our critique, we contend (1) that the Cosmides-Tooby argument in favor of domain-specific reasoning mechanisms, as opposed to general-purpose reasoning modules, fails in at least three ways; (2) that the Cosmides-Tooby argument in favor of evolutionarily selected Darwinian algorithms, as opposed to inductively acquired availability algorithms, also fails in three ways; and (3) that the general theory proposed by Cosmides and Tooby, their so-called "social contract" hypothesis, is founded on an incorrect characterization of social exchanges in real life and therefore does not concern genuine social contracts at all. We will argue for each of these theses in turn, but we shall begin by providing a brief sketch of the central terms and issues involved.

I   Issues and Terms

The debate in which Cosmides and Tooby are participating is concerned primarily to characterize the mind in terms of its information-processing capabilities. The participants in this debate are concerned with neither the physical bases of mental phenomena nor the relationship between mental and physical phenomena. They are cognitive psychologists who take their inspiration from the modern digital computer and whose aim is to uncover the "program" or set of "programs" which governs the processes constituitive of human thought. (See, for example, Johnson-Laird 1988 and Cosmides and Tooby 1991; for critiques, see Fetzer 1990b, 1991 and Searle 1992).

One of the fundamental questions among cognitive psychologists today is whether the module that governs human reasoning is comprised of algorithms that are relatively context-free and thus general-purpose or of algorithms that are context-sensitive and thus domain-specific. All of the parties agree that the mind is modular and that most significant mental phenomena are produced by modules that are more or less functionally discrete. This is a general view inherited from Noam Chomsky and Jerry Fodor. (See, for example, Fodor 1975 and Fodor and Pylyshyn 1988; for discussion, see Fetzer 1991, 1992.) All parties also agree that there must be a module governing processes of reasoning that is more or less functionally autonomous. The fundamental issue, then, is whether this particular module operates according to rule-like procedures which are general-purpose and thus plastic (if not somewhat inefficient) in their applications or according to procedures that are domain-specific and thus less plastic (though presumably more efficient) in their applications.

Prior to Cosmides and Tooby, there were two general positions on this fundamental issue. Theorists such as Henle (1962), Braine (1978), and Rips (1990) argued that the reasoning module is governed by general-purpose algorithms. Their specific thesis, while rather opaque, is that the rules of propositional logic, which are sensitive to only the formal properties of sentences, constitute a reasoning module that is paradigmatically context-free and general-purpose. We shall refer to this view as the *mental logic hypothesis*. Other theorists, including Manktelow and Over (1979), Griggs and Cox (1982), Johnson-Laird (1982), Pollard (1982), Wason (1983), and Cheng and Holyoak (1985), however, argued that the reasoning module is governed by frequency-based algorithms. Their specific thesis, while more deeply entrenched in our philosophical tradition if no less opaque, is that the rule-like procedures by which we reason are inductively acquired associations between various types of items. Such associations, much as in traditional empiricist epistemology, are acquired during the course of each person's lifetime. We shall refer to this general view as the *availability hypothesis*.

In light of Wason 1966, the mental logic hypothesis became increasingly difficult to sustain. Wason employed his selection task (explained below) to support the claim that content—the specific subject matter about which one is reasoning—affects the perceived correctness of anyone's reasoning. When content is unfamiliar or abstract, it appears that subjects reason in ways that fail to accord with basic forms of logical inference. Unfamiliar or abstract content, for example, apparently causes subjects to affirm the consequent or deny the antecedent in deductive reasoning. When content is familiar and concrete, however, subjects tend to commit logical errors much less frequently. The evident influence of content is now called the content effect. Discovery of the content effect, which is now believed to be quite robust, cast considerable doubt on the mental logic hypothesis, since the mental logician claims that reasoning is governed by the forms and rules of logic, rules which, it is assumed, are procedures that operate independently of specific content. Even as the credentials of the mental logic hypothesis diminished, however, those of the availability hypothesis increased. For the availability theorist claims that reasoning is governed by rules acquired from experience and, because our experiences concern familiar and concrete matters, rules derived from experience offer a tight fit between phenomena and explanation.

The Cosmides-Tooby view purports to reject both the mental logic and the availability hypotheses in favor of a social contract hypothesis, the principal foundation for what is now called "evolutionary psychology". (For lengthy discussions of their "evolutionary psychology", see Cosmides and Tooby 1987; Tooby and Cosmides 1989; Tooby and Cosmides 1992; Cosmides and Tooby 1992.) The social contract hypothesis asserts that human reasoning in real-life social exchanges is governed by algorithms which have evolved via natural selection. It is conjectured that these algorithms, as causal adaptations of natural selection, are reasonably envisioned as sensitive to specific domains of organism-environment interactions. Selected mechanisms for food choice, for example, are plausibly domain-specific to the extent that they were selected as a consequence of the adaptive advantage conferred upon the adapted organism in the face of specific types of foods. (However, this position may or may not be especially compelling, since some mechanism might have been selected due to its efficacy in responding to some specific demand and yet, nevertheless, be a general-purpose mechanism. The particular demands to which it answered during its selection need not exhaust its actual powers. But we shall not pursue this matter here.)

Cosmides and Tooby also conjecture that the bulk of our mental hardware was shaped by selective forces operative during the Pleistocene era, when our ancestors were primarily hunters and food-gatherers. (For discussions of this speculation, see, for example, Cosmides 1989, pp. 194–96; Cosmides and Tooby 1989, pp. 57–59; Tooby and Cosmides 1989, pp. 34–35; Cosmides and Tooby 1991.) Assuming this, they infer that the mind must incorporate resources, selected during the Pleistocene era, which enabled our ancestors to engage in social exchange situations. For those of our ancestors who successfully engaged in exchange situations—situations in which cost-benefit relations are constructed between two or more parties—were likely to have enjoyed a reproductive advantage over those who failed to so engage. (This too is uncompelling. Even if some specific type of trait or behavior might have conferred selective advantage during our genealogical past, no specific conclusion seems to follow from that. We cannot deduce what actually happened from the fact that a certain evolutionary outcome was probable or even highly probable. Cosmides and Tooby 1989, p. 52, however, explicitly maintain that these deductions are both possible and scientifically important.)

Cosmides and Tooby additionally conjecture that, in order for them to have successfully engaged in social exchanges, our ancestors must have acquired an algorithm enabling them to detect those who would cheat against an established contractual agreement. (See Cosmides 1989, pp. 195–200; Cosmides and Tooby 1989, pp. 84–92.) Those able to detect cheaters, it is conjectured—and this is among their most crucial hypotheses—were likely to have enjoyed greater reproductive success than those unable to detect cheaters. Thus, Cosmides and Tooby maintain, on the basis of social-contract theory, that subjects today are likely to reason according to a psychological mechanism, now part of our species-wide hardware, which causes us to actively scan for and to detect cheating in social exchanges.

As against the mental logic hypothesis, therefore, Cosmides and Tooby argue that reasoning is governed not by general-purpose algorithms but rather by evolutionarily-derived domain-specific algorithms. As against the availability hypothesis, they argue that reasoning is governed not by the strength of acquired associations between various items but instead by evolutionarily-derived sensitivity to cost-benefit relations. The conclusion they derive is that only social contract theory affords the proper foundation for understanding evolved psychological mechanisms, which in turn implies that human behavior should be studied within the framework supplied by evolutionary psychology. Given this understanding of the issues, we turn to the arguments offered in defense of their position.

II The Argument for Domain Specificity

Cosmides and Tooby claim that human reasoning is governed by domain-specific rather than by general-purpose rules. The general form of their argument can be presented as a simple argument by elimination,[i] namely:

Figure A.1   The Argument for Domain Specificity

Premise P1:	H1 (general-purpose) vs. H2 (domain-specific)
Premise P2:	not-H1 (general-purpose)
Conclusion C:	therefore, H2 (domain-specific)

We shall argue, however, that the conclusion of this argument is entirely unwarranted. Specifically, we shall contend (1) that H1 is excessively narrowly defined and that its putative elimination on the basis of P2 is therefore inferentially unjustified, (2) that the experiments intended to support P2 either fail to eliminate H1 or else actually provide evidence supporting H1, which suggests that P2 might be empirically false, and (3) that the formulation of P1 is based upon a misconceived dichotomy and that the strategy with which Cosmides and Tooby hope to establish their conclusion therefore appears to be cast into doubt as a conceptual confusion. We shall argue for each of these points in turn.

1 H1 Has Not Been Eliminated

Although Cosmides and Tooby do not explicitly articulate their position in the precise form of this argument, it is nevertheless clear that their general strategy is to eliminate the general-purpose hypothesis and to conclude that the domain-specific hypothesis is correct. Thus, Cosmides and Tooby presumably take P1 for granted. They do not entertain the possibility of any third alternative. Perhaps it seems obvious that the rules governing human reasoning must be either general-purpose (and temporarily adapted to specific circumstances) or else domain-specific (and permanently adapted to specific circumstances). They also take for granted that the forms and rules of propositional logic are the paradigm for general-purpose reasoning module. Indeed, they argue for P2 and against the hypothesis that humans reason via general-purpose rules by arguing that humans do not reason in accordance with the forms or rules of propositional logic.

They do not, however, test human reasoning against all of propositional logic. Their tests are extremely narrow in scope, focusing entirely on the material conditional. English language sentences with an "if . . . then __" structure, when represented in propositional logic, are translated into material conditional form. The symbol '→' (the arrow) is often used to represent that "if. . . then __" structure, where a material conditional is a specific instance of a sentence having that structure or form. Such a material conditional, therefore, is a molecular sentence (which is made up of other sentences) having at least two (atomic or molecular) parts. If we label the " . . . " space as p and the "__" space as q, then the form of a material conditional can be represented as that of "$p \rightarrow q$".

The if-sentence (which fills in the p-space) is known as the *antecedent* and the then-sentence (which fills in the q-space) is known as the *consequent*. Material conditionals are examples of truth-functional sentences, because nothing about what those sentences may mean or might describe makes any difference to the truth or falsity—known as the *truth value*—of material conditionals apart from the truth values of their component sentences. Material conditionals are understood to be *false* only when their antecedents are true and their consequents are false together. In every other combination of truth values for the component sentences—true antecedent and true consequent; false antecedent and true consequent; false antecedent and false consequent— material conditionals are understood to be *true*. This is a definitional property of such sentences.

Cosmides and Tooby achieve their narrow focus by adapting the Wason selection task. The selection task is intended to test its subjects' facility with "if . . . then __" sentences of English. The content of constituent sentences might vary but the structure of the task is always the same. In its original form the selection task asks subjects to consider the following sentence:

If a card has a vowel on one side then it has an even number on the other side.

This sentence refers to four cards displaying the following sides up:

[E]   [4]   [K]   [7]

Each card has a letter on one side and a number on the other. Subjects are instructed to turn over those cards, and only those cards, that need to be turned over to determine decisively whether the sentence is true or false (Wason 1966, pp. 145–47). It is assumed that, if human reasoning is governed by general-purpose rules, such as the rules of propositional logic, then the correct response to the Wason selection task ought to be one that suitably correlates with the definition of material conditionals.

Because a conditional is false just in case the antecedent is true and the consequent is false, the "correct" response to the Wason selection task is supposed to be to turn over both the first and the last cards, that is, the 'E' and the '7' cards. This is because only the 'E' (not the 'K') makes the antecedent true and only the '7' (not the '4') makes the consequent false.

Since the rule is satisfied in every other case, in order to determine ("decisively") whether it has been violated, these are the cases that have to be eliminated. If the '7' has a vowel on its other side, for example, or if the 'E' has an odd number of its other side, then the rule has been violated, but otherwise not. The emphasis here is on how it might be falsified.

The results secured by Wason (1966), Wason and Johnson-Laird (1972), and several others since, suggest that subjects do not reason according to the definition of the material conditional. In some domains dealing with abstract or unfamiliar problems, for example, subjects do poorly, while in other domains dealing with concrete and familiar problems, subjects do well. Reasoning thus seems to be governed by mechanisms that are sensitive to the specific content about which one is reasoning. Cosmides and Tooby, along with many other cognitive psychologists, interpret this result as evidence that human reasoning is not governed by general-purpose algorithms. These content effects are supposed to be strong evidence that there is no general-purpose reasoning module.[ii]

This last move is permissible, however, only insofar as propositional logic is the only or (at least) the best example of a general-purpose reasoning module. But it is not the only and it is certainly not the best. Consider, first, that propositional logic is hardly the only candidate. Logic is a tree with many branches, where each branch is designed to capture the valid forms of reasoning of some specified kind. Leaving inductive logic aside, deductive logic includes not only propositional but also classical term (or "syllogistic") logic, modern predicate logic, and many varieties of modal logic. So the general-purpose hypothesis, H1, tacitly conceals a whole family of alternative hypotheses for various kinds of logical reasoning:

H1a: There is a general-purpose syllogistic logic reasoning module;

H1b: There is a general-purpose propositional logic reasoning module;

H1c: There is a general-purpose predicate logic reasoning module;

.
.
.

Any of these might serve as a general-purpose reasoning module, yet, apart from the propositional reasoning module, Cosmides and Tooby have tested for none of them. (Even independently of Cosmides and Tooby's adaptation of it, moreover, the Wason selection task is problematic in several ways, some of which are discussed below in Appendix A.)

Secondly, consider that propositional logic is the most impoverished and is therefore hardly the best branch of logic against which to test human reasoning. There are, for example, many valid forms of reasoning from classical term logic that cannot be expressed adequately in propositional logic. The obviously valid, "All men are mortal; Socrates is a man; therefore, Socrates is mortal", when represented in propositional logic, exemplifies the argument form, "p and q, therefore r", which is obviously not valid. Moreover, it is silly to test actual human reasoning against mere material conditionals. For material conditionals, against which Cosmides and Tooby's tests are directed, are artificial artifacts of elementary logic which are seldom encountered in ordinary discourse, where the content of the antecedent and of the consequent make a difference to the truth of most conditionals. Causal conditionals are an appropriate illustration.

Properly understood, material conditionals are suitably introduced as an abbreviatory device for sentences that mean "either not-p or q", where false antecedents by themselves automatically guarantee the truth of any material conditions conditional. This follows because any material conditional with a false antecedent cannot have both a true antecedent and a false consequent, no matter what the value of its consequent. For example,

(MC1) If $2 + 2 = 5$, then snow is white;

and

(MC2) If $2 + 2 = 5$, then snow is not white;

are both true material conditionals, since they both have false antecedents. In this respect, material conditionals stand in striking contrast with non-material conditionals, such as subjunctive conditionals, for example, because a false antecedent does not ensure the truth of any subjunctive conditional. For example, the following two conditionals,

(SC1) If Bill Clinton were a bachelor, then he would be married;

(SC2) If Bill Clinton were a bachelor, then he would be unmarried;

are not both true merely because they both have false antecedents. Although Bill Clinton is not a bachelor, it remains true hypothetically that, if he were a bachelor, he would be unmarried, by virtue of the meaning of the terms involved. Subjunctives make assertions about what would be the case on the hypothetical assumption that their antecedents are satisfied, even when that assumption happens to be historically false.

Some subjunctives are true by virtue of their grammar alone, while others are true by virtue of the meaning of their constituent terms, as in the case of (SC2). These are justified on logical grounds. Others, however, concern properties and relations that obtain in the physical world and are true or false as manifestations of laws of nature. For example,

(SC3) If this were made of copper, then it would conduct heat;

(SC4) If this were made of copper, then it would conduct electricity;

are not both true merely because the object under consideration happens to be a wooden match. (SC3) and (SC4) are true, not simply by virtue of the meaning of their constituent terms, but by virtue of laws of physics. Conditionals of this kind are true on ontological grounds. The varieties of conditionals that are justified as manifestations of laws of nature include both deterministic and probabilistic causal conditionals. (For discussions of these various kinds of conditionals, see Fetzer 1981, 1990b, and 1993.)

Reasoning with material conditionals, such as (MC1) and (MC2), tends to be artificial or "non-sense" reasoning, while reasoning with subjunctive and causal conditionals, such as (SC3) and (SC4), tends to be eminently sensible. Sensible reasoning, no doubt, is important to our survival, but nonsense reasoning, almost certainly, is not. So the second premise of the Cosmides-Tooby argument seems to be overly narrow. Their claim that human reasoning is not governed by a general-purpose reasoning module is unsupported, precisely because they have failed to rule out several viable alternative versions of H1 and, moreover, have failed to rule out alternatives that are demonstrably superior to the one they consider. As a consequence, their putative elimination of the general-purpose reasoning mechanism hypothesis is not inferentially justified.

2 P2 May Be False

Cosmides and Tooby adapt the Wason selection task to test the social-exchange hypothesis against the mental logic hypothesis. A social-exchange situation is one in which someone receives a benefit on the condition that he or she agrees to pay a specified cost. As Cosmides and Tooby define them, the only way to cheat against (or to violate) a social-exchange rule is to benefit and fail to pay. (See Cosmides 1989, p. 197; Cosmides and Tooby 1989, p. 84.) Cosmides and Tooby's adaptation of Wason's selection task employs rules of the following general form:

(SE) If someone receives the benefit, then s/he pays the cost.

If the logic of social-exchange rules deviated from that of material conditionals, then presumably the conditions under which they would be violated or falsified would differ. According to Cosmides and Tooby, (SE) is violated when someone receives the benefit but does not pay the cost. When interpreted as a material conditional, however, (SE) is falsified when both its antecedent B ("someone receives the benefit") is true and its consequent P ("someone does not pay the cost") is false. Just as a material conditional with antecedent p and consequent q is false only when p & $\sim q$ is true (' $\sim$ ' means not), a social exchange rule with benefit B and cost P is violated only when B & $\sim P$ is true. The logic of social-exchange rules appears to correspond strikingly to that of material conditionals rather than deviate from it. There appears to be no evidence here to establish that social exchange has a logic that differs from that of propositional logic, which is Cosmides and Tooby's target; consequently, nothing here indicates that the social-exchange hypothesis is preferable to the mental logic hypothesis. Indeed, Cosmides and Tooby's account of social exchange not only fails to falsify the mental logic hypothesis but may even appear to confirm it.

The central innovation of Cosmides 1989, therefore, is a test intended to overcome the above impasse. Cosmides switches the order in which the constituent sentences of (SE) occur. She now formulates rules with the alternative general general form:

(SSE) If someone pays the cost, then s/he takes the benefit.

The correct social-exchange response to (SSE), according to Cosmides, is supposed to be precisely the same as the correct social exchange response to (SE). The order in which constituent statements occurs is asserted to be of no significance to the algorithms that are postulated by social contract theory, just because "social contract algorithms are, by hypothesis, content-dependent: a 'look for cheaters' procedure should always pick the 'cost not paid' card and the 'benefit accepted' card, regardless of what logical category they happen to fall into" (Cosmides 1989, p. 216). Logical forms are presumably irrelevant to the operations of social contract algorithms; the mere co-occurrence of benefiting and not-paying suffices to cause them to fire. So (SE) as a social exchange rule is violated just when 'B & $\sim P$' is the case. Notice the correct logical response to (SSE) is not the same as the correct logical response to (SE): (SSE) is false only when 'P & $\sim B$' is the case, while (SE) is false instead when 'B & $\sim P$' is the case. The switch from (SE) to (SSE), according to Cosmides, thus provides a difference in prediction between the social contract and the mental logic hypotheses (Cosmides 1989, pp. 198–99).

This predictive difference, however, is merely apparent. To illustrate, we shall make two assumptions. First, we will assume that the mental logician, the advocate of a general-purpose reasoning module, is free to enhance the power of the reasoning module by adding elements from logical systems other than propositional ones. We assume, for example, that the reasoning module may contain elements from deontic systems, which concern the logic of principles of obligations and of entitlements. Second, we assume, along with Cosmides and Tooby, that the mind is modular and thus composed not only of the reasoning module but also modules governing the input of perceptual information, the translation of perceptual information into an appropriate internal idiom, the triggering of various motor routines, and so on. On the basis of these two assumptions, conjoined with the mental logic hypothesis, it is easy to construct experimental predictions that are exactly the same as those made by Cosmides and Tooby. We shall offer three distinct examples.

(a) The First Way

Consider first the powers of modules other than the reasoning module. Imagine yourself the subject in one of Cosmides's switched conditional experiments. You are presented with a brief story concerning the practices of an unfamiliar people, a rule concerning some of its customs, and the explicit instructions to look for violators of the rule (Cosmides 1989, p. 211). The rule that you are given is an instance of the general form,

(SSE) If someone pays the cost, then s/he accepts the benefit.

How might you respond? We suggest you will be confused. You know perfectly well what the concept of "violating" or of "cheating" involves. Indeed, given our widely shared grasp of the notion, we know that (SE) is a rule against which cheating is possible while (SSE) is no rule at all. Specifically, we all know that someone who benefits and fails to pay is a cheater while someone who pays and fails to accept the benefit is not a cheater but a fool (or, perhaps, an altruist, a possibility to which we shall return; but observe that an altruist is no more of a cheater than is a fool). Thus, when confronted with (SSE), which is not a rule, you are inappropriately instructed to look for cheaters. Hence, your confusion.

We conjecture that, given the instructions to look for cheaters, this confusion will be resolved swiftly. For you will be motivated to reinterpret (SSE) as a genuine rule, that is, as something against which it is possible to cheat. In particular, you will be caused to reinterpret (SSE) as

(USE) (Only) if someone pays the cost, s/he accepts the benefit.

Having noticed that (SSE) is not a rule against which cheating is possible and, having been given your instructions, you will be inclined to reinterpret (SSE) as (USE). Indeed, it is plausible to claim that the "only if" is already implicit in (SSE), because otherwise the instruction to look for violators of (SSE) makes no sense. This reintepretation, moreover, may be the outcome of your translation module. For this module receives at least two bits of incoming information, that is, an "if . . . then __" sentence of English and the instructions to look for violators of that "if . . . then __" sentence. Both (SSE) and (USE) are possible representations of that incoming "if . . . then __" sentence, but only one of them, namely (USE), also accounts for the instruction to look for violators, given that only one of them, namely (USE), appears to be something against which it is possible to cheat. We conjecture, then, that the translation module would tend to produce (USE) and not (SSE). The problem this raises for Cosmides and Tooby should be obvious. For the reinterpretation of (SSE) to (USE) in effect unswitches the switched conditional. (USE), but not (SSE), after all, is logically equivalent to the unswitched conditional in (SE). The statement "Only if P, B" is logically equivalent to "If B, then P". Given this logical equivalence, subjects who respond to (SSE) by reinterpreting it as (USE) are thereby responding to the unswitched conditional in (SE) or to some equivalent of (SE). From the point of view of the hypothetical reasoning module, therefore, there is no difference between (SE) and (SSE). This means that the predictive difference of which Cosmides (1989) boasts is illusory, since the mental logician, by appeal to the powers of the translation module, can predict the very same results as Cosmides predicts.

(b) The Second Way

An alternative conjecture may seem to be even more plausible as an instance of the importance of translation. Plausibly, when placed in the experimental setting previously described, you would reinterpret (SSE) as a *biconditional* (going both ways) having the following form:

(BSE) You take the benefit if and only if you pay the cost.

J.L. Austin, the brilliant ordinary-language philosopher, observed that, when a social contract is extended by means of a sentence of the form,

(ABC) If you give me B, then I will give you P

the conditions which are contextually implied include all the following:

(i)   if you give me B then I will give you P;
(ii) by virtue of my adhering to the conditions of this contract, my belief that you have given (or will give) me B will be the cause of my giving you P; and,
(iii) if you do not give me B then I will not give you P.

If this is correct, however, then it is not at all implausible to suppose that you will be caused by your own translation module (which, in a case of this kind, reflects your understanding of English) to read (SE) as asserting (BSE). For the force of (SE), interpreted in the light of (i) and the contrapositive of (iii), which turns out to be "if I give you P, then you will give me B", is the very biconditional asserted by (BSE).

The consequences for Cosmides and Tooby should be obvious. When (SE) is reinterpreted as (BSE), then the mental logician can, once again, formulate the very same predictions as those offered by Cosmides and Tooby. For (SE), when read as (BSE), consists of the conjunction of two conditionals—namely, '$B \rightarrow P$' and '$P \rightarrow B$'. Since you were instructed to look for violators, and since you know that it is impossible to violate or cheat against '$P \rightarrow B$' (remember, 'P & $\sim B$' might make you a fool or an altruist, but not a cheater), you will very likely be caused to process the other conjunct. But the correct logically falsifying response to '$B \rightarrow P$' is 'B & $\sim P$', which is the same response predicted by Cosmides and Tooby. Once again, the predictive difference of which Cosmides (1989) boasts appears to be missing.

(c) The Third Way

There is yet another way the mental logician's predictions may match those of the social contract theorist, one which does not appeal to the powers of any other module. We assume only that the reasoning module itself is somewhat more powerful than Cosmides and Tooby allow.

To illustrate, again imagine yourself to be a subject in one of Cosmides's switched conditional experiments. You are again presented with a story, a rule—an instance of (SE)—and the instruction to look for violators. We now assume, however, that your reasoning module is comprised of the forms and rules of deontic logic and that your translation module has the capacity to represent natural language utterances and inscriptions in the formal elements appropriate to deontic logic. Your module thus contains not only the forms and rules of propositional logic but also the forms and rules for representing and manipulating statements concerned with *obligations* and *entitlements.*

We conjecture that, equipped with a sensitivity to such deontic elements, you will detect in (SE) an implicit appeal to permissiblity. So instead of representing (SE) as a material conditional of the form, '$P \rightarrow B$', your enhanced translation module will represent it as

(PSE) $P \rightarrow \mathbf{E}(B)$

where the operator '$\mathbf{E}$' indicates entitlement and where (PSE) asserts "if someone pays, then s/he is entitled (permitted) to take the benefit". We conjecture, however, that the deontic algorithm, whenever it receives a statement concerning entitlements, automatically triggers procedures for entitlements and obligations and, whenever it receives a statement concerning obligations, automatically triggers procedures for obligations and entitlements. When faced with (SE), for example, your algorithm triggers not only procedures for (PSE), but also procedures for

(OSE) $B \rightarrow \mathbf{O}(P)$

where the operator '**O**' indicates *obligation* and thus where (OSE) asserts "if you take the benefit, then you are obligated to pay the cost". Indeed, it is plausible to claim that (SE) triggers procedures within the algorithm for both (PSE) and (OSE), because of the obvious conceptual connection between permissions and obligations. If paying entitles you to a benefit, entitlement of some sort appears required to receive the benefit, unless, of course, you happen to be cheating! It is plausible to infer, therefore, that entitlement is necessary to socially approved behavior, when rules of this kind are norms. This makes it reasonable to suppose further that, should you receive the benefit prior to enjoying such an entitlement, you would thereby be obligated to pay a subsequent cost. (Whether you actually do pay a subsequent cost, of course, would depend upon whether or not your behavior happens to be detected and the rules are enforced!) The same reasoning works the other way too, insofar as being obligated to pay a cost, as specified in a social-exchange rule, requires that there exist certain entitlements subsequent to fulfillment of such obligations.

The problem for Cosmides and Tooby once again should be clear. Insofar as a subject's algorithm triggers procedures for both (PSE) and (OSE), it thereby triggers procedures for (OSE). But insofar as you are caused to look for violators of (OSE), you will be caused to look for situations in which someone benefits and does not pay—that is, precisely those cases in which 'B & ~P' obtains. The mental logician, once again, can make the very same predictions as those made by social-contract theorists such as Cosmides and Tooby.

The ways in which the mental-logic hypothesis might be varied seem to be enormous. Advocates of a general-purpose reasoning module have resources that extend well beyond anything for which Cosmides and Tooby have tested. In particular, we might sustain the claim that we reason according to the forms and rules of propositional logic merely by drawing on the powers of some other module, or we could reformulate the mental-logic hypothesis and claim that humans reason according to the rules and forms of deontic logic. Cosmides and Tooby have simply failed to disconfirm the mental-logic hypothesis. They have also failed to rule out the claim that humans reason according to general-purpose principles. The second premise of their overall argument has not been supported experimentally and might plausibly be supposed to be false.

3   P1 May Be False

To this point, we have focused our attention on Cosmides's and Tooby's failure to support their second premise. But the first requires scrutiny as well. Recall the first asserts that humans reason according to either general-purpose or domain-specific algorithms, where this, apparently, presumes a dichotomy between general-purposiveness and domain-specificity. It is unlikely, however, that this dichotomy can be sustained.

Cosmides unpacks the general-purpose–domain-specific distinction in terms of yet another distinction, namely, a distinction between logical form and propositional meaning or content. She seems to reason in the following fashion. If, on the one hand, human reasoning is governed by general purpose algorithms and, more specifically, if the paradigm of a general-purpose system is propositional logic, then human reasoning is determined exclusively on the basis of logical form and of logical rules. The meaning or content of the sentences we produce or the sentences to which we respond, on this view, is not relevant to the functioning of our reasoning module. On the other hand, if human reasoning is governed by domain-specific algorithms and, more specifically, by the effects of content, then reasoning is determined exclusively on the basis of meaning or content. The logical form of the sentences we produce or of the sentences to which we react is instead not relevant to the functioning of our reasoning module (Cosmides 1989, p. 216; Cosmides and Tooby 1992, pp. 187–190).

This is the distinction that cannot be sustained. To illustrate, consider Cosmides's characterization of the mental-logic hypothesis. Taken literally, she is claiming that we are caused to process any sentence on the basis of its logical form alone. But imagine that a mugger corners you in a dark alley, puts a gun to your head, and says,

(X)   If you move, I will shoot you.

On Cosmides's construal, the "if . . . then __" structure (for users of the English language, at least), appropriately translated into some formal sentence, somehow causes the algorithm for the material conditional to switch on and thereby engage procedures based on the truth definition for the arrow ' → '. But now imagine that instead of (X) the mugger had uttered

(Y)   You move and I will shoot you.

In this case, the ". . . and __" structure (for English-language users again), appropriately translated, somehow causes the algorithm for the "and" connective to switch on and thereby engage procedures based on the definition for the ampersand '&'. But the truth definition for '&' is distinct from the definition for '→' and therefore we ought to expect that, in at least some cases, subjects will respond to (Y) differently than they respond to (X). Consider too that the mugger may have said:

(Z) Don't move! (else I will shoot you)

where the first half of (Z) is a command, not a proposition. We might in fact symbolize (Z) as a disjunction and apply the truth definition for the wedge connective 'v', but the truth definition for 'v' is distinct from the definitions for both '&' and '→'. Moreover, insofar as the first disjunct is not an assertion and hence is neither true nor false, we cannot assume that any conclusions derived from (Z) must be either true or false. Once again, therefore, we ought to expect that subjects' responses to (Z) would differ from their responses to either (Y) or to (X).

But intuitively this seems to be misguided. We would expect that most subjects respond to (X), (Y), and (Z) in the very same way because, under the circumstances, there is no cognitive difference between these three sentences. We know that there are no such differences precisely because we attend to the meaning or to the content of these utterances. To claim that we or our translation modules can distinguish between these three statements without any consideration of meaning or content is nonsense.

The underlying confusion concerns a rather mundane fact about logic. Cosmides is correct to claim that the truth value of a sentence is a function of its logical form, but only when we are considering that sentence—technically, as a well-formed formula (wff)—*within a logical system*! A wff is a string of symbols arranged in accordance with the syntactic rules of the system. The truth of any wff that is composed of other wffs is entirely a function of the relevant syntactic rules, provided the truth values of the atomic wffs is given. But standards of logical correctness of this kind, which are based on syntactic rules, such as the truth-functional definitions of the arrow, the ampersand, and the wedge, apply to well-formed strings within the system and not to sentences outside the system. As a consequence, they do not apply—at least, not without interpretation—to the natural language sentences employed in the Wason selection task. In particular, the standards of correctness represented by truth-functional definitions do not apply to the switched or to the unswitched conditionals that are employed in Cosmides's social exchange experiments. Cosmides and Tooby apparently have confused sentences within a logical system, namely wffs, with sentences of natural language. They are therefore mistaken in their assumption that the truth-functional definition for the material conditional is the appropriate standard of correctness for the natural language conditionals that are employed in their experiments.

Cosmides and Tooby have conspicuously omitted an account of the process of translation of sentences from a natural language into a formal language. Subjects in their experiments, of course, are presented with natural-language sentences, and no doubt *how those subjects translate the natural language utterances or inscriptions into some formal idiom* would determine what kinds of logical operations could or could not be performed within that idiom. Nothing within Cosmides's and Tooby's theoretical discussions address this problem, and nothing within their experiments controls for the effects of the translation module. Without such controls, however, the results of these experiments can no more appropriately be attributed to the reasoning module specifically than they can appropriately be attributed to the translation module itself.

The critical upshot, therefore, is that the translation of natural language utterances or inscriptions into the language of a formal system requires careful attention to the very thing that Cosmides and Tooby disavow—namely, the meaning, the propositional content, of the natural language sentences. One must decide what type of logical system—classical term, propositional, predicate, modal, and so forth—and what type of construction within the specific system best represents those specific natural-language sentences. As everyone who has actually done some logic could testify, these decisions cannot be made without careful (and sometimes subtle) distinctions about the meaning of those sentences. (Further examples of these difficulties in Cosmides's other work may be found in Appendix B.)

In view of these considerations, we are now forced to wonder in what the distinction between general-purposiveness and domain-specificity is supposed to consist. There cannot be mental algorithms that operate according to the forms and rules of any logical system unless there are additional algorithms which, by careful attention to the meaning of incoming sentences, felicitously translate those sentences into an appropriate internal idiom. The human mind, *if it contains general-purpose rules analogous to the rules of some logical system*, must on that basis possess mechanisms which are sensitive to domain-specific meanings. Otherwise successful translations from natural to formal idioms would be impossible and the general-purpose rules would remain idle. (This may account for Fodor's emphasis upon an innate language of thought; see especially Fodor 1975, Fodor and Pylyshyn 1988, and Fetzer 1992.) There are no grounds for the claim that the mind must consist either of general purpose mechanisms or of domain-specific algorithms, but not both. Premise P1 of the Cosmides-Tooby argument appears to be false.

Considerations (1) through (3) above support the claim that the general argument advanced by Cosmides and Tooby fails. They have adopted an excessively narrow definition of the general-purpose hypothesis, H1, and have not provided appropriate evidence in support of their second premise, P2. Indeed, other evidence that we have considered suggests that P2 is false. Their first premise, P1, which appears to depend upon taking for granted a misconceived dichotomy, likewise appears to be false.

We conclude that the Cosmides/Tooby hypothesis that humans reason according to domain-specific rather than general-purpose algorithms cannot be estabished by means of the arguments which they provide.

III   The Argument for Darwinian Algorithms

Cosmides and Tooby also maintain that human reasoning is governed by selectively evolved Darwinian algorithms rather than by means of inductively acquired availability algorithms. The general form of their reasoning once again may be represented as a simple argument by elimination:

Figure A.2   The Argument for Darwinian Algorithms

Premise P3:	H3 (availability) vs. H4 (Darwinian)
Premise P4:	not-H3 (availability)
Conclusion D:	Therefore, H4 (Darwinian)

We shall argue, once again, that the conclusion of this argument is not warranted. Specifically, we will contend (1) that, as before, H3 is also excessively narrowly defined and that its putative elimination on the basis of P4 is therefore inferentially unjustified, (2) that experiments which are intended to support P4 either fail to eliminate H3 or fail to provide evidence for H4, which means that P4 is not adequately supported, and (3) that P3 rests upon a distinction that appears to be theoretically unprincipled and that the strategy with which Cosmides and Tooby attempt to defend their conclusion is therefore cast into doubt. We shall argue for each thesis in turn.

1   H3 has Not been Eliminated

Once again, Cosmides and Tooby may not explicitly articulate the above argument, but it is reasonably clear that their general strategy is indeed to demonstrate the untenability of the availability hypothesis and thereby imply that the Darwinian hypothesis is correct. Thus P3 is taken for granted; no third alternative is considered. Moreover, they also take for granted that, while the availability hypothesis may occur in importantly different versions, every version assumes that "the subject's actual past experiences create associational links between terms mentioned in the selection task" (Cosmides and Tooby 1992, p. 184; see also Cosmides 1989, pp. 201–07). That is, they take for granted that the availability hypothesis is reducible to the postulation of associative links between regularly conjoined terms. Indeed, they argue for P4 and thus against the availability hypothesis by maintaining that subjects in social exchange situations that involve unfamiliar (and therefore previously unassociated) terms elicits a statistically significant portion of correct responses.

According to Cosmides and Tooby, the availability hypothesis maintains that a subject's reponses on the Wason selection task are determined by the strengths of associative links that have been established during the subject's personal experiences, which are assumed to be directly proportional to the number of exposures that that person has had to each such pairing. The strength of association relating the content described by p and the content described by q is proportional to the relative frequency with which q-content has occurred in relation to p-content during that person's life history. If p-content has occurred n times and q-content has occurred m times in relation to p-content, then the strength of the association r for the person linking q with p should be equal to $m/n = r$. This hypothesis represents a psychologized and personalized version of what is often referred to as the *straight rule* of induction (see Salmon 1967 or Fetzer 1991). According to the straight rule, if m/n observed As have been Bs, then infer that m/n As are Bs, provided that a large number of As have been observed under a wide variety of conditions.

According to Cosmides (1989) and Cosmides and Tooby (1992), predictions made on the basis of the availability hypothesis are unsupported by the experimental data, while predictions made on the basis of the social contract hypothesis are so supported. In particular, Cosmides (1989) reports on experiments involving both social-exchange situations and unfamiliar terms. Situations are assumed to involve social exchange insofar as there exist cost-benefit exchanges between two or more individuals; some, for example, are situations in which only men with tattoos on their faces— an indication that they are married—are allowed to eat a sumptuous kind of root which is believed to be an aphrodisiac. Situations involve unfamiliar terms insofar as the items involved in the exchange are novel notions; for example, the type of root involved is called "cassava root" which, because it is a fictitious entity concocted by Cosmides, is not likely to be familiar. The availability hypothesis predicts that subjects will tend to score poorly on such tests when compared to tests in which the terms involved are familiar; the social-contract hypothesis predicts that subjects will tend to score well in situations involving a social exchange, whether familiar or unfamiliar. Predictions based on the social contract hypothesis, but not those based on the availability hypothesis, were confirmed by Cosmides's experiments. Cosmides and Tooby thus conclude that the second premise of their argument has been demonstrated.

But this conclusion is drawn much too hastily. It follows only if every version of the availability hypothesis actually does depend on a straightforward projection of the inductively acquired associations between terms. But they do not. Contrast straight rule induction with, for example, the *counter-inductive rule*. According to counter-induction, if we observe As to be frequently associated with Bs, we infer that any future As will be proportionately less associated with Bs. More precisely, if m/n observed As have been Bs, then counter-induction would have us infer that $1 - m/n$ As are Bs. Or again contrast straight rule induction with the *a priori rule*, according to which observed associations between As and Bs provide no evidence for inferences concerning unobserved instances of A or of B. More precisely, if m/n As have been observed to be Bs, then infer that k As are Bs, where k is an arbitrary constant whose values represent proportions. (See Salmon 1967 and Fetzer 1991, Chapter 7.)

These alternative rules are but a few of the available competitors, among which abductive rules and Bayesian inference are of particular interest.[iii] This suffices to show that the availability hypothesis, H3, tacitly conceals a whole family of alternative hypotheses for different kinds of reasoning:

H3a: There is a domain-specific straight rule reasoning module;

H3b: There is a domain-specific counter-inductive reasoning module;

H3c: There is a domain-specific a priori reasoning module;

.

.

.

The existence of alternative inductive rules such as these establishes that, even if Cosmides's and Tooby's experiments did support their claim that humans do not reason according to the straight rule, they would still not establish the truth of their second premise P4, because hypothesis H3 is excessively narrowly defined. As a consequence, their agument has not successfully eliminated the availablility alternative.

2   P4 is Inadequately Supported

This last argument, of course, concerns the full range of inferences that someone might make on the basis of an inductively acquired association between terms; it is precisely the full range of options that Cosmides and Tooby overlook. We now wish to shift attention from the kinds of inferences made on the basis of such associative links to the associative links themselves. We want to examine, in particular, the types of items which are capable of entering into these associative relations.

In explicating the availability hypothesis, Cosmides and Tooby refer to the work of investigators such as Griggs and Cox (1982), Johnson-Laird (1982), Manktelow and Over (1979), Pollard (1982), and Wason (1983), while these latter theorists, in turn, refer to the earlier work of Tversky and Kahneman, including, especially, Tversky and Kahneman 1973. It is Tversky and Kahneman who introduce what they call an "availability heuristic" as a procedure for making inferences from certain properties, objects, or states of affairs to certain other properties, objects, or states of affairs on the basis of their "availability", that is, on the basis of the ease with which the mind moves from the first item to the associated second item. They put the point this way:

> A person is said to employ the availability heuristic whenever he estimates frequency or probability [of some property, object, or state of affairs] by the ease with which instances or associations could be brought to mind. (Tversky and Kahneman 1973, p.208)

In one group of experiments, for example, the subjects were exposed to a list of names of nineteen famous women and twenty not so famous men. After their exposure, subjects' recall was significantly greater for the names of famous women and, more interesting, most subjects claimed (falsely) that the lists contained a greater number of women's names than men's (Tversky and Kahneman 1973, pp. 220–21).

Note, however, that the contraints on the kinds of items that are capable of entering into an associative relationship are relatively minimal. It is necessary only that candidate links co-occur with other candidate links in ways that are *regular* and *experientially accessible* to us. Of course, we must experience any candidate link in conjunction with its future associate link with sufficient frequency. But this makes the range of possible links extremely broad, extending from the very particular to the very general. For example, in addition to specific tokens (names and instances) of particular objects, such as the Manchester train and the city of Manchester (Wason and Shapiro 1971), general types of particular objects, such as modes of transport and towns or cities, may also qualify; and, in addition to specific tokens of particular relations, such as the relationship between an envelope's being sealed (as opposed to unsealed) and the amount of postage required (Johnson-Laird 1982), types of relations, such as the relation between differential services and differential costs, may also qualify; and so on.

These possibilities, moreover, are more than merely logical possibilities; they are genuine psychological possibilities. Pollard (1982), for example, argues that availability works not only on matters of content but also on matters of context. While Pollard does not put the point this way, one implication of his thesis is that types of context themselves are (at least in some cases) associative links that generate availability. He argues, in fact, that factoring types of contexts into the availability heuristic tends to explain why certain instances of the Wason selection task facilitate a content effect so strongly and why other instances facilitate little or no content effect. Instead of these associations being straightforward links between pairs of objects, at least some associations obtain between, on the one hand, a type or set of types of contexts and, on the other, a pairing of objects or a pairing of states of affairs or whatever. In this way, the availability theory may be enriched to include inductively acquired *generalizations* of categories of properties, objects, and states of affairs.

The view that these general categories of properties, objects, and states of affairs qualify as associative links raises several difficult questions. What, for example, makes such items "experientially-accessible" to us? Indeed, under what conditions is anything "experientially accessible" at all? These appear to be serious issues that availability theorists need to confront. As we shall now argue, however, these are also issues social-contract theorists have to face. They confound one view no more than the other.

Recall that Cosmides and Tooby performed experiments employing both social-exchange situations and *unfamiliar* terms. They claim that, if the situation is social exchange and the social contract hypothesis is correct, we should predict a facilitation of the content effect, but if the situation involves unfamiliar terms and the availability hypothesis is correct, we should predict little or no facilitation of the content effect. Now consider the question, Why is the unfamiliarity of the items involved any less of a problem for the social contract hypothesis than it is for the availability hypothesis? In virtue of what considerations, after all, do the postulated social-contract algorithms operate when the terms involved are not familiar? By hypothesis, social-contract algorithms are putative products of our evolutionary history; if we haven't experienced certain items in our selective past, however, then how, on the social contract hypothesis, can we reason about them in the present or the future? The social-contract hypothesis along with the availability hypothesis would seem to predict little or no facilitation when the terms items involved are not familiar.

Cosmides and Tooby attempt to respond to this type of worry with the following claim:

If people do have inference procedures that are specialized for reasoning about social contracts, then these ought to function, in part, as frame or schema builders, which structure new experiences. This means they should operate in unfamiliar situations. No matter how unfamiliar the relation or terms of a rule, if the subject perceives the terms as representing a rationed benefit and a cost/requirement in the implicational arrangement appropriate to a social contract, then a cheater detection procedure should be activated. Social contract algorithms need to be able to operate in new contexts if one is to be able to take advantage of new exchange opportunities. (Cosmides and Tooby 1992, p. 185)

Our selective histories, according to Cosmides and Tooby, have produced algorithms which, in some way or another, contain generalized schemata that "structure new experiences". Perhaps so—but if so, then Cosmides and Tooby ought to admit that *exactly the same claim may be made by the availability theorist*. Nothing within the availability theory as such, not to mention nothing within Cosmides's and Tooby's characterization of the availability theorist, precludes or otherwise rules out the possibility that generalized schemata that "structure" new experiences are among the kinds of items that can become associated in our minds.

If the postulation of general schemata were implausible for availability hypotheses, which perhaps it is, then it ought to be equally implausible for social-contract hypotheses. Moreover, if the availability theorist is faced with the challenge of explicating the notion of experiential-accessibility, especially as it applies to generalized items, including frames or schemata, then so too is the social contract theorist. There is nothing involved here that supports one of these hypotheses at the expense of the other.

It is quite reasonable, moreover, to understand the *pragmatic-reasoning schemata* introduced by Cheng and Holyoak (1985) as a more general version of the availability hypothesis. Indeed, Cosmides describes the Cheng and Holyoak hypothesis as "an instance of" the availability view (see Cosmides 1989, p. 191). Cheng and Holyoak themselves distinguish their proposal both from the "syntactic, context-free rules of inference" and from the "memory of specific experiences"; they claim instead that reasoning is governed by "abstract knowledge structures induced from ordinary life experiences . . ." (Cheng and Holyoak 1985, p. 395). These are envisioned as general structures that are sensitive to specific types of domains and relations, including permissions, obligations, and causation, which are inductively acquired on the basis of each organism's history.

One way to understand the actual construction or inductive acquisition of these schemata is via associations between particulars, associations between generals and particulars, or even associations between associations. We do not claim this view is correct. Nor do we claim it is what Cheng and Holyoak actually propose. What we claim is that it implies a possible development of the availability thesis that produces the same predictions and that suffers the same conceptual unclarities as the social-contract hypothesis. (Cosmides 1989 contains a sustained attack on Cheng and Holyoak 1985, claiming, for example, that the only permission schemata to successfully facilitate the content effects are—unrecognized by Cheng and Holyoak, alas!—really social-exchange situations. Cheng and Holyoak 1989 provides a detailed rebuttal that, in our judgment, weighs rather heavily against Cosmides's position.)

We conclude, therefore, that the possibility of generalized schemata enables the availability theorist to make exactly the same predictions as those made by Cosmides and Tooby. Insofar as such schemata are accessible to the social contract theorist, they are similarly accessible to the availability theorist. If the problematic notion of experiential accessibility poses a stumbling block to the availability theorist, then it is likewise an obstacle to the social contract theorist. In these respects, predictions that are based on availability theory would appear to be ill-founded only if predictions based on social contract theory are likewise ill-founded. The availability theory, even in the excessively narrowly formulation that Cosmides and Tooby would impose upon it, therefore, has not yet been shown to have been experimentally eliminated. As a consequence, premise P4 has clearly not been established on the basis of appropriate empirical evidence.

3   P3 May Be Incoherent

We have thus far focused on Cosmides's and Tooby's failure to support their second premise, but our reflections on this failure point toward an obvious but fundamental problem with their first premise as well. The first asserts that humans reason according to either inductively acquired availability algorithms or evolutionarily acquired Darwinian algorithms. This distinction, moreover, is unpacked by Cosmides and Tooby in terms of *familiarity*. On the availability hypothesis, correct reasoning requires familiarity with the items involved, but on the social contract hypothesis, correct reasoning does not require such familiarity. (See Cosmides 1989, pp. 201ff; Cosmides and Tooby 1989, pp. 90–92; Cosmides and Tooby 1992, pp. 184–87.) But our most recent reflections suggest that this way of unpacking the availability-Darwinian distinction cannot be theoretically sustained.

Cosmides and Tooby correctly perceive that, on their view, it is not clear how humans are able to reason about unfamiliar items, about properties, objects, or states of affairs not experienced during the selective history of our species. How, for example, were Darwin or his contemporaries able to reason correctly about the mechanisms of evolution by natural selection, assuming that none of our earlier ancestors had discovered those mechanisms? For that matter, how are Cosmides and Tooby able to reason correctly about the postulations of their theory, especially social exchange algorithms, assuming this is the first discovery of such mechanisms? Cosmides's and Tooby's appeal to frames or schemata, while woefully undeveloped, clearly appears to be a move away from pure domain-specificity and toward domain or categorical-generality. Thus, at the time Darwin discovered the mechanisms of selection, such mechanisms were unfamiliar as *specific tokens* or as *particular ideas*, but, in relation to his hardwired "frames" or "schemata", those precise mechanisms were presumably familiar as instances of certain *domains* or *categories*. This, then, is how the social-contract theorist accounts for the apparently unfamiliar—namely, by maintaining that, thanks to our frames and schemata, such unfamiliarity is merely apparent.

As we have argued above, however, the availability theorist can make an exactly parallel move and nevertheless preserve the central claim concerning associationism. Such a move, while equally undeveloped, is again an obvious move away from pure domain-specificity and toward domain or categorical-generality. The availability theorist, therefore, may account for the apparently unfamiliar in the very same way as Cosmides and Tooby—namely, by claiming that such unfamiliarity is merely apparent.

Once this last move is granted, however, the distinction implied by the first premise, P3, of the Cosmides-Tooby argument collapses. For the availability-Darwinian distinction putatively hinges on the claim that availability algorithms respond only to what is familiar, while Darwinian algorithms do not. But this is false. Both types of algorithms may be characterized as mechanisms that respond to what is familiar, if only familiar in terms of the general "frames", "schemata", or "structures". The alleged distinction between the availability hypothesis and the social exchange Darwinian hypothesis, at least as bruited by Cosmides and Tooby, is therefore lost. Consequently, the overall strategy of the Cosmdies-Tooby argument is likewise lost.

Considerations (1) through (3) support the claim that the argument in favor of Darwinian algorithms fails. Cosmides and Tooby have (again) adopted an excessively restricted conception of the (in this case) availability hypothesis, H3, and have failed to offer even weak evidence in support of their second premise, P4. Moreover, the first premise, P3, appears to rest upon an untenable distinction. We conclude, therefore, that the Cosmides-Tooby claim that humans reason according to evolutionarily derived Darwinian algorithms does not follow from and cannot be established on the basis of the arguments they have advanced.

IV The Logic of Social Exchange

Cosmides and Tooby claim that the general form of any social-exchange rule—namely, the assertion that "if someone receives a benefit, then s/he pays the cost"—is adequately represented symbolically by the sentence,

(SE) $B \to P$

where (SE) belongs to some system of propositional logic (Cosmides 1989, pp. 198–99). It is this formulation that is employed in their appropriation of the Wason selection task to social-exchange situations. As against (SE), we shall (1) sketch out in rudimentary form the logic of social exchange rules, (2) argue that (SE) is an incorrect representation of genuine social exchange rules, and (3) conclude that Cosmides and Tooby's theory, while offered as a theory of social-exchange rules, is actually founded upon a hopeless characterization of genuine social exchanges and that, as a consequence, it cannot properly qualify as a theory of social exchange at all.

1 The Logic of Social Exchange

We assume that social exchange situations, properly understood, involve relations of obligations and entitlements (or permissions). They also involve appeals to hypothetical situations concerning *what obligations and entitlements would obtain if something were the case*, which can only be adequately formalized by means of subjunctive conditionals. We tentatively assume that each of the following four assertions are involved in a correct conceptual characterization of any social exchange, namely:

[LL] (a) If a person were to receive a benefit, then s/he would be *obligated* to pay the cost.

(b) If it is not the case that a person were to receive a benefit, then it is not the case that s/he would be obligated to pay the cost.

(c) If a person were to pay the cost, then s/he would be *entitled* to receive the benefit.

(d) If it is not the case that a person were to pay the cost, then it is not the case that s/he would be entitled to receive the benefit.

On purely intuitive grounds, it is plausible to claim that (a) though (d) are necessary elements of any social exchange. For example, if anyone believes that taking a benefit confers on the taker an obligation to bear a certain cost, then if one takes the benefit, as in (a), that person there-by obligates himself to paying the specified cost. If a person does not take the benefit, as in (b), however, then no obligation is incurred. Similarly for (c) and (d). However, a person might still receive a benefit to which they are not entitled by virtue of the generosity (or the "charity") of another (a benefactor), which appears to be inconsistent with (d) and also seems to qualify as a violation of (a). We are *ordinarily* expected to pay for benefits which we enjoy, but special cases might be exceptions.

Let us assume that (a) through (d) are appropriate conceptions, even as we concede that special cases may have to be considered further. We are then in a position to develop aspects of the logic of rules for social exchange. Translated into deontic formal idiom using ' $\Rightarrow$ ' (the double arrow) as the subjunctive, (a) through (d) can be fashioned as follows:

(A) B $\Rightarrow$ **O**(P)   [If you were to receive the benefit, then you would be obligated to pay the cost]

(B) ~B $\Rightarrow$ ~**O**(P)   [If it is not the case that you were to receive the benefit, then it is not the case that you would be obligated to pay the cost]

(C) P $\Rightarrow$ **E**(B)   [If you were to pay the cost, then you would be entitled to the benefit]

(D) ~P $\Rightarrow$ ~**E**(B)   [If it is not the case that you were to pay the cost, then it is not the case that you would be entitled to the benefit]

where the operator '**O**' asserts that "it is obligatory that . . ." and the operator '**E**' asserts "it is entitled or permitted that . . .". More adequate formal representations of these four English sentences would employ the use of quantifiers and would make explicit reference to context (a matter we consider further below), but most of our arguments do not require them.

Two consequences are of special importance here. First, observe that the conjunction of (A) and (B) produces the following biconditional:

(E) B $\Leftrightarrow$ **O**(P)   [You would get the benefit if and only if you were obligated to pay the cost]

which, once again, may suggest the importance of exceptions to the rule, while (C) and (D), when conjoined, yield a second biconditional, namely,

(F) P $\Leftrightarrow$ **E**(B).   [You would pay the cost if and only if you were entitled to the benefit]

Both biconditionals appear to be necessary to a correct characterization of any real-life *social-exchange situation*. (Indeed, the explanation for exceptions to (A) and (D) in the case of benefits conferred upon persons due to the generosity of others would be that, strictly speaking, they are not "social-exchange situations" at all, since such parties are not entering into contractual agreements as they are ordinarily understood. Similar cases of this kind would include giving gifts.) Both are derived from elements necessary to social exchange situations—the first from what is obligatory and the second from what is permissible. Moreover, each of (A) through (F) connects an action descripton, which describes something a person actually might do, with a deontic assertion, which refers to a state of entitlement or of obligation. Each of them, in other words, relates actions (actual or possible) to certain kinds of situations within which those act-ions might take place, where within those situations those actions would qualify as entitlements or as obligations. We shall return to this point.

Evidently, there are four types of actions that may be performed in a social exchange situation. One may benefit and pay < B, P >, in which case (let us say) one is a *buyer*. One may benefit and not pay < B, ~P >, in which case (presumably) one is a *cheater*. One may also pay and not benefit < ~B, P >, in which case one is a *fool*, an *altruist*, or perhaps the *victim of cheaters*. Or one may not pay and not benefit < ~B, ~P >, in which case one is a mere *window shopper*. To illustrate, let us consider the consequences of each type of action in relation to our biconditionals.

The first case < B, P >, together with (E) and (F), entails the following ("the buyer"):

"P" with "$P \Leftrightarrow E(B)$" entails "$E(B)$";

"$E(B)$" with "B" entails doing what one is entitled to do;

"B" with "$B \Leftrightarrow O(P)$" entails "$O(P)$";

"$O(P)$" with "P" entails doing what one is obligated to do.

Here one does what one is entitled to do and what one is obligated to do; one is thus an honest participant in a contractual arrangement.

The second case < B, ~P >, together with (E) and (F) entails the following ("the cheater"):

"B" with "$B \Leftrightarrow O(P)$" entails "$O(P)$";

"$O(P)$" with "~P" entails not doing what one is obligated to do [which is a *violation* of our deontic rules];

"~P" with "$E(B) \Leftrightarrow P$" entails "~$E(B)$", not being entitled to a benefit;

"~$E(B)$" with "B" entails doing what one is not entitled to do [which is a *violation* of our deontic rules].

Here one fails to do what one is obligated to do and does what one is not entitled to do. Such a person is thus a genuine cheater.

The third case $< ~B, P >$, together with (E) and (F) entails the following ("the fool", "the altruist", or "the victim"):

"~B" with "$B \Leftrightarrow O(P)$" entails "~$O(P)$";

"~$O(P)$" with "P" entails doing something one is not obligated to do [which is not a violation of the deontic rules];

"P" with "$P \Leftrightarrow E(B)$" entails "$E(B)$", being entitled to a benefit;

"$E(B)$" with "~B" entails not doing what one is entitled to do [which is not a violation of the rules].

Here one does what is not obligatory and does not do what is permitted; one is clearly not a cheater. One's actions are beyond the duties of any social exchange and, as a consequence, the categorization of one's action depends heavily upon one's motivation. One might pay and fail to take a benefit from foolishness, out of altruism, or involuntarily as a victim.

The fourth case $< ~B, ~P >$, together with (E) and (F) entails the following ("the window shopper"):

"~B" with "$B \Leftrightarrow O(P)$" entails "~$O(P)$";

"~$O(P)$" with "~P" entails not doing something that one is not obligated to do [which is *not* a violation of the deontic rules];

"~P" with "$P \Leftrightarrow E(B)$" entails "~$E(B)$", not being entitled to a benefit;

"~$E(B)$" with "~B" entails not doing something that one is not entitled to do [which is *not* a violation of the deontic rules].

Here one neither does what one is not obligated to do nor what one is not entitled to do; one simply refrains from engaging in a social contract altogether. One is thus merely a window shopper.

The range of available actions in any social-exchange situation is therefore diverse; one is not constrained simply to adhere to or to deviate from the rules. For present purposes, however, notice that the second type of action, cheating, occurs in two distinct forms. Corresponding to (E), cheaters *fail to do what they should do*—they violate an obligation; corresponding to (F), *they do what they should not do*—they violate the denial of a permission. Correct descriptions of genuine social exchange situations therefore require specifying both the relevant obligation and the relevant permission. Having developed the logic of social exchange rules this far, we turn to Cosmides's and Tooby's representation of what they take to be the general form of social contract rules.

2 Cosmides and Tooby's Account

Cosmides and Tooby claim that real-life social exchange rules are properly represented by a single material conditional, namely,

(SE) $B \rightarrow P$.

This is to assume that social-exchange rules are correctly represented in purely propositional terms, absent any deontic operators. Assuming this, Cosmides and Tooby further argue that this single material conditional, as opposed to some material biconditional, correctly represents social exchange rules. They reason in the following way: Suppose (toward a contradiction) that the material biconditional '$P \rightarrow B$', without deontic operators, represents the social-exchange rule; then there will be two distinct ways to "violate" the rule, one corresponding to each conditional; one might benefit and not pay (the cheater) or pay and not benefit (the fool); but a fool is not a genuine violator of the rule; hence the conditional '$P \rightarrow B$' is not relevant to cheating after all and thus '$P \rightarrow B$' does not turn out to represent the rule. (See Cosmides and Tooby 1989, pp. 82–84.)

This argument is valid. It does show that social-exchange rules cannot be properly formalized as material biconditionals. Contrary to Cosmides and Tooby, this argument does not also show that social-exchange rules can (or "must") properly be represented as material conditionals. The inference from "social-exchange rules are not material biconditionals" to "therefore social-exchange rules must be material conditionals" is valid *only if* it is also assumed that "social exchange rules are either material biconditionals or material conditionals, and these are the only options". But this last assumption is patently false in at least two different ways.

First, a correct characterization of genuine social exchange rules requires (E) and (F) above, that is, at least two non-truth-functional biconditionals. Assuming that the sketch in (1) of the logic of social exchanges is correct, subjunctive conditionals, which imply but are not implied by corresponding material conditionals, are necessary. But even if the sketch presented in (1) were mistaken, that is, even if subjunctive conditionals were not necessary,

Cosmides and Tooby would still be mistaken. For the use of subjunctive conditionals is at least a plausible way to represent the logic of social exchanges, which itself implies that non-truth-functional options are available, contrary to Cosmides's and Tooby's presupposition.

Secondly, and much more significantly, neither non-deontic conditionals nor non-deontic biconditionals can represent the logic of social exchange adequately. For (SE), as a sentence of propositional logic, is nothing but a descriptive sentence. It asserts only that if someone in fact benefits, then that same someone in fact pays. (SE) if true asserts that '$B \rightarrow P$' is indeed the case. Consider now the cheater. A cheater is someone who benefits and fails to pay, who creates situations in which 'B & $\sim P$' is the case. Merely because someone has derived a benefit and has not paid a cost, however, *it does not follow that that person has done anything that they should not have done!* Recipients of generosity are not invariably cheating! Without further premises implying deontic principles of obligation and entitlement, "cheating" cannot occur as a normative conception.

Notice that, if (SE) were true, there would no benefiters who are not also payers; hence, there would be no cheaters. Cosmides and Tooby intend (SE) to imply that those who benefit and do not pay are on that ground alone "cheating". However, when people benefit without paying (including beneficiaries of charity and recipients of gifts), they may or may not be cheating: "cheating" requires benefiting without paying *when you are not entitled to benefit without paying* or *when you are obligated to pay for that benefit!* Thus, when the general form of social-exchange rules is expressed propositionally—*without deontic elements*—cheating becomes a logical impossibility. (The necessity for deontic elements generalizes to any application of the Wason selection task to phenomena involving obligations and permissions. See Appendix A for additional discussion.)

This shows that real-life social exchanges cannot be properly represented exclusively in non-deontic truth-functional logic. Yet a non-deontic truth-functional representation is exactly what Cosmides and Tooby employ. As a result, they have not adequately represented social exchanges either in their theory or in their experiments. The phenomenon they describe and attempt to explain is not what they claim. Despite its name, their theory is not a theory of social-exchange reasoning, which lies beyond its scope.

3 Some Ramifications

Cosmides and Tooby, no doubt, will object. In discussing the claim that subjects appear to read obligations and permissions into social-exchange rules (from Manktelow and Over 1987), Cosmides and Tooby agree but then go on to maintain that such behavior is predicted by their theory:

[The fact that subjects apparently read in deontic elements] is, in fact, a prediction of social contract theory: A cost is something one is obligated to pay when one has accepted a benefit, whereas a benefit is something that one is entitled to take (but need not) when one has paid the required cost. Thus, the interpretive component of the social contract algorithms should cause subjects to "read in" the appropriate "musts" and "mays", even when they are not actually present in the problem. . . . (Cosmides and Tooby 1992, p. 190)

Now it is altogether unclear how or why social contract algorithms can be said to contain an "interpretive component" that somehow reads in the appropriate deontic elements when Cosmides and Tooby have explicitly claimed that social contract algorithms operate independently of logical form. The important message here, however, is that our criticism is not about the nature or operation of mental algorithms. Our criticism is that Cosmides and Tooby have incorrectly characterized what is involved in any *bona fide, real-life social exchange*. We must distinguish between claims regarding the internal workings of postulated mental mechanisms and claims concerning the logical properties of social exchange situations.

At this point, the importance of *considerations of context* becomes plain. Cosmides and Tooby have mischaracterized these logical properties in at least two important ways. The first is their omission of deontic elements concerning obligations and entitlements. The second is their omission of considerations concerning context. Genuine social exchange situations create contexts C, such as contractual agreements, within which these obligations and entitlements arise, obligations and entitlements that do not not arise within other contexts C*, which may involve charitable contributions, gift-giving and the like. As a consequence, *there can be situations—possibly numerous situations—in which persons receive benefits without paying and nevertheless are not cheating!* But if that is indeed the case, then real-life social exchange situations are not even remotely adequately characterized by Cosmides and Tooby, which is a profound defect in their theory, no matter what algorithms they might postulate.

Admittedly, the explict acknowledgment of contextual considerations also implies that our own formulations could be improved by incorporating explicit reference to kinds of context C in which they properly apply. More exact formulations of (E) and (F) might assume the following form:

(E*) $C(B) \Leftrightarrow O(P)$ [You (sh)ould get the benefit in a context of this kind if and only if you were obligated to pay the cost]

(F*) $C(P) \Leftrightarrow E(B)$ [You (sh)ould pay the cost in a context of this kind if and only if you were entitled to the benefit] where corresponding qualifications are required of our other principles.[iv] Considerations of neither kind, however, are reflected by Cosmides and Tooby's account. We thus infer that their theory of reasoning founders on notions that are ill-described, ill-defined, and above all ill-fitted to the discovery of how humans reason in genuine real-life social-exchange situations. The theory is putatively about social exchanges, but in fact it is not. It may be about real phenomena in need of scientific explanation, but if that is indeed the case, it ought to be cast in a less misleading and more illuminating form. It is not a theory of *bona fide* social exchanges.

V Closing Observations

We conclude with two general observations. First, in Sections II and III above, we argued that both the mental logic and availability hypotheses, properly and charitably understood, can produce predictions identical to those produced by the social-contract hypothesis. Thus, we are left to wonder exactly what it is about the social-contract theory that is original and important or (more to the point) both significant and possibly true.

To illustrate the force of this question, consider that, on the one hand, the mental-logic hypothesis requires some analogue of what Cosmides and Tooby call the "interpretive component", while, on the other hand, the availability hypothesis requires an analogue of what Cosmides and Tooby call "frames" or "schemata". The mental logic hypothesis requires an interpretive component in order to account for translations between natural and formal language; the availability hypothesis requires frames or schemata in order to account for our facility with unfamiliar items. The Cosmides-Tooby hypothesis, on their own admission, requires both an interpretive component and some variety of generalized frames or schemata. Insofar as social contract theory is forced to import elements from those theories it aspires to overthrow, exactly what in the social contract hypothesis is supposed to be new or exciting? The addition of considerations from the theory of evolution by natural selection hardly suffices, for both the mental logic and the availability hypotheses are compatible with certain adaptationist assumptions. In what way, then, does the Cosmides-Tooby hypothesis qualify as a genuine contribution to inquiry concerning human reasoning?

Secondly, the fact that both mental logic and social contract hypotheses can, when necessary, appeal to the powers of some "interpretive" component or of some "translation" module and the fact that both the avail- ability and the social contract hypotheses can, when necessary, appeal to the powers of some "frames" or "schemata" surely casts doubt upon the general enterprise of cognitive psychology as a mode of experimental inquiry—

at least as it is practiced by Cosmides and Tooby. We need to construct experiments in which the possible effects of various modules besides the reasoning module are properly controlled within a framework of genuine scientific alternatives.

To illustrate, advocates of any of the three competing hypotheses may fix the powers of one module, formulate predictions, and run their experiments. If those experiment fail to confirm the predictions made, their proponents only need alter this or that bit of their theory—for example, by redescribing the powers of some other module—and thereby adjust the predictions to fit the data obtained. Indeed, an advocate of mental logic, when faced with Cosmides's (1989) data, can make any one of the three adjustments discussed in Section III above and thereby produce predictions identical to those made by Cosmides. The problem is that, for all we are told about the powers of other modules or even about the reasoning module itself, there are an indefinite number of other *ad hoc* adjustments available.

The question thus becomes whether anything within the information-processing paradigm of human reasoning adds up to a principled form of scientific inquiry. Surely there must be some general theoretical and methodological principles and procedures whose function is to prohibit theorists from adjusting the putative powers of this or that postulated module in non-arbitrary ways. And surely those principles and procedures apply within the domain of evolutionary psychology as well as in other domains. Perhaps a return to the study of the nature of science itself will provide a framework for considering these questions, further clarifying what qualifies as a coherent theory and what qualifies as an informative experiment.[v]

Appendix A: The Wason Selection Task

The Wason selection task, even apart from Cosmides and Tooby's appropriation, is problematic in several ways. Here we briefly mention those that seem most severe.

(a) It is apparently assumed that the conditional sentence involved in the selection task—for example, "if a card has a vowel on one side, then it has an even number on the other side"—has to be correctly understood as a material conditional. Subjects whose reaction to the conditional sentence deviates from the truth definition for the material conditional are said to have reasoned incorrectly. But this assumption rests on a naive understanding of logic. The above conditional cannot even be represented properly by means of the limited resources of propositional logic alone. What is additionally required, at a bare minimum, are predicates and quantifiers. For the subject of the antecedent is "a card", while the subject of the consequent is merely "it". Thus, in order to ensure that the "it" refers back to the "card", we apparently need to symbolize that sentence as follows:

(UG) $(x)(Vx \rightarrow Ex)$

which asserts that "for any object, if it has a vowel on one side, then it has an even number on the other side". (For more discussion, see Fetzer 1990a.) Since rules such as those employed in the Wason selection task cannot even be properly formalized within propositional logic, those who would employ it for the purpose of testing propositional reasoning might want to reconsider the rationale for its employment within that context.

(b) The instructions given in the Wason selection task are ambiguous in a highly significant way. They instruct subjects to turn over just those cards required to show that the conditional sentence "is true or false". (They are evidently meant to be read, "is true or is false".) But this is ambiguous between those cards required to establish the falsity of the sentence and those required to establish the truth of the sentence. To demonstrate that the sentence is false, for example, only two cards are relevant, but to conclusively establish the truth of the sentence (if possible), arguably all four cards are relevant. The idea is that there are both direct and indirect ways in which evidence can be confirmatory.

As Carl G. Hempel (see Hempel 1965) explained in relation to material conditionals, observations of non-black non-ravens apparently qualify as confirming the hypothesis, "All ravens are black". The assumptions that are required for this consequence to follow are: (i) that instances that satisfy the antecedent and the consequent of a conditional confirm it; (ii) that instances that satisfy the antecedent but not the consequent of a conditional disconfirm it; and (iii) that instances that do not satisfy the antecedent of a conditional neither confirm nor disconfirm; and (iv) that sentences that are materially equivalent (that are true or false under all and only the same conditions) are confirmed by all and only the same class of instances. Insofar as "All ravens are black" is materially equivalent to "All non-black things are non-ravens", the existence of a white shoe, a yellow cow, and so on, which satisfy both the antecedent and the consequent of "All non-black things are non-ravens", and thus confirm it, must also confirm "All ravens are black". This oddity has been widely discussed and is known as *the paradox of confirmation*.

One response to the paradox of confirmation is to assume that evidence that does not disconfirm an hypothesis counts as confirming it, perhaps as *indirect* ("weak") rather than as direct ("strong") evidence, as would occur when that hypothesis survives a serious attempt at its refutation. (See Fetzer

1981, 187–196). Given a conception of confirmation of this kind, turning over all four cards, including those that cannot establish the falsity of that conditional sentence, nevertheless provides empirical evidence that each card is of the letter or number type as well as indirect evidence that the sentence is true. If subjects take their task to be establishing the truth of a generalization rather than its falsity, then whether or not we should expect their responses to deviate from searching exclusively for falsifying instances seems to depend on their interpretation of the instructions and our appraisal of the paradox (Fetzer 1990a).

(c) In Section IV, we argued that social-exchange rules, properly understood, cannot be represented adequately with sentences in propositional logic. Deontic operators are indispensable. We should like to speculate, however, that this point might generalize to several applications of the Wason selection task. For deontic operators are necessary insofar as the tasks involve specific types of rule. Theorists who employ the selection task must take care to discern whether their particular rules describe relations involving obligations and entitlements. The relevant range of obligations and entitlements is presumably much broader than those that were operative during past "economic interactions" between our Pleistocene ancestors. It may include agreements concerning etiquette, matters of practical expediency, matters of morally appropriate or of religiously permitted behaviors, and so on. To the extent that deontic operators are involved in the phenomena tested in the Wason selection task, representing the relevant relations merely in terms from propositional logic confounds the conclusions one might be tempted to draw.

We do not claim that (a) through (c) constitute insurmontable problems for those who would employ the Wason selection task. We claim only that, unless and until these problems are resolved, it is difficult to say exactly what it is that the Wason selection task actually tests. Cognitive psychologists who would draw substantive conclusions from such tests may want to fulfill their obligation to come to grips with these problems.

Appendix B: Logical Infelicities

Apart from the errors that we have exposed above, Cosmides and Tooby commit several mistakes either in their characterization of or in their use of certain logical claims. Such mistakes appear to cast further doubt on the putative results of their experiments. We shall mention only two.

(a) Cosmides 1985 appears to misuse negation. Consider the following formulation of various varieties of social contract conditionals (Cosmides 1985, pp. 56–66):

(AA) If you take the benefit, then you must pay the cost;

AN) If you take the benefit, then you must not pay the cost;

(NA) If you do not take the benefit, then you must pay the cost;

(NN) If you do not take the benefit, then you must not pay the cost.

The only difference between these four is the placement of negatives. As an example of type (AA), Cosmides advances the example, "If a person is drinking beer, then the person must be over nineteen," in relation to which is the following (NN), "If a person is not drinking beer, then the person must not be over nineteen" (Cosmides 1985, p. 66). If (NN) is intended to represent a sentence obtained by negating the antecedent and the consequent of (AA) within propositional logic, however, then this is a mistake involving a simple misplacement of the negations. Its correct counterpart is, "If it is not the case that a person is drinking beer, then it is not the case that the person must be over nineteen." Similarly for (AN) and for (NA). Cosmides does not realize that the negation of a "must" sentence is an "it-is-not-the-case-that-one-must" sentence rather than a "must not" sentence. (See Fetzer 1990a; compare Griggs and Cox 1983.)

(b) Cosmides (1989) similarly misses an obvious and important logical non-equivalence. Cosmides maintains that a social-exchange rule is violated when and only when someone benefits without paying, namely,

(i) $B \,\&\, {\sim}P$

This means there is a general way not to violate a social exchange rule, namely,

(ii) ${\sim}(B \,\&\, {\sim}P)$

This is as it should be, since (ii) is logically equivalent to the unswitched conditional form of a social exchange rule, namely,

(SE) $B \rightarrow P$

The problem, however, is that Cosmides introduces a "switched" version of the social exchange rule, namely,

(SSE) $P \rightarrow B$

where (SSE) is not logically equivalent to (ii). (SSE) is not equivalent to a general statement of the conditions under which social exchange rules could be violated, and therefore it is not a "social exchange rule" at all. Instead of (ii), (SSE) is equivalent to

(iii) $\sim(P \ \& \ \sim B)$

which asserts that one does not both pay and not take the benefit. But as we have already seen (Section IV above), paying and not taking the benefit is not cheating. It may be an instance of foolishness, or perhaps of altruism, or even of victimization, but not of cheating.

Cosmides has thus missed the non-equivalence of (ii) and (iii). Had she noticed it, she might have thereby seen the inequivalence between (SE) and (SSE). The consequence for her investigations is that experiments employing (SSE) fail to employ a genuine social-exchange rule and thus fail to test the social contract hypothesis. Such experiments do not test Cosmides's or any other theory of social exchange situations. (For fuller discussion, see Davies and Foster manuscript.)

NOTES

[i] The logical structure of their position can be cast in various different forms, depending upon which aspects should be emphasized. Since they affirm domain-specificity and assume it entails non-domain-generality, it could equally well be formulated as an instance of *modus ponens*:

Premise P1*:   If H1* (domain-specificity), then not-H2* (general purpose)
Premise P2*:   H1* (domain-specificity)
Conclusion C*:   Therefore, not-H2* (general purpose)

Their appeals to the Wason selection task, *inter alia*, to undermine the tenability of the general-purpose alternative suggests that *elimination* is more illuminating, but nothing important hangs on which is adopted.

[ii] These content-specific effects have been interpreted, perhaps even more widely, as evidence for a frequency effect (availability being due to previous exposure to specific items), and frequency effects are typically held to be due to general-purpose mechanisms, as one referee has pointed out—a construction that also undermines Cosmides and Tooby.

[iii] The abductive and Bayesian alternatives are more reasonable than the counter-inductive and *a priori* rules, no doubt, but the former are simpler to explain than the latter and work better within this context.

[iv] Alternatives to (E*) and (F*) might assume the following form instead:

(E**) C $\Rightarrow$ [B $\Leftrightarrow$ O(P)]   [If you were in a context of kind C, you (sh)ould get benefit B if and only if you were obligated to pay cost P]

(]F**) C $\Rightarrow$ [P $\Leftrightarrow$ **E**(B)]   [If you were in a context of kind C, you (sh)ould pay cost P
if and only if you were entitled to benefit B]

These formulations, like (E*) and (F*), however, are tentative and approximate, since more precise characterizations would require quantifiers and predictates and the development of a more complete semantic analysis than we have provided here.

  ^{v} This paper appeared in *Biology and Philosophy* 10 (1995). The four earlier notes are responses to criticisms from an anonymous referee.

Bibliography

Ackermann, R. 1965. *Theories of Knowledge.* New York: McGraw-Hill, 1965.

Alexander, R. 1987. *The Biology of Moral Systems.* Hawthorne: Aldine De Gruyter.

Angier, N. 1997. Survey of Scientists Finds a Stability of Faith in God. *New York Times* (3rd April), p. A10.

————. 2000. Do Races Differ? Not Really, DNA Shows. *New York Times* (22nd August, 2000), on the web.

Beckoff, M. and D. Jamieson, eds. 1996. *Readings in Animal Cognition.* Cambridge, Massachusetts: MIT Press, 1996.

Bernstein, L., *et al.* 1978. *Concepts and Challenges in Physical Science.* Fairfield: Cebco, 1978.

Betzig, L., M. B. Mulder, and P. Turke. 1988. *Human Reproductive Behavior: A Darwinian Perspective.* Cambridge: Cambridge University Press, 1988.

Block, N. 1995a, On a Confusion about a Function of Consciousness. *Behavioral and Brain Sciences* 18, pp. 227–247.

————. 1995b), How Many Concepts of Consciousness? *Behavioral and Brain Sciences* 18, pp. 272–284.

Bonner, J.T. 1980. *The Evolution of Culture in Animals.* Princeton: Princeton University Press, 1980.

Braine, M. 1978. On the Relation Between the Natural Logic of Reasoning and Standard Logic. *Psychological Review* 85, pp. 1–21.

Brandon, R. 1982. The Levels of Selection. In P. Asquith and T. Nickles, eds., *PSA 1982, Volume 1* (East Lansing: Philosophy of Science Association), pp. 315–322.

Brandon, R., and R. Burian, eds. 1984. *Genes, Populations, Organisms: Controversies over the Units of Selection.* Cambridge, Massachusetts: MIT Press, 1984.

Cann, R., M. Stoneking, and A. Wilson 1987. Mitochondrial DNA and Human Evolution. *Nature* 325 (1st January), pp. 31–36.

Chalmers, D. 1996. *The Conscious Mind.* New York: Oxford University Press, 1996.

Cheney, D.L. and R.M. Seyfarth 1990. *How Monkeys See the World.* Chicago: University of Chicago Press, 1990.

Cheng, P., and K. Holyoak. 1985. Pragmatic Reasoning Schemas. *Cognitive Psychology* 17, pp. 391–416.

Cheng, P., and K. Holyoak. 1989. On the Natural Selection of Reasoning Theories. *Cognition* 33, pp. 285–313.

Chomsky, N. 1959. Review of B.F. Skinner's *Verbal Behavior. Language* 35, pp. 26–58.

———. 1988. *Language and the Problem of Knowledge.* Cambridge, Massachusetts: MIT Press, 1988.

Cleland, C. 1993. Is the Church-Turing Thesis True?. *Minds and Machines*, pp. 283–312.

Coates, P. 1997. Meaning, Mistake, and Miscalculation. *Minds and Machines* 7, pp. 171–197.

Cosmides, L. 1985. Deduction or Darwinian Algorithms? An Explanation of the 'Elusive' Content Effect on the Wason Selection Task. Cambridge, Massachusetts: Ph.D. Dissertation, Department of Psychology and Social Relations, Harvard University.

———. 1989. The Logic of Social Exchange: Has Natural Selection Shaped How Humans Reason? Studies with the Wason Selection Task. *Cognition* 31, pp. 187–276.

Cosmides, L., and J. Tooby. 1987. From Evolution to Behavior: Evolutionary Psychology as the Missing Link. In Dupré 1987, pp. 277–306.

Cosmides, L., and J. Tooby. 1989. Evolutionary Psychology and the Generation of Culture, Part II. *Ethology and Sociobiology* 10, pp. 51–97.

Cosmides, L., and J. Tooby. 1991. Reasoning and Natural Selection. *Encyclopedia of Human Biology*. Volume 6 (New York: Academic Press), pp. 493–503.

Cosmides, L., and J. Tooby. 1992. Cognitive Adaptations for Social Exchange. In J. Barkow, L. Cosmides, and J. Tooby, eds., *The Adapted Mind: Evolutionary Psychology and the Generation of Culture* (New York: Oxford University Press), pp. 117–182.

Cummins, R., and G. Schwarz. 1991. Connectionism, Computation, and Cognition. In T. Horgan and J. Tienson, eds., *Connectionism and the Philosophy of Mind* (Dordrecht: Kluwer, 1991), pp. 60–73.

Davies, P.S., J.H. Fetzer, and T.R. Foster. 1995. Logical Reasoning and Domain Specificity: A Critique of the Social-Exchange Theory of Reasoning. *Biology and Philosophy* 10, pp. 1–37. Reprinted as Appendix below.

Davies, P.S., and T. Foster. 1989. Switched Conditionals and Empty Experiments: A Critique of Cosmides. Unpublished manuscript.

Dawkins, M.S. 1993. *Through Our Eyes Only? The Search for Animal Consciousness.* Oxford: Freeman.

Dawkins, R. 1976. *The Selfish Gene.* Oxford: Oxford University Press, 1976.

———.1982. *The Extended Phenotype.* Oxford: Oxford University Press.

Dennett, D. 1991. *Consciousness Explained.* Cambridge, Massachusetts: MIT Press.

———. 1996. *Kinds of Minds.* New York: Basic Books.

Dietrich, E. 1991. Computationalism. *Social Epistemology* 4, pp. 135–154.

Donald, M. 1991. *Origins of the Modern Mind.* Cambridge, Massachusetts: Harvard University Press.

Donn, J. 2000. 'Out-of-Africa' Evolution Theory Gets Boost from DNA Study. *Duluth News Tribune* (7th December), p. 7A.

Dupré, J., ed. 1987. *The Latest on the Best: Essays on Evolution and Optimality.* Cambridge, Massachusetts: MIT Press, 1987.

Elgar, M.A. 1986a. The Establishment of Foraging Flocks in House Sparrows: Risk of Predation and Daily Temperature. *Behavioural Ecology and Sociobiology* 19, pp. 433–38.

————. 1986b. House Sparrows Establish Foraging Flocks by Giving Chirrup Calls if the Resources are Divisible. *Animal Behavior*, pp. 169–174.

Facione, P., D. Schere, and T. Attig. 1978. *Values and Society.* Englewood Cliffs: Prentice-Hall.

Facione, P., D. Scherer, and T. Attig. 1991. *Ethics and Society.* Second edn. Englewood Cliffs: Prentice Hall.

Fetzer, J.H. 1981. *Scientific Knowledge.* Dordrecht: Reidel, 1981.

————. 1984. Philosophical Reasoning. In J.H. Fetzer, ed., *Principles of Philosophical Reasoning.* Totowa: Rowman and Allanheld, 1984), pp. 3–21.

————. 1985. Science and Sociobiology. in J.H. Fetzer, ed., *Sociobiology and Epistemology.* Dordrecht: Reidel, pp. 217–246.

————. 1986. Methodological Individualism: Singular Causal Systems and Their Population Manifestations. *Synthese* 68 1986. pp. 99–126.

————, ed. 1988a. *Aspects of Artificial Intelligence.* Dordrecht: Kluwer.

————. 1988b. Signs and Minds: An Introduction to the Theory of Semiotic Systems. In Fetzer 1988a, pp. 133–161.

————. 1988c. Program Verification: The Very Idea. *Communications of the ACM* (September), pp. 1048–063.

————. 1989. Language and Mentality: Computational, Representational, and Dispositional Conceptions. *Behaviorism*, pp. 21–39.

————. 1990a. Evolution, Rationality, and Testability. *Synthese* 82, pp. 423–439.

————. 1990b. *Artificial Intelligence: Its Scope and Limits.* Dordrecht: Kluwer.

————. 1991. *Philosophy and Cognitive Science.* New York: Paragon House.

————. 1991/96. *Philosophy and Cognitive Science.* Second edn. St. Paul: Paragon House.

————. 1991d. Primitive Concepts: Habits, Dispositions, and Laws. In J.H. Fetzer, D. Shatz, and G. Schlesinger, eds., *Definitions and Definability* (Dordrecht: Kluwer), pp. 51–68.

————. 1992. Connectionism and Cognition: Why Fodor and Pylyshyn are Wrong. In A. Clark and R. Lutz, eds., *Connectionism in Context* (New York: Springer), pp. 37–56.

————. 1992b. Is Evolution an Optimizing Process? Unpublished manuscript.

————. 1993. *Philosophy of Science.* New York: Paragon House.

————. 1994a. Mental Algorithms: Are Minds Computational Systems? *Pragmatics and Cognition* 2 1994. pp. 1–29.

————. 1994b. What Makes Connectionism Different? *Pragmatics and Cognition* 2, pp. 327–348.

———. 1995. Minds and Machines: Behaviorism, Dualism, and Beyond. *Stanford Humanities Review* 4, pp. 251–265.

———. 1996a. *Philosopy and Cognitive Science*, Second edn. New York: Paragon House.

———. 1996b. Ethics and Evolution. In James Hurd, ed., *Investigating the Biological Foundations of Human Morality* (Lewiston: Mellen).

———. 1997a. Intelligence vs. Mentality: Important but Independent Concepts. In A. Meystel, ed., *Proceedings of the 1997 International Conference on Intelligent Systems and Semiotics*. Gaithersburg: National Institute of Standards and Technology, pp. 493–98.

———. 1997b. Thinking and Computing: Computers as Special Kinds of Signs. *Minds and Machines* 7, pp. 345–364.

———. 1998a. Group Selection and the Evolution of Culture. In V. Falger, P. Meyer, and J. van der Dennen, eds., *Research in Biopolitics: Sociobiology and Politics* (Stamford: JAI Press), pp. 3–15.

———. 1998b. People Are Not Computers: (Most) Thought Processes Are Not Computational Problems. *Journal of Experimental and Theoretical AI* (October–December), pp. 371–391.

———. 2001. *Computers and Cognition: Why Minds Are Not Machines*. Dordrecht: Kluwer.

Fetzer, J.H., and R. Almeder. 1993. *Glossary of Epistemology and Philosophy of Science*. New York: Paragon House.

Fetzer, P.L. 1997. *The Ethnic Moment: The Search for Equality in the* American Experience. Armonk: Sharpe.

Fisher, R.A. 1930. *The Genetical Theory of Natural Selection*. Oxford: Clarendon.

Fodor, J. 1975. *The Language of Thought*. Cambridge, Massachusetts: MIT Press.

Fodor, J., and Z. Pylyshyn. 1988. Connectionism and Cognitive Architecture: A Critical Analysis. *Cognition* 28, pp. 3–71.

Fossey, D. 1983. *Gorillas in the Mist*. Boston: Houghton Mifflin.

Friedman, M. 1974. Explanation and Scientific Understanding. *Journal of Philosophy* 71, pp. 5–19.

Funderburk, C., and R. Thobaben. 1997. *Political Ideologies*. Third edn. New York: Addison Wesley Longman.

Galef, B. 1986. Social Identification of Toxic Diets by Norway Rats (*Rattus norvegicus*). *Journal of Comparative and Physiological Psychology* 100, pp. 331–34.

———. 1991. Information Centre of Norway Rats: Sites for Information Exchange and Information Parasitism. *Animal Behavior* 41, pp. 295–301.

Girgerenzer, G., and K. Hug. 1992. Domain-Specific Reasoning: Social Contracts, Cheating, and Perspective Change. *Cognition* 43, pp. 127–171.

Glymour, C. 1998. What Went Wrong? Reflections on Science by Observation and *The Bell Curve*. *Philosophy of Science* 65, pp. 1–32.

Goldberg, C, 1999. On Web, Models Auction Their Eggs to Bidders for Beautiful Children. *New York Times* (23rd October), p. A10.

Goodin, R., and P. Pettit, eds. 1993. *A Companion to Contemporary Political Philosophy*. Oxford: Blackwell.

Goodman, M., and R. Snyder, eds. 1993. *Contemporary Readings in Epistemology.* Englewood Cliffs: Prentice-Hall.

Gould, S.J. 1981. *The Mismeasure of Man.* New York: Norton.

———. 1994. Curveball. *The New Yorker* (28th November). Reprinted in Jacoby and Glauberman 1995, pp. 3–13.

———. 1996. *The Mismeasure of Man.* Revised and Expanded. New York: Norton.

Griffin, D. 1984. *Animal Thinking.* Cambridge, Massachusetts: Harvard University Press.

———. 1992. *Animal Minds.* Chicago: University of Chicago Press.

Griggs, R., and J. Cox. 1982. The Elusive Thematic-Materials Effect in Wason's Selection Task. *British Journal of Psychology* 73, pp. 407–420.

Griggs, R., and J. Cox. 1983. The Effects of Problem Content and Negation on Wason's Selection Task. *British Journal of Psychology* 73, pp. 407–420.

Hamilton, W.D. 1964. The Genetical Evolution of Social Behavior. *Journal of Theoretical Biology* 7, pp. 1–52.

Hartung, J. 1995. Love Thy Neighbor: The Evolution of In-Group Morality. *Skeptic Magazine* 3, pp. 86–99.

Haugeland, J. 1981. Semantic Engines: An Introduction to Mind Design. in J. Haugeland, ed., *Mind Design.* Cambridge, Massachusetts: MIT Press, pp. 1–34.

Hempel, C.G. 1952. *Fundamentals of Concept Formation in Empirical Science.* Chicago: University of Chicago Press.

———. 1962. Rational Action. Reprinted in N. Care and C. Landesman, eds., *Readings in the Theory of Action* (Bloomington: Indiana University Press, 1962), pp. 281–305.

———. 1965. *Aspects of Scientific Explanation.* New York: Free Press.

———. 1966. *Philosophy of Natural Science.* Englewood Cliffs: Prentice-Hall.

Henle, M. 1962. On the Relation between Logic and Thinking. *Psychological Review* 69, pp. 366–378.

Herrnstein, R. 1973. *IQ in the Meritocracy.* Boston, Massachusetts: Little, Brown.

Herrnstein, R., and C. Murray. 1994. *The Bell Curve.* New York: Free Press.

Holcomb, H.R. 1994. *Sociobiology, Sex, and Science.* Albany: SUNY Press.

———. 1996. Review of Kevin MacDonald, *A People that Shall Dwell Alone. Human Ethology Bulletin* (June), pp. 14–18.

Huxley, T.H. 1897. *Evolution and Ethics and Other Essays.* New York: Appleton.

Jacoby, R., and N. Glauberman, eds. 1995. *The Bell Curve Debate.* New York: Times Books.

Jensen, A. 1979. *Bias in Mental Testing.* New York: Free Press.

———. 1998. *The g Factor: The Science of Mental Ability.* New York: Praeger.

Johnson-Laird, P. 1982. Thinking as a Skill. *Quarterly Journal of Experimental Psychology* 34A, pp. 1–29.

———. 1988. *The Computer and the Mind.* Cambridge, Massachusetts: Harvard University Press.

Johnston, D. 1999. Gap Between Rich, Poor has Grown Wider. *Duluth News-Tribune* (5th September), p. 17A.

256   Bibliography

Kirkham, R.L. 1992. *Theories of Truth*. Cambridge, Massachusetts: MIT Press.

Kleene, S.C. 1967. *Mathematical Logic*. New York: Wiley.

Kliban, B. 1982. *Two Guys Fooling Around with the Moon*. New York: Workman.

Kolata, G. 2005. P.S.A. Test No Longer Gives Clear Answers. *New York Times* (20th June), pp. E1, E9.

Lumsden, C., and E.O. Wilson. 1981. *Genes, Mind, and Culture*. Cambridge, Massachusetts: Harvard University Press.

Lumsden, C., and E.O. Wilson. 1983. *Promethean Fire: Reflections on the Origin of Mind*. Cambridge, Massachusetts: Harvard University Press.

Madsen, K.R. 1960. *Theories of Motivation*. Copenhagen: Munksgaard Press.

Manktelow, K., and D. Over. 1979. Facilitation of Reasoning by Realism: Effect or Non-effect? *British Journal of Psychology* 70, pp. 477–488.

Manktelow, K., and D. Over. 1987. Reasoning and Rationality. *Mind and Language* 2, pp. 199–219.

Marshall, J., *et al*. 1971. Effects of Kinds of Questions and the Atmosphere of Investigations on Accuracy and Completeness of Testimony. *Harvard Law Review* 84 (1971), pp. 1620–643.

Mayr, E. 1984. *The Growth of Biological Thought*. Cambridge, Massachusetts: Harvard University Press.

Michalos, A. 1969. *Principles of Logic*. Englewood Cliffs: Prentice-Hall.

———. 1973. Rationality between the Maximizers and the Satisficers. *Policy Sciences* 4, pp. 229–244.

Millikan, R.G. Forthcoming a. On Cognitive Luck: Externalism in an Evolutionary Frame.

———. Forthcoming b. The Mind in Its Ecological Niche, Its Language Community.

Murray, C. 1996. Afterword. In Herrnstein and Murray 1996, pp. 553–575.

Nei, M., and A. Roychoudhury. 1993. Evolutionary Relationships of Human Populations on a Global Scale. *Molecular Biology and Evolution* 10, pp. 927–943.

Nei, M., and G. Lavishits. 1989. Genetic Relationships of Europeans, Asians, and Africans, and the Origin of Modern *Homo sapiens*. *Human Heredity* 39, pp. 276–281.

Newell, A., and H. Simon. 1976. Computer Science as Empirical Inquiry: Symbols and Search. Reprinted in J. Haugeland, ed., *Mind Design* (Cambridge, Massachusetts: MIT Press, 1981), pp. 35–66.

Nozick, R. 1981. *Philosophical Explanations*. Cambridge, Massachusetts: Harvard University Press.

Penrose, R. 1995. *Shadows of the Mind*. London: Vintage.

Petrinovich, L., P. O'Neill, and M. Jorgensen. 1993. An Empirical Study of Moral Intuitions: Toward an Evolutionary Ethics. *Journal of Personality and Social Psychology* 64, pp. 467–478.

Pinker, S. 1994. *The Language Instinct*. New York: Morrow.

———. 1997. *How the Mind Works*. New York: Norton.

Plotkin, H. 1994. *Darwin Machines and the Nature of Knowledge*. Cambridge, Massachusetts: Harvard University Press.

Pollard, P. 1982. Human Reasoning: Some Possible Effects of Availability. *Cognition* 10, pp. 65–96.

Popper, K.R. 1963/68. *Conjectures and Refutations*. New York: Harper and Row.

———. 1978. Natural Selection and the Emergence of Mind. *Dialectica* 32, pp. 339–355.

Ramsey, W., and S. Stich 1991. Connectionism and Three Levels of Nativism. In W. Ramsey, S. Stich, and D. Rumelhart, eds., *Philosophy and Connectionist Theory* (Hillsdale: Erlbaum), pp. 287–310.

Richards, R. 1987. *Darwin and the Emergence of Evolutionary Theories of Mind and Behavior*. Chicago: University of Chicago Press.

Rimer, S., and P. Healy. 2005. Furor Lingers as Harvard Chief Gives Details of Talk on Women. *New York Times* (18th February) online edition.

Rips, L. 1990. Reasoning. *Annual Review of Psychology* 41, pp. 321–353.

Ristau, Carolyn. 1991. Aspects of the Cognitive Ethology of an Injury-Feigning Bird, The Piping Plover. In Carolyn Ristau, ed., *Cognitive Ethology*. Hillsdale: Erlbaum), pp. 1–126.

Rosenthal, E. 2005. For Fruit Flies, Gene Shift Tilts Sex Orientation. *New York Times* (3rd June), pp. A1, A19.

Rothstein, R. 2000. What Limits? I.Q. and Brain Research. *New York Times* (20th December), p. A22.

Ruse, M., and E.O. Wilson. 1985. The Evolution of Ethics. *New Scientist* 17, pp. 50–52.

Ruse, M., and E.O. Wilson. 1986. Moral Philosophy as Applied Science. *Philosophy* 61, pp. 173–192.

Rushton, J.P. 1995a. *Race, Evolution, and Behavior*. New Brunswick: Transaction.

———. 1995b. J. Philippe Rushton Responds. *Skeptic* 3, pp. 22–25.

———. 1997. Race, Intelligence, and the Brain: The Errors and Omissions of the 'Revised' Edition of S.J. Gould's *The Mismeasure of Man*. *Personality and Individual Differences* 23:1, pp. 169–180.

Rushton, J.P., and C.D. Ankney. 1996. Brain Size and Cognitive Ability. *Psychonomic Bulletin and Review* 3:1, pp. 21–36.

Rushton, J.P., and A. Jensen. 2005. Thirty Years of Research on Race Differences in Cognitive Ability. *Psychology, Public Policy, and Law* 11:2 (June), pp. 235–294.

Salmon, W. 1967. The Foundations of Scientific Inference. Pittsburgh: University of Pittsburgh Press.

Sarich, V., and A. Wilson. 1967. Immunological Time Scale for Hominid Evolution. *Science* 158 (14th September), pp. 1200–03.

Saul, S. 2005. U.S. to Review Drug Intended for One Race. *New York Times* (13th June), pp. A1, A12.

Savage-Rumbaugh, S., and R. Lewin. 1994. *Kanzi: The Ape at the Brink of the Human Mind*. New York: Doubleday.

Scheffler, I. 1965. *Conditions of Knowledge*. Chicago: University of Chicago Press.

Schoenemann, P.T. 1999. Syntax as an Emergent Characteristic of the Evolution of Semantic Complexity. *Minds and Machines* 9.

Schoenemann, P.T., and W. Wang 1996. Evolutionary Principles and the Emergence of Syntax. *Behavioral and Brain Sciences* 19, pp. 646–47.

Schwartz, S., ed. 1977. *Naming, Necessity, and Natural Kinds*. Ithaca: Cornell University Press.

Scoccia, D. 1990. Utilitarianism, Sociobiology, and the Limits of Benevolence. *Journal of Philosophy* LXXXVII, pp. 329–345.

Searle, J. 1992. The Rediscovery of the Mind. Cambridge, Massachusetts: MIT Press.

Sheets-Johnstone, M. 1990a. *The Roots of Thinking*. Philadelphia: Temple University Press.

———. 1990b. Taking Evolution Seriously. Unpublished manuscript.

Sherry, D.F. 1982. Food Storage, Memory, and Marsh Tits. *Animal Behavior* 30, pp. 631–33.

———. 1984. Food Storage by Black-Capped Chickadees: Memory for Location and Content of Catches. *Animal Behavior* 32, pp. 451–464.

Shettleworth, S.J., and J.R. Krebs 1986. Stored and Encountered Seeds: A Comparison of Two Spatial Memory Tasks. *Journal of Experimental Psychology: Animal Behavior Processes* 12, pp. 248–256.

Sober, E. 1984. *The Nature of Selection*. Cambridge, Massachusetts: MIT Press.

Stolberg, S. 2000. A Genetic Future Both Tantalizing and Disturbing. *New York Times* (1st January), p. C7.

Thompson, N., R.K. Malenky, and N. Badrian 1984. Sexual Behavior of *Pan paniscus* under Natural Conditions in the Lomako Forset, Equateur, Zaire. In R.L. Susman, ed., *The Pygmy Chimpanzee* (New York: Plenum), pp. 347–368.

Tooby, J., and L. Cosmides. 1989. Evolutionary Psychology and the Generation of Culture, Part I. *Ethology and Sociobiology* 10, pp. 29–49.

Tooby, J., and L. Cosmides. 1990. The Past Explains the Present: Emotional Adaptations and the Structure of Ancestral Environments. *Ethology and Sociobiology* 11, pp. 375-424.

Tooby, J., and L. Cosmides. 1992. The Psychological Foundations of Culture. In J. Barkow, L. Cosmides, and J. Tooby, eds., *The Adapted Mind: Evolutionary Psychology and the Generation of Culture* (New York: Oxford University Press), pp. 19–136.

Tversky, A., and D. Kahneman. 1973. Availability: A Heuristic for Judging Frequency and Probability. *Cognitive Psychology* 5, pp. 207–232.

Vernon, M. 1971. *The Psychology of Perception*. New York: Penguin.

von Eckhardt, B. 1993. *What Is Cognitive Science?* Cambridge, Massachusetts: MIT Press.

Wade, N. 2000. The Human Family Tree: 10 Adams and 18 Eves. *New York Times*. Science Times (2nd May), pp. D1, D5.

———. 2005. Researchers Say Intelligence and Disease May Be Linked to Ashkenazic Genes. *New York Times* (3rd June), p. A21.

Wason, P. 1966. Reasoning. In B. Foss, ed., *New Horizons in Psychology* (Harmondsworth: Penguin), pp. 135–151.

———. 1983. Realism and Rationality in the Selection Task. In J. St. B.T. Evans, ed., *Thinking and Reasoning: Psychological Approaches* (London: Routledge), pp. 44–75.

Wason, P., and D. Shapiro. 1971. Natural and Contrived Experience in a Reasoning Problem. *Quarterly Journal of Experimental Psychology* 23, pp. 63–71.

Wason, P., and P. Johnson-Laird. 1972. The Psychology of Reasoning. Cambridge, Massachusetts: Harvard University Press.

Webster 1988. *Webster's New World Dictionary*. Third College edn. New York: Simon and Schuster.

Wilkinson, G.S. 1984. Reciprocal Food-Sharing in the Vampire Bat. *Nature* 308, pp. 181–84.

Wilkinson, R. 1996. *Unhealthy Societies*. New York: Routledge.

Williams, G.C. 1966. *Adaptation and Natural Selection*. Princeton: Princeton University Press.

———. 1992. *Natural Selection: Domains, Levels, and Challenges*. New York: Oxford University Press.

———. 1996. *Adaptation and Natural Selection*. Reprinted with a new preface. Princeton: Princeton University Press.

Williams, G.W. 1989a. Review of Robert Richards, *Evolution and the Emergence of Evolutionary Theories of Mind and Behavior*. *Evolutionary Biology* 2, pp. 385–87.

———. 1989b. A Sociobiological Expansion of *Evolution and Ethics*. In J. Paradis and G.C. Williams, eds., *Evolution and Ethics* (Princeton: Princeton University Press), pp. 179–214.

Wilson, D.S. 1980. *The Natural Selection of Populations and Communities*. Menlo Park: Cummings.

———. 1983. The Group Selection Controversy: History and Current Status. *Annual Review of Ecology and Systematics* 14, pp. 159–187.

———. 1989. Levels of Selection: An Alternative to Individualism in Biology and the Human Sciences. *Social Networks* 11, pp. 257–272.

Wilson, D.S., and E. Sober 1994. Reintroducing Group Selection to the Human Behavioral Sciences.. *Behavioral and Brain Sciences* 17, pp. 585–654.

Wilson, E.O. 1971. *The Insect Societies*. Cambridge, Massachusetts: Harvard University Press.

———. 1975. *Sociobiology: The New Synthesis*. Cambridge, Massachusetts: Harvard University Press.

———. 1978a. *On Human Nature*. Cambridge, Massachusetts: Harvard University Press.

———. 1978b. Foreword. In A. Caplan, ed., *The Sociobiology Debate* (New York: Harper and Row), pp. xi–xiv.

———. 1980. *Sociobiology: The Abridged Edition*. Cambridge, Massachusetts: Harvard University Press.

———. 1992. *The Diversity of Life*. New York: Norton.

————. 1999. *Consilience*. New York: Vintage.

Wittgenstein, L. 1958. *Philosophical Investigations*. Oxford: Blackwell.

Wolff, E. N. 1996. *Top Heavy*. New York: Free Press.

Index

Definition 2, ranges of behavior, 108
Definition 3, ranges of behavior, 108
Definition 4, culturgens, 109
Definition 5, epigenetic rules, 109
Definition 6, epigenetic rules, 109
Definition 7, mentality as semiotic ability, 112
Definition 8, (sexual) species, 113
Definition 9, societies, 113
Definitions, 104
definitions, circular, 37
definitions, ostensive, 38
definitions, regressive, 37
definitions, verbal, 39
Dennett, D., xiii, 41–43, 162
Dennett's conceptions, 162–63
denotations, 89
deontic systems, 220
deontological collectively and distributively, 182
deontological moral values, 178
deontological theories, 173–74
Descartes, R., 28, 68, 154
description, 43
descriptions, 16
deterministic causal processes, 198–99
deterministic mental dispositions, 44
Deuteronomy, 170
dictatorships, benevolent, 208
Dietrich, E., 77–78
digital machines, xiii, 72, 77
directive function variables, 15, 24
disciplined step-satisfaction, 77, 80–81
dispositional paradigm, 91
dispositional properties, 7
dispositions, 93, 102–103, 143, 187, 191–92, 203
dispositions, linguistic, 38–39
distributive justice, 203
Diversity of Life, The, 100
DNA studies, 125
domain specificity, argument for, 214–228
domain-specific reasoning modules, 200, 211
Donald, M., 46–51, 62, 72
Dr. Spock, 170
dreaming, 49

dreams and daydreams as non-computational, 78–79
drugs, hallucinogenic, 46
dynamogenic function variables, 24

East Asian population, 119
E. coli bacteria, 8–9, 12–13, 44, 109, 156
education, benefits of, 161
egoism, psychological, 171
Elgar, M.A., 32
emergent properties, 193, 196
empirical procedures, 21
empirical studies of ethical behavior, 180
Empiricism, 154
entitlements, 223, 236–240, 242, 246
environmental explanations, xvi
environmental factors, 7, 105–114, 135
epigenetic rules, xiv, 101–04, 106–114, 121, 134, 197–99, 202
episodic stage, 46–47
epistemic interdependence, 8
equivalence, misuse of, 245–46
ethical behavior, empirical studies of, 180
ethical egoism, 171–73, 175
ethics, 4, 173, 182
Eugenio, 5
European American, 119
evolution of communication, 163
evolution of consciousness, 32
Evolution of Culture in Animals, The, 8, 155
evolution of group traits, 192
evolution, causal mechanisms of, 6
evolution, laws of, 6
evolutionary biology, 105
evolutionary epistemology, 148–49
evolutionary epistemology, 151
evolutionary ethics, 182
evolutionary explanations, 93–94
evolutionary origins of intelligence, 123
evolutionary psychology, xiv, 200–02, 211
evolutionary rationality, 154
evolutionary theory, different versions of, 6
exaptations, 27
exclamation functions, 62
exclamatory sentences, 48
exclamatory/imperative, 62